Bioregional Financing Facilities

Advance Praise

"Our institutions are no longer serving us. We must give birth to institutions that support a new kind of economy, a new kind of philosophy, a new kind of ontology, a new way of being on this planet. And Bioregional Financing Facilities can play a critical role in supporting that transition."

- Lynne Twist, Philanthropist, Author, & Co-founder of the Pachamama Alliance

"A comprehensive articulation of some of the many possibilities to re-align financial capital with social and natural capital. It is rich with working examples from around the world that follow Jane Jacob's observation that economic development that mimics ecological development, a constant process of "differentiation emerging from generality", offers hope of a more reliable prosperity."

- Spencer Beebe, Co-founder of Salmon Nation Trust and Ecotrust

"The regenerative economy I imagine MUST be built on a foundation of bioregionally adapted, landscape scale regeneration. Bioregional Financing Facilities are the critical missing infrastructure. A brilliant and timely clarion call!"

- John Fullerton, Impact Investor & Founder of the Capital Institute

"In the early 1970s there was an epochal evolutionary emergence of transcultural ecocentric principles manifesting in the Gaia Principle, ecological economics, and bioregionalism, fundamentally framing and addressing the anthropogenic planetary metacrisis characterized as the Sixth Great Extinction. Of these, Bioregionalism held the deepest possible integrative context for the critically necessary systems decentralization required.

In the 50+ years of my work in the bioregional movement, I never imagined that anything like Bioregional Financing Facilities would come forth in my lifetime (or ever). BFFs provide a specific, fully integrated, comprehensive pathway for taking ecological economics and bioregionalism from the realm of the theoretical and visionary to operational implementation. In this astonishing work the epochal spiral comes around again in a living architecture of manifestation."

David Haenke, Founder, Ozark Area Community Congress & Co-organizer of North America Bioregional Congresses

"This is an important book. There is a lot of money sloshing around the world, with an increasing amount being directed to solving the compounding crises facing us. This is good. But as Samantha and Leon point out, who decides how it will be spent and thus how the solutions are shaped is critically important. We're out of time to wait for governments, multilateral financial institutions, banks, donors, and others to get it right. They won't. Creating locally based, Bioregional Financing Facilities is an approach too long ignored. By spelling out how to do this, the authors have done all of us who seek a finer future a great service. This is an idea that just might work and make a real difference."

- Hunter Lovins, President and Founder of Natural Capitalism Solutions, Author of "A Finer Future"

"To manifest the potential of regenerative cultures supported by regenerative economies, we have to pay attention to plurality, scale, and scale-linking. When we shift from the pattern of abstraction and generalization that caused the meta- and polycrisis, to unleashing the potential of people and place in the specific contexts of bioregions, we begin to see the poly-potential that is embedded in the long-term survival pattern of human beings as regenerative keystone species in the ecosystems they dwell in.

This book opens the vitally important discourse about what kind of Bioregional Financing Facilities need to be established urgently to enable divestment from globalized patterns of degeneration and reinvest in bioregional regeneration. While the exact legal formats for such institutions will be specific to the jurisdiction of each country, this book describes 4 types of financing facilities that need to be present to enable people to heal places and in doing so contribute to restoring planetary health."

- Daniel Christian Wahl, Author of Designing Regenerative Cultures

"Bioregional Finance Facilities are an aikido move to bring finance into right relationship with place, people and planet. Samantha and Leon have drawn a roadmap to shift the relationship between financial institutions and mechanisms from extractive and degenerative, to reciprocal and regenerative."

- Gregory Landua, CEO and Co-founder, Regen Network

Bioregional Financing Facilities

Reimagining Finance to Regenerate Our Planet

Samantha Power

Leon Seefeld

Dedication

We dedicate this book to the regenerators – the individuals, communities, organizations, and networks actively engaging in biocultural regeneration efforts in landscapes, seascapes, and watersheds around the world. We give thanks for the work that you do which, reminds us all that humanity can be a keystone species.

The next big thing in finance
is a lot of little things.

TABLE OF CONTENTS

Foreword

This book makes an argument for the decentralization of financial resource governance, and the organization of project portfolios for systemic change, to enable financial capital to reach the people and initiatives best positioned to contribute to global regeneration. It makes the case for the urgent development and piloting of a new structure to support this decentralization – the Bioregional Financing Facility (BFF) – which every bioregion on Earth could create to support its transition to a regenerative economy. We believe that BFFs can help align financial flows with living systems principles and Indigenous wisdom, to serve the thriving of all life on Earth – a purpose shared by all of us who contributed to this book.

We recognize that the current financial system was designed to serve colonialism, imperialism, and capitalism. Over centuries, these forces have produced a massive concentration of financial resources tied to the extractive activities destroying the possibility for life on Earth to continue to thrive. As awareness of the polycrisis grows, a wave of capital is forming that is attempting to avert further ecological, social, and economic collapse. And yet, there is a significant risk that if this capital flows through a financial architecture rooted in the same life-denying and inequitable power structures and logic based on abstraction, it will simply perpetuate, and perhaps even accelerate, the existing extractive processes.

An effective and proportionate response to the ecological crisis requires urgent, large-scale regeneration of the biosphere rooted in ecological integrity, cultural revitalization, the centering of Indigenous wisdom, and the recognition of the interdependence of everything on Earth. This will only be possible through local actions taken by the many small groups all over the world that are living in "right relationship" with place – in both rural and urban settings. These groups are active stewards and many have Indigenous and traditional practices for land management that can be interwoven with Western scientific insights and technology to support critically impactful biocultural regeneration and repair.

Indeed, we believe that the recognition and empowerment of the sovereignty of Indigenous peoples must be foundational in our response to the ecological crisis. We must learn from these original stewards about the roles of relationality, reciprocity, responsibility, respect, reverence, redistribution, reconnection, and critically, regeneration, in all that we design and build – including evolutions of the global financial system.

There is currently a lack of connective tissue between those that hold and manage the large pools of financial resources seeking regenerative impact, and the coalitions of actors on the ground carrying out critical regeneration activities. Bioregional Financing Facilities can become this connective tissue – using a systemic investment lens to facilitate the flow of resources and regeneration benefits between these two currently disconnected groups of actors to support regeneration free of externalities, exploitation, and oppression. BFFs can serve as semi-permeable membranes between institutions rooted in the status quo economic paradigm and the emerging bioregional economies applying fundamentally different economic logic and value systems. The authors and team of advisors believe that BFFs are a critical piece of the financial architecture needed to respond to the ecological crisis, in particular, and the polycrisis more broadly.

In these pages, we aim to raise awareness among investors and policymakers of the urgency and importance of decentralizing financial resource governance to achieve global climate and nature goals, and to mitigate further ecological, economic, and social collapse. We also hope to catalyze Bioregional Organizing Teams and Indigenous communities around the world to design and implement these facilities, and develop project portfolios for systemic change, so that they may raise and deploy financial capital that supports their transition to regenerative economies. We aim to motivate a network of philanthropists, public grant providers, and investors to capitalize these facilities through a strategic, integrated capital approach. Additionally, we hope to inspire innovators, futurists, designers, and artists from across disciplines and worldviews to develop new financial and governance tools, business models, and ownership structures that can support the realization of the value of biocultural regeneration at multiple scales.

This proposal for Bioregional Financing Facilities is woven from many long, diverse threads: five hundred years of anticolonial resistance and decolonial creativity; movements for economic, ecological, and social justice and liberation; and the inspired efforts of peoples around the world organizing autonomously for the regeneration of the biosphere and their local-global communities. It is informed by persistent innovation in the fields of economics, finance, ecology, evolutionary biology, and systems theory. BFFs were born out of and can support the web of interdependent efforts of the broader regenerative movement.

Money is one of the strongest attractors in the world today. You are likely reading this book, at least in part, for this reason. Money confers power and choice. It holds the potential to be both a great destroyer, and a great organizer. As a result, finance – how money is designed and flows – is a key leverage point for systems change and largely determines how our systems impact our ecological basis of survival.

We believe deeply that BFFs can wield and reshape finance to empower regeneration. And, perhaps more importantly, for all those who will be attracted to engage with BFFs – either as a lever for systems change or a source of funding – we believe this new class of financial institution can catalyze more life-affirming worldviews and deeper place-based relationships with all life in a bioregion. Finance is just a vehicle. Planetary regeneration is our journey.

We value your willingness as you explore this book to engage with us on the possibilities for these new institutions in serving the flourishing of all life on Earth.

Authors: Samantha Power (The BioFi Project and Finance for Gaia) *and Leon Seefeld* (Dark Matter Labs / Dark Matter Capital Systems)

Advisors: Stuart Cowan, Ph.D. (Buckminster Fuller Institute), *Edward West* (Applied Alchemy / The BioFi Project), *Indy Johar* (Dark Matter Labs / Dark Matter Capital Systems), *Raj Kalia* (Dark Matter Labs / Dark Matter Capital Systems), *Jan Hania* (Biome Trust), *Matthew Monahan* (Biome Trust / Ma Earth), *Karl Burkart* (One Earth), *and Justin Adams* (Ostara)

Key Messages

Policymakers, institutional and individual wealth holders, and the general public are increasingly recognizing the severity of the current ecological collapse and the risk of further collapse cascading across our interdependent economic, political, and social systems.

Large pools of capital have been committed to 'nature' to respond to this crisis. However both traditional and novel institutional financing mechanisms and methodologies risk perpetuating the same extractive processes and power structures driving the crisis.

Many important regenerative projects and initiatives are led by people with deep relationships to place who are best positioned to both utilize this capital and support the design of contextually-sensitive financing practices more likely to produce regenerative outcomes.

However, these projects and initiatives, many of which are small scale and informal, are often structurally excluded from capital sources or considered illegible to capital holders.

Communities around the globe are building networks of bioregional collaboration and solidarity, creating Bioregional Learning Centers and Bioregional Hubs that grow capacity for place-based learning and coordination towards regenerative economies.

We propose *"Bioregional Financing Facilities" (BFFs)* as an institutional template to empower these networks by connecting pools of capital to regenerative projects and initiatives, and structuring these capital flows in alignment with living systems principles and Indigenous wisdom.

Bioregional Financing Facilities drive:
→ the decentralization of financial resource governance
→ the design of project portfolios for systemic change
→ and the transition to a regenerative economy.

They become the connective tissue between:
→ centralized financial resources
→ and the mycelial network of regeneration.

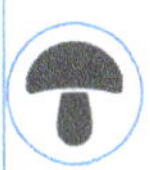

BFFs can enable financial capital to support the strengthening of relationships between community members, between stewards and the lands and waters they tend, and amongst all of the more-than-human life and living processes in those lands and waters.

The warning signs from the Earth we are experiencing can be seen as an invitation to remember our interconnectedness with all life on the planet and begin embedding relationality, reciprocity, responsibility, respect, reverence, redistribution, reconnection, and critically, regeneration, in all that we design and build at this juncture – including our financial systems.

A note on language: In this book, we have chosen to use the terms *"investment"* and *"investing"* to describe all processes of providing financial resources. This builds on an understanding that all forms of financial capital provision (equity, debt, donations, grant-making, etc.) ideally yield returns, as in the traditional notion of investment yielding financial returns to the investor. However, in our broader usage of the term, we recognize that some investment (such as traditional impact investment) can be designed to yield financial returns for the investor in addition to multi-capital returns for a broader community, and that other investment (such as grants) can be designed to yield non-financial returns (such as social connection and inspiration) for the investor and a diversity of multi-capital returns for a broader community.

Many diverse multi-capital frameworks and definitions – including Indigenous concepts – have been proposed in recent years to offer language for breaking from the perception that money is the only form of capital flowing around and through us. The authors celebrate this diversity of frameworks as an insight into the diverse nature of value itself and do not recommend the global use of a single homogenous multi-capital framework. However, this book focuses on the 4 Returns Framework[1] (financial, social, ecological, inspiration) due to its accessibility and demonstrable success. At times this book draws upon language from the seminal Eight Forms of Capital[2] (intellectual, spiritual, social, material, financial, living, cultural, and experiential).

1   Commonland: 4 Returns Framework & 4 Returns Platform
2   Ethan Roland and Gregory Landua: Regenerative Enterprise: Optimizing for Multi-Capital Abundance
    (Chapter 3: The Eight Forms of Capital)

Executive Summary

1. Introduction

We are living in the midst of widespread and recognized destruction of the living world. The ecological crisis, the crisis faced by Indigenous nations, multiple geopolitical crises, the economic crisis, the refugee and migrant crisis, the energy crisis, the inequity crisis, and social crises are deeply interconnected and mutually reinforcing. In face of this "polycrisis," a key realization is now spreading: the global economy cannot survive the ecological and social destabilization on the horizon. This recognition among economic and financial policymakers, the financial sector, and real sector corporations marks a shift away from the false, myopic, and devastating view that the economy is separate from the biosphere. Developing modes of being aligned with Indigenous values in rallying communities to respond in service to life will be key in adapting humanity's response to the polycrisis.

As awareness and understanding grow, and regulatory pressure increases, actors from across the financial sector are beginning to direct financial capital towards supporting biocultural regeneration. While on the surface this might seem promising, there is significant risk that if these resources flow through the existing financial architecture, they could lead to further commodification, privatization, financialization, and centralization of natural assets and wealth. The structural characteristics of the economy that are driving the crisis have remained largely unaddressed. Therefore, closing the "nature finance gap" alone is not sufficient. Where those resources are spent, how financing is structured, and who gets to make those decisions is as important as the quantum of capital. In particular, how those resources support the transformation of systems, relationships, and worldviews will determine whether they are successful in addressing the ecological crisis and poly-crisis that we collectively face.

Biocultural regeneration – A holistic and interconnected approach to revitalizing and restoring ecosystems, biodiversity, and cultural practices in a given spatial context. It recognizes the interdependence of nature and culture, emphasizing the importance of Indigenous and traditional knowledge and practices in stewarding ecosystems. Broadly speaking, regeneration is the process of a system regaining its needed energies, resources, and relationships to vitalize and sustain. Contrasted with "*sustainability*", which is oriented towards preserving and minimizing negative impacts, regeneration is oriented towards restoring and revitalizing systems that have been degraded.

2. The Case for Bioregional Financing Facilities

In an attempt to slow and reverse the ecological crisis, and in the absence of sufficient or expedient action by global actors, nation state governments or the private sector, communities around the world have started to organize living economies, ecological management, and governance systems at the bioregional scale.

Bioregions are defined by ecological, geographical, and/or cultural boundaries as opposed to human-made, jurisdictional ones. Despite the immense promise and potential of bioregional-scale organizing, strategic planning, and implementation, these initiatives are chronically underfunded around the world. A participatory, transparent, place-based approach is needed to identify those people and projects that must urgently be provided financial resources to enable their important work. There is a lack of connective tissue (trunk and branches in Figure I.) between those that hold and manage the large (and increasingly concentrated) pool of financial resources (leaves of the tree) and the coalitions of actors on the ground (regenerators) carrying out these critical regenerative activities (roots and mycelial network[3]).

Regenerators - The individuals, communities, organizations, and networks actively engaging in biocultural regeneration efforts. The specifier *"on-the-ground"* refers to those working in consistent, embodied, and intimate relationship with ecosystems and landscapes.

---

3   The complex network of fungal hyphae that extends through soil or other substrates, facilitating nutrient transfer and communication between and across species within soil ecosystems.

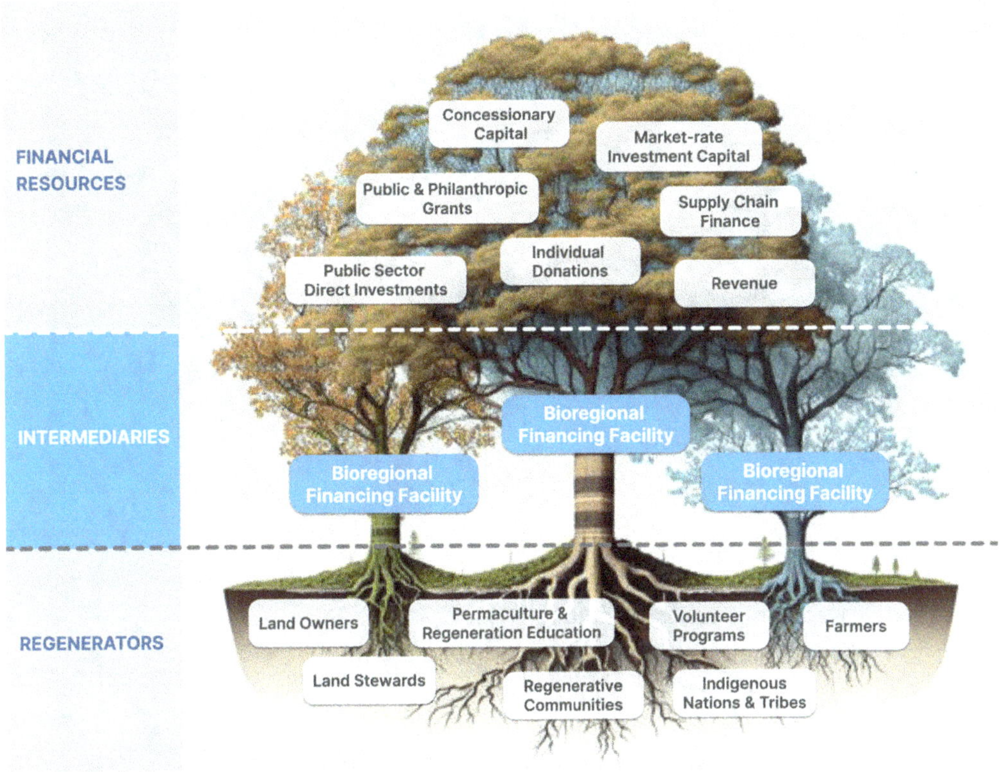

In this critical moment, the authors propose a new layer in the global financial architecture through the creation of Bioregional Financing Facilities to serve every bioregion on Earth. Bioregional Financing Facilities can drive the decentralization of financial resource governance, the design of project portfolios for systemic change, and the transition to a regenerative economy. They have the potential to become the connective tissue between financial resources and on-the-ground regenerators. They can do this by enabling strategic, integrated capital raised from a variety of sources to flow to aggregated portfolios of systemically coordinated and supported regenerative projects on the ground. In return, regeneration benefits can flow back to investors in a community-determined, non-extractive way. We believe this infrastructure is needed to put finance in service to life and Indigenous wisdom.

Note: The categories of financial resources and regenerators included here are illustrative, but not comprehensive.
Art by Cory Brown.

Figure II: What are Bioregional Financing Facilities?

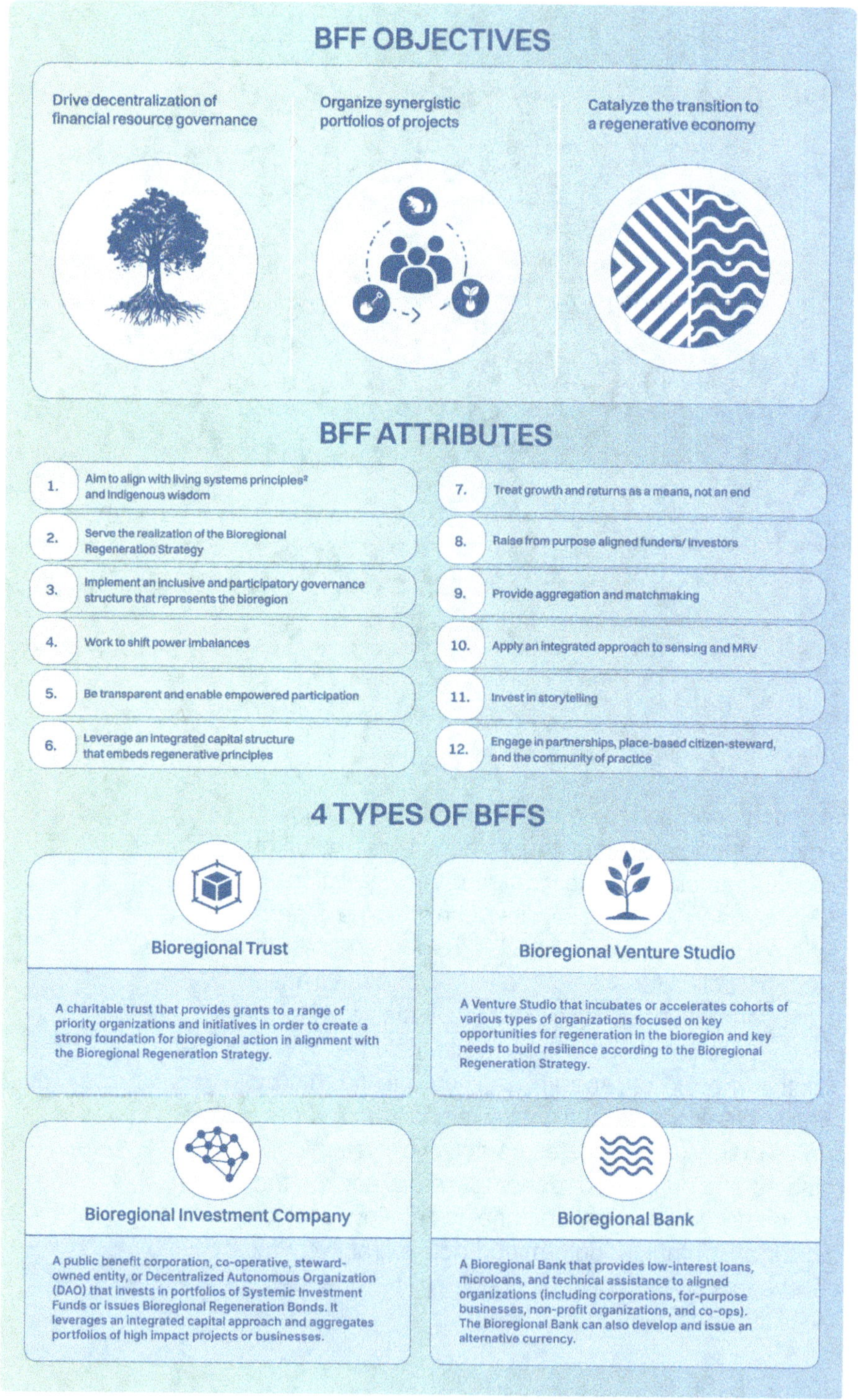

BFF OBJECTIVES

Drive decentralization of financial resource governance

Organize synergistic portfolios of projects

Catalyze the transition to a regenerative economy

BFF ATTRIBUTES

1. Aim to align with living systems principles[a] and Indigenous wisdom
2. Serve the realization of the Bioregional Regeneration Strategy
3. Implement an inclusive and participatory governance structure that represents the bioregion
4. Work to shift power imbalances
5. Be transparent and enable empowered participation
6. Leverage an integrated capital structure that embeds regenerative principles
7. Treat growth and returns as a means, not an end
8. Raise from purpose aligned funders/ investors
9. Provide aggregation and matchmaking
10. Apply an integrated approach to sensing and MRV
11. Invest in storytelling
12. Engage in partnerships, place-based citizen-steward, and the community of practice

4 TYPES OF BFFS

Bioregional Trust

A charitable trust that provides grants to a range of priority organizations and initiatives in order to create a strong foundation for bioregional action in alignment with the Bioregional Regeneration Strategy.

Bioregional Venture Studio

A Venture Studio that incubates or accelerates cohorts of various types of organizations focused on key opportunities for regeneration in the bioregion and key needs to build resilience according to the Bioregional Regeneration Strategy.

Bioregional Investment Company

A public benefit corporation, co-operative, steward-owned entity, or Decentralized Autonomous Organization (DAO) that invests in portfolios of Systemic Investment Funds or issues Bioregional Regeneration Bonds. It leverages an integrated capital approach and aggregates portfolios of high impact projects or businesses.

Bioregional Bank

A Bioregional Bank that provides low-interest loans, microloans, and technical assistance to aligned organizations (including corporations, for-purpose businesses, non-profit organizations, and co-ops). The Bioregional Bank can also develop and issue an alternative currency.

As Bioregional Financing Facilities are designed to serve each unique Bioregional Regeneration Strategy, their structures will be diverse. Diverse, decentralized organizations can support increased systemic resilience and improve the effectiveness of BFFs as connective tissue[4]. Therefore, we do not seek to be overly prescriptive in how BFFs should be designed. Instead we lay out twelve high-level attributes our research tells us each facility could work towards, and eventually meet, in order to effectively support the realization of the BFF objectives:

1. Aim to align with living systems principles[5] and Indigenous wisdom

2. Serve the realization of the Bioregional Regeneration Strategy

3. Implement an inclusive and participatory governance structure that represents the bioregion

4. Work to shift power imbalances

5. Be transparent and enable empowered participation

6. Leverage an integrated capital structure that embeds regenerative principles

7. Treat growth and returns as a means, not an end

8. Raise from purpose aligned funders/investors

9. Provide aggregation and matchmaking

10. Apply an integrated approach to sensing and MRV

11. Invest in storytelling

12. Engage in partnerships, place-based citizen-stewardship, and the community of practice

4   Nunes: *Neither Vertical Nor Horizontal*
5   In a way that recognizes the interconnectedness of everything on Earth (rocks, minerals, water, plants, fungi, animals, air, etc.). Recognition of this interconnectedness is foundational in Indigenous traditions from around the world and is also laid out in Western science in the Gaia Hypothesis.

3. The Enabling Environment for Bioregional Financing Facilities

To effectively serve bioregional regeneration, Bioregional Financing Facilities should be designed and implemented once there is already a strong foundation of organizing and activation in the bioregion. This foundation will most likely include a dedicated team which is in charge of stewarding the community organizing, weaving, and activation. Supported by the Bioregional Organizing Team, a wider group of local stakeholders embarks on a journey to regenerate ecological integrity in their bioregion. All regeneration efforts are eventually aligned with the co-created Bioregional Regeneration Strategy. A series of steps that organizing teams may want to follow for their multi-stakeholder process is outlined in the five phases of Preparation, *Mapping and Analysis, Convening and Activation, Co-initiation and Co-creation, and finally Co-evolution*.[6]

Building on the concept of Bioregional Learning Centers, we suggest the development of Bioregional Hubs. These grassroots hubs can foster the critical wealth of community resources and connectivity from which BFFs can sprout and support the transition to regenerative bioregional economies by focusing on financial capital flows.

One bioregion may have multiple hubs, each supporting a specific community or with a focus on a certain aspect of the bioregional system. Hubs may already exist or may be adapted from existing institutions. Important roles that Bioregional Hubs can perform to support the development of BFFs will include:

— Stewarding the co-creation and implementation of the Bioregional Regeneration Strategy
— Listening, ongoing, and comprehensive systems mapping, and research
— Capacity building and upskilling
— Identification and incubation/acceleration of regenerative business cases
— Transparent and real-time progress tracking and data collection
— Curating interfaces with global networks of Bioregional Hubs and Learning Centers

Table I. Illustrative regenerative actions and returns (inspired by the 4 Returns Framework[7])

INSPIRATION

Actions:
> Connecting people to place and ecology
> Revitalizing a sense of beauty
> Experiencing positive change
> Collective visioning through art

Returns:
> Sense of purpose
> Sense of connection to place & ecology, identity, and belonging
> Return of hope

ECOLOGICAL

Actions:
> Rewilding
> Restoring water cycles
> Wildlife corridors
> Ecological conservation
> Carbon sequestering and emission reduction
> Regenerative agriculture & forestry

Returns:
> Soil health improvement
> Increased biodiversity
> Restored water cycles and improved water quality
> Resilience against extreme weather
> Mitigation of natural hazards
> Increased food security and sovereignty

SOCIAL

Actions:
> Revitalization of spiritual practices, healing rituals and language
> Youth engagement and empowerment
> Education
> Food, music, storytelling, arts & culture
> Bioregional and watershed identity
> Connecting interrelated social issues within a bioregional lens
> Bioregional learning

Returns:
> Social connections
> Human health (physical, mental, spiritual, etc.)
> Knowledge
> Skills
> Safety

ECONOMIC AND FINANCIAL

Actions:
> Building regenerative food industries
> Establishing local, community-owned renewable energy production
> Empowering local entrepreneurship
> Promoting social entrepreneurship
> Establishing ecotourism
> Bioregional frameworks and place-based economy
> Supporting the transition to relational economies

Returns:
> Direct & indirect local job creation
> Land value uplift
> Profit and economic prosperity
> Local investment opportunities
> Financial return on investment
> Lower value-at-risk

Note: This table is not comprehensive.

4. Designing, Building, and Implementing Bioregional Financing Facilities

Once a Bioregional Organizing Team has brought together key bioregional actors to develop a Bioregional Regeneration Strategy as part of the Co-initiation & Co-creation phase, Bioregional Financing Facilities can be set up[8] to fund and finance the realization of the vision laid out in the strategy.

BFFs do this by working hand in hand with the Bioregional Organizing Team and Bioregional Hub to enable the decentralization of financial resource governance, the design of synergistic project portfolios, and the transition to a regenerative economy. Whereas Bioregional Hubs work to bring together and empower a bioregional regeneration network by facilitating regenerative flow of all capital types, BFFs focus specifically – but not exclusively – on facilitating the regenerative flow of financial capital. Together, the Bioregional Organizing Team, Bioregional Hub, and BFFs form the three legs of a stool that supports bioregional regeneration.[9]

Figure III. The three legs of bioregional regeneration

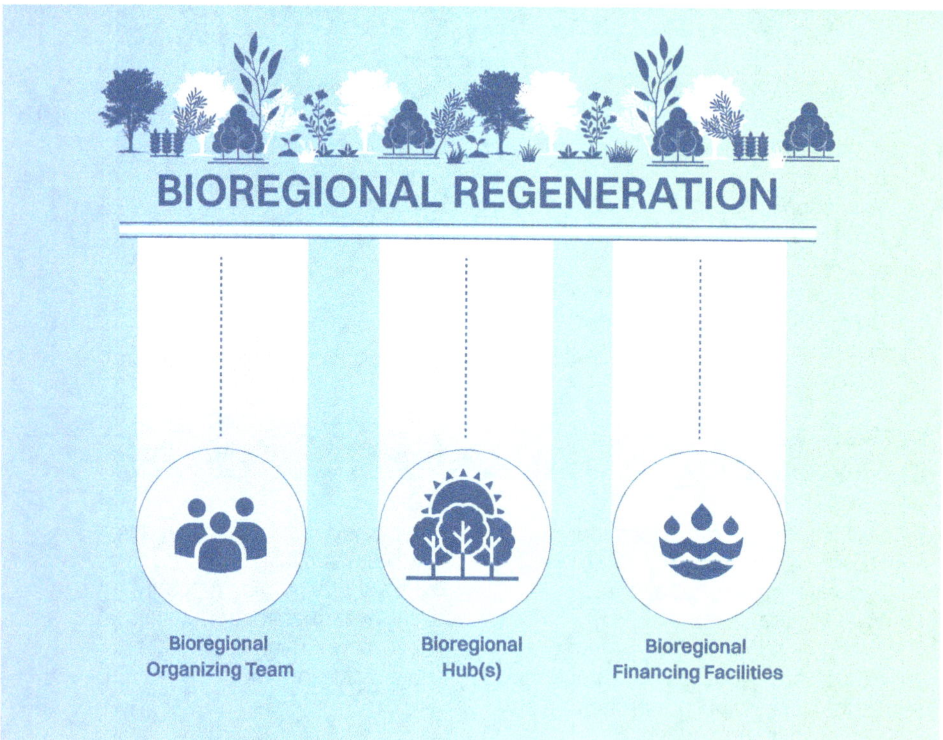

8   Or evolved from an existing aligned institution.
9   Noting that their role is to realize synergies and build networks between the many critical actors in a bioregion.

Bioregional Financing Facilities support the transition to an economy that is less, rather than more, dependent on both financial capital overall and financial capital from outside the region, and where financial flows better align with real flows of value. BFFs will work on creating regenerative flows at multiple levels – at the level of organizations it invests in, and at various levels in nested systems. This includes supporting regenerative organizations in the bioregion with technical assistance, and the development of the enabling environment conditions needed for regenerative organizations to succeed; deepening and expanding markets for regenerative activities; creating regenerating pools of funding to support management of common assets; raising the right type of investment capital; leveraging derisking approaches; and creating cutting edge, integrated MRV strategies. We recommend the Bioregional Financing Facilities are implemented in a phased approach as laid out in Table II.

Table II. An overview of the four types of BFFs (Part 1/2)

<table>
<tr><td colspan="2">PHASE 1</td></tr>
<tr><td>1. Bioregional Trust </td><td>2. Bioregional Venture Studio </td></tr>
<tr>
<td>

A trust that acts as a catalytic grant fund – providing grants to a range of priority organizations and initiatives in order to create a strong foundation for bioregional action. It can also set up and manage bioregional eco-credit programs, Common Asset Trusts, and Ecological Institutions.

Capital Raising
> Philanthropic and public grant capital (could be sub-national, national, or multilateral), as well as individual donations (including through crowdfunding)
> Bioregional Tithing program[10]
>

Capital Allocation
> Provides grants to fund key processes laid out in steps 2-5 of the Multi-stakeholder Bioregional Regeneration (Table 4)
> Provides grants to priority projects or organizations aligned with the Bioregional Regeneration Strategy
> Provides grants to Bioregional Hubs and Bioregional Organizing Teams
> Funds the development of a bioregional MRV platform (to be developed together with a Bioregional Hub)
> Sets up the Bioregional Venture Studio, Bioregional Investment Company and Bioregional Bank

Both Capital Raising and Allocation
> Works with citizen groups to develop, bundle, and sell bioregional scale eco-credits (including to companies operating in the bioregion)
> Sets up Common Asset Trusts – holding the rights to manage key ecosystems in the bioregion as commons
> Sets up Ecological Institutions – supporting greater sovereignty and economic legibility of bodies of nature

</td>
<td>

A non-profit, public benefit corporation, co-operative, steward-owned entity, or DAO that supports the development of a cohort of synergistic regenerative organizations to drive systems change. These organizations provide dealflow for the Investment Company.

Capital Raising
> Philanthropic grants
> Public sector grants (could be sub-national, national, or multilateral)
> Supply chain finance
> Concessional capital

Capital Allocation
> Invests in and incubates cohorts of early-stage organizations that work together to change a specific system and generate cascading benefits

</td>
</tr>
</table>

10   Credit to Edward West of Applied Alchemy.

Table II. An overview of the four types of BFFs (Part 2/2)

3. Bioregional Investment Company

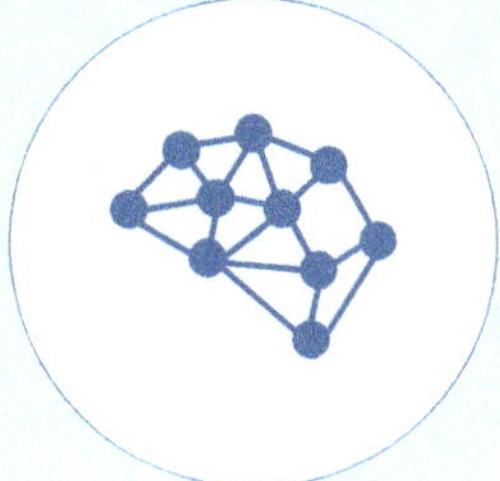

A public benefit corporation, co-operative, steward-owned entity, or DAO that develops a portfolio of Systemic Investment Funds and Bioregional Regeneration Bonds. It leverages an integrated capital approach, aggregates portfolios of high impact projects or businesses.

Capital Raising
> Market-rate investment capital
> Concessional capital
> Philanthropic grants
> Public sector grants (could be sub-national, national, or multilateral)
> Supply chain finance
>

Capital Allocation
Systemic Investment Funds
> Invests in diversified portfolios of projects & businesses designed to create systemic impact

Bioregional Regeneration Bonds
> Same objectives as the funds, but through a fixed income security

4. Bioregional Bank

A bank that provides low-interest loans, microloans, lines of credit, and technical assistance to aligned organizations. It can also provide retail banking services to individuals and can develop and issue a complementary or nature-based currency.

Capital Raising
> Concessional capital
> Public sector grants (could be sub-national, national, or multilateral)
> Philanthropic grants
> Guarantees
> Deposits
>

Capital Allocation
> Provides low interest loans to aligned organizations
> Provides technical assistance
>

Currency Creation
> Develops and issues complementary or nature-based currency

Figure IV. Schematic structure of Bioregional Financing Facilities

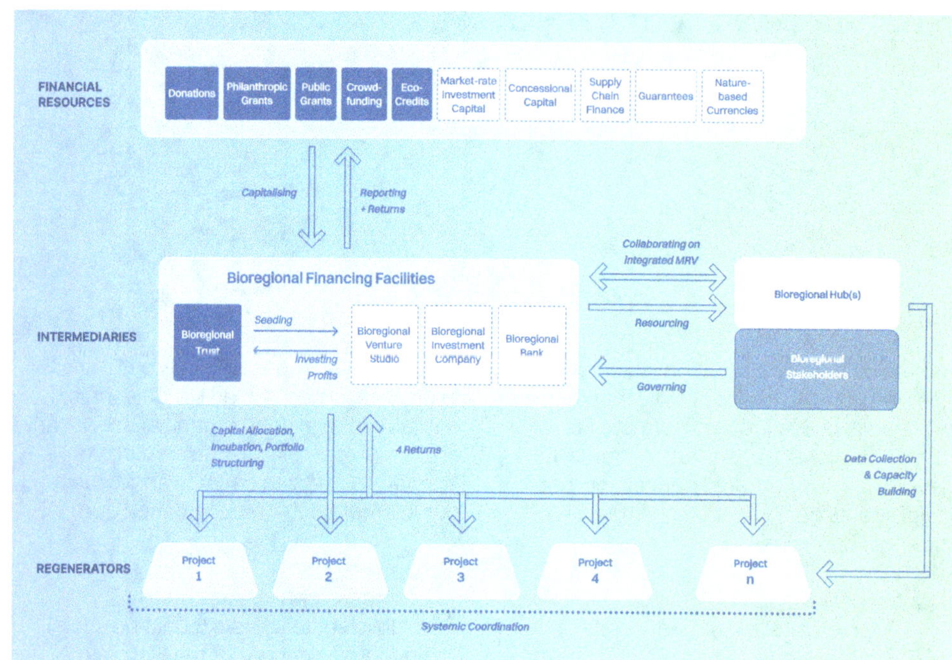

Bioregional Financing Facilities are capitalized through the whole spectrum of types of financial capital, including public and philanthropic grant capital, concessional and market-rate investment capital, as well as supply chain finance and eco-credit revenues. Other critical financial tools are public direct investment, tax revenue, subsidies, and the issuance of Bioregional Regeneration Bonds.

Bioregional Financing Facilities build on the emerging concept of systemic investing as an evolution of impact investing. They seek to establish a financial architecture that recognizes the complexity inherent to systemic transformation, and the fundamental interconnectedness of interventions. They help to build synergistic and systemic investment portfolios, creating positive spillover values which enable mutually rein-forcing and positive feedback loops of systemic value generation across projects.

BFFs provide a pathway for even multinational corporations – that often seem to operate everywhere and nowhere at the same time – to come back into relationship with the very real places and people they are dependent on and are in turn impacting. BFFs enable them to move towards healing and reciprocity through how they invest.

5. BFF Governance and Capital Allocation

The governance structure of BFFs underpins their ability to both decentralize financial resource governance and catalyze the transition to a regenerative economy. As BFFs represent an intentional attempt to encode an institution with worldviews, values, logic, and context that are fundamentally distinct from those of existing financial institutions, governance will be a challenging area requiring great care and collective experimentation. The assumptions and habits of governance learned through participation in traditional institutions may not serve BFFs, and both intra- and interpersonal friction in the learning process will likely emerge. It is critical for BFFs to cultivate a healthy unlearning/learning culture where they can carefully consider and experiment with what values are encoded in their governance, who participates, and what frameworks, processes, and tools are applied.

At the highest level, we encourage BFFs to implement an inclusive, participatory governance structure that represents the bioregion and is built upon a solid relational foundation of trust. BFFs governance design does not emerge from a vacuum, but rather from the rich context of the learnings and relationships built throughout bioregional organizing efforts and the creation of a Bioregional Regeneration Strategy, which can clarify specific, place-based understandings of the values that are to be upheld governance. In particular, we recommend careful consideration of the "R Values" that many Indigenous communities center in their governance (Section 4.1).[11] We offer many proven and emergent frameworks, processes, and tools that can support BFFs in both governance design and practice.

Finally, we encourage BFFs to explicitly design their governance towards three key aims: shift power imbalances, work with existing authorities, and build right relationship with other BFFs across regions and scales. This is hard, messy work with no easy answers that fit all contexts. However, we trust that through experiments in creating BFFs around the world, the collective intelligence of place can be harnessed to inform and support an entire network of BFFs – allowing common patterns of trustworthy governance structures to emerge.

---

11   For example: relationality, reciprocity, responsibility, respect, reverence, regeneration, redistribution, and reconnection

6. Innovative Mechanisms for Financing Bioregional Regeneration

A series of innovative financial tools and approaches is emerging that can help to capitalize BFFs and support the transition of a bioregional economy. Some worth mentioning include:

— Decentralized Autonomous Organizations and Web3-based eco-credits
— (Digital) Nature-based Currencies
— Local Market Networks & Bioregional Vouchers
— Bioservices Banks
— Participatory grant-making through quadratic and Conviction Voting
— Quadratic Funding and Equity Crowdfunding as proxies for capital allocation
— Place-based Bioregional Tithing, voluntary taxation, and Business Improvement Districts
— Advance Market Commitments for bioregional regeneration
— Profit Pooling and whole-economy health as triggers for investor returns

Many of the themes explored in this book are aligned with the values and patterns driving the decentralized finance or "DeFi" movement. The authors believe that the potential of existing protocols, tools, technologies, and templates in the Web3 space to bolster the bioregional movement and supercharge grassroots regeneration, has – as yet – not been realized.

Table III. Case Studies

CASE STUDIES

1. Salmon Nation – Envisioning a Nature State
2. Bioregional Weaving Labs in South East Ireland – An Example for a Multi-Stakeholder Process and Bioregional Regeneration
3. The Bioregional Learning Center in South Devon – Modeling Bioregional Hubs
4. Hawai'i Investment Ready Initiative – An Intermediary for Investing in a Resilient Economy for all Hawai'i
5. Spruce Root – An Indigenous-led CDFI Catalyzing a Regenerative Economy
6. Regen Network and Eco-credits – A Novel Funding Mechanism for Regeneration
7. Golden Bay and the Wellbeing Protocol – Participatory Grant-making through Quadratic and Conviction Voting in Practice
8. Regenerate Cascadia – Coordinated and Coherent Bioregional Organizing
9. The Edge Prize – Scaling What's Possible by Supporting Regenerative Innovators
10. Hylo – A Coordination Platform for the Future of Bioregional Organizing
11. ReCommon – Regenerative Common Land Trusts
12. Regenerosity – Flowing Capital to Grassroots Regenerators

7. Additional Case Studies: Stories of Bioregional Organizing and Bioregional Finance in Action

In addition to the multiple case studies throughout this book, five more case studies are presented in the annex. Each of the case studies tells diverse stories of combining dedicated social processes and thoughtful technological innovations to create strong foundations for BFFs. While each is substantial as a standalone case study, they represent, as a set of interdependent stories, a collective case study in how creative efforts across bioregions are resourcing each other and the global movement.

8. Next Steps and Call to Action

A series of recommendations and calls to action are presented for important stake-holder groups: Bioregional Organizers; Regenerators and Indigenous Communities, Nations, and Tribes; Investors; Philanthropists; Policymakers; Multilaterals and Development Agencies; Innovators and Futurists; Designers; Economists; and Financial Services Consultants. While many of these actions may on the surface look like to-do list items to check off, we suggest that they are all – including the most technocratic and technical – actually suggestions for forming and nurturing relationships of care, trust, healing, reciprocity, clear communication, and mutual learning.

Most of these recommended actions are not merely speculative. They have been sourced from a diverse set of active practitioners around the world. Thus, our list may also be seen as a celebration of the strength and maturity of existing bioregional organizing, coordination, and financing efforts. And yet, there is still much to do, and innovation to pursue, for this movement to cohere, and for BFFs to be established as effective, trustworthy institutions.

The recommended actions should not be understood as prescriptive or linear. Not all actions will look the same, or be needed across all contexts, and they do not need to follow an ordered sequence from first to last. We understand bioregional regeneration is a complex, dynamic flow of actions and relations across multiple nested scales within a landscape and our global networks, and we see these actions as supporting that process.

Finally, we encourage you to consider that by reading this book, you are already an active – even essential – participant in this movement, whether or not you resonate with everything written or identify as a key stakeholder. We encourage you to hold your professional or place-based identities lightly, and approach this book with curiosity towards the relationships and actions — listed and unlisted — that feel most compelling to you. Perhaps look up from the screen or the page every once in a while — you may be surprised by what is available right now, in your place.

9. Conclusion

Bioregional Financing Facilities have the ability to take capital from an extractive and destructive economic system and grow new, regenerative, bioregional economies that can autonomously engage in economic reciprocity with their neighbors. Our financial architecture must serve this recognition. There is an order to the changes now emerging from the disorder of our current social and economic systems: capital is finding its way to flow back to life and the humans stewarding it.

1. Introduction

1. Introduction

1.1 The state of the planet

We are living in the midst of widespread and recognized destruction of the living world. The scale and causes of this destruction are widely known and well-documented: approximately 75 percent of the Earth's ice-free land surface and 66 percent of its marine environment have been significantly altered as of 2019[12], and at least 20 percent of its land surface is now degraded[13]. The average global populations of mammals, birds, fish, reptiles, and amphibians declined by 68 percent from 1970 to 2016, with South America seeing a 94 percent decline[14]. Nearly 1 million animal and plant species (of 8 million recorded species) are now threatened with extinction;[15] extinction rates are tens to hundreds of times higher than they averaged over the past 10 million years.[16]

2023 was the warmest year in the 174-year observational record, with the global mean near-surface temperature reaching approximately 1.40 (± 0.12) °C above the 1850–1900 average[17]. A recent study found that the Atlantic meridional overturning circulation (AMOC), or the Atlantic Ocean current, is showing early signs of collapse[18]. The global pollution crisis has escalated to unprecedented levels, as evidenced by the ubiquitous occurrence of microplastics. These microplastics have been detected in clouds, aquifers, bottled water[19], and even in the human placenta,[20] representing what has been called a "slow-motion oil spill" through all the waters on Earth.[21] Additionally, research shows that per- and polyfluoroalkyl substances (PFAS) or resistant "forever chemicals," widely used in consumer products, are constantly cycling through the ground, air, and water and can now be found in even the most remote regions on Earth.[22] 14 of the 18 assessed categories of ecosystem services have deteriorated since 1970[23] and 6 of 9 planetary boundaries have now been

12   Intergovernmental Science-Policy Platform on Biodiversity and Ecosystem Services (IPBES, 2019): Summary for policymakers of the global assessment report on biodiversity and ecosystem services.
13   United Nations Convention to Combat Desertification (UNCDD): Global Land Outlook 2nd Edition
14   World Wildlife Fund.: Living planet report
15   IPBES, 2019
16   Pimm et al.: The biodiversity of species and their rates of extinction, distribution, and protection
17   World Meteorological Organization (WMO): 2023 Shatters Climate Records, With Major Impacts
18   Westen, Kliphuis, and Dijkstra: Physics-based early warning signal shows that AMOC is on tipping course
19   National Public Radio: Researchers find a massive number of plastic particles in bottled water
20   Ragusa et al.: Plasticenta: First evidence of microplastics in human placenta
21   Ocean Conservancy: Plastic Pollution is like a Slow-Motion Oil Spill
22   Stockholm University: It's raining PFAS: even in Antarctica and on the Tibetan plateau rainwater is unsafe to drink.
23   IPBES, 2019
24   Richardson et al.: It's raining PFAS: even in Antarctica and on the Tibetan plateau rainwater is unsafe to drink.
25   Global Footprint Network
26   Stockholm Resilience Center: Planetary Boundaries
27   Doughnut Economics Action Lab: About Doughnut Economics

exceeded.[24] Approximately 1.7 Earths would be required to maintain the world's current living standards with current economic systems.[25] Humanity's demands far exceed the Earth's ability to meet them, and this gap is widening.

The authors feel a profound sense of loss as we continue to witness the destruction of the interconnected web of irreplaceable, intelligent life that took billions of years to evolve. We increasingly live in and visit places where what we each hold sacred seems to be disappearing. The authors believe that Indigenous peoples have a critical role to play in leading not only ecological regeneration, but also in cultural regeneration – helping humanity to reconnect with our role as planetary stewards.

> "There are no unsacred places;
> there are only sacred places
> and desecrated places."
>
> – *Wendell Berry*

Indigenous peoples are stewarding an estimated 80 percent of the world's biodiversity on only 20 percent of the world's land,[34] and are often doing so without land tenure and under constant threat from extractive interests.[35] They continue to face systemic racism, oppression, and

Indigenous - Produced, growing, living, or occurring natively or naturally in a particular region or environment.[28]

Indigenous peoples - A term holding immense complexity that is best defined within specific context.[29] However, for general interpretation throughout this book, we suggest the term be understood as members "of a community retaining memories of life lived sustainably on a land-base, as part of that land-base,"[30] particularly peoples practicing non-colonial knowledge systems rooted in relationships of reciprocity with more-than-human life, and as a term of self-identification used by those with "a special relationship with their traditional territory and an experience of subjugation and discrimination under a dominant cultural model."[31]

Biodiversity - Biodiversity or biological diversity is the variety and variability of life on Earth. Biodiversity is a measure of variation at the genetic (genetic variability), species (species diversity), and ecosystem (ecosystem diversity) level[33]

Note: In some geographic contexts, 'First Nations' is used as a more specific term.[32]

28 Merriam-Webster: Indigenous
29 We encourage great care with this term and caution against simplistic categorizations that ignore historical contexts of interrelatedness between peoples, and between all peoples and the entire land-base of Earth. We encourage deep listening and relationship-building with sources of Indigenous knowledge and dialogue in your contexts.
30 This quotation is sourced from Tyson Yunkaporta's book *Sand Talk: How Indigenous Thinking Can Save the World*, which is an excellent resource for engaging with the depth and complexity of this term.
31 Wikipedia: Indigenous peoples
32 'First Nations' is often used to identify Indigenous peoples of Canada (who are neither Inuit nor Métis) and to identify people with familial heritage from, and membership in, the ethnic groups that lived in Australia before British colonization.
33 UNEP: What is biodiversity?
34 UN Convention of Biological Diversity: Indigenous Communities Protect 80% Of All Biodiversity
35 International Institute for Sustainable Development: Indigenous Peoples: Defending an Environment for All and "Who Owns the World's Land?"

Figure 1. Planetary boundaries

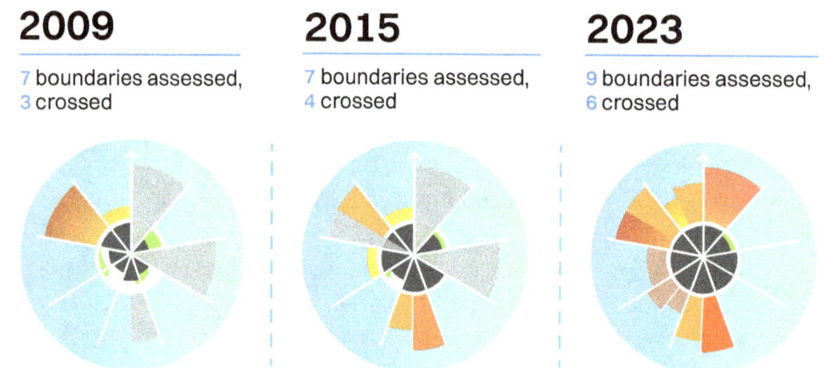

Building on the planetary boundaries framework, the **Doughnut Model**[27] (*see Figure 2*.) by Kate Raworth argues that a safe and just operating space for humanity is not only constrained by ecological ceilings but also a social foundation that needs to be sufficiently strengthened to reach sustainable prosperity. The social foundation, according to Raworth, comprises 12 factors: Food Security, Health, Education, Income and Work, Peace and Justice, Political Voice, Social Equity, Gender Equality, Housing, Networks, Energy, and Water. The social factors are more difficult to measure quantitatively on a planetary scale. Hence, the Doughnut Model is often used for local or place-based rather than planetary analyses.

Figure 2. The Doughnut Model

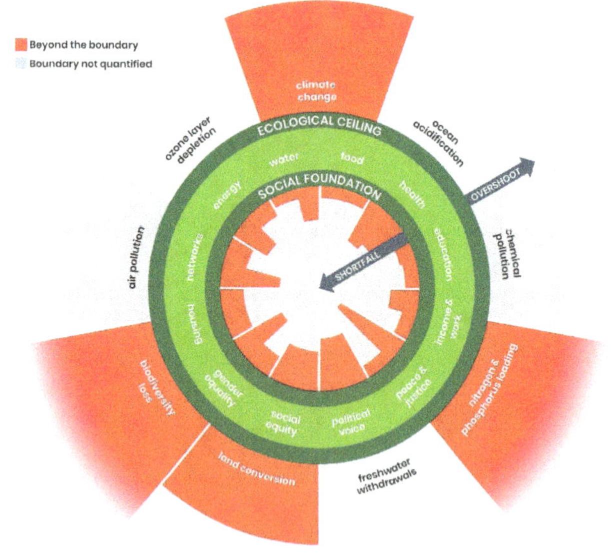

economic inequity. And yet, they act as stewards of ecosystems that provide essential ecological services underpinning the foundations of the modern world (e.g. biodiversity conservation – including of life-saving medicines, evapotranspiration, carbon storage, and broader climate regulation).[36] These services are being consumed by high-income individuals and people living in high-income countries at a significantly higher per capita rate than peoples practicing traditional or Indigenous ways of life.

Access to resources, tools, and technologies by Indigenous peoples to support their well being (including formal education and modern healthcare) often comes with pressure to enter into capitalist systems and compromise their ways of life.[37] The pressure of capitalism on Indigenous communities has often stoked violence. An estimated 1,910 environmental defenders have been killed since 2012 – many of whom were Indigenous.[38] Very few jurisdictions require companies that operate in or near Indigenous territories (particularly in the Global South) to obtain free, prior, and informed consent for commercial activities affecting these peoples, or to apply the principles laid out in the United Nations Declaration on the Rights of Indigenous Peoples (UNDRIP) as part of their supply chain due diligence.[39]

36   FAO and FILAC: Forest governance by Indigenous and tribal peoples
37   Atossa Soltani of the Amazon Sacred Headwaters Alliance speaks about this in the following interview: Ma Earth.
     Biocultural Jaguar Credits.
38   In 2012 Global Witness started tracking this type of violence.
39   Mongabay: International hesitancy to adopt environmental regulations threatens Indigenous rights

1.2 The polycrisis and collapse

The world right now is characterized by a number of deeply interconnected and mutually reinforcing crises, which together are driving the unfolding phenomenon increasingly referred to as "the polycrisis". Some of these are:

— the **ecological** crisis, encompassing climate change, biodiversity collapse, soil degradation, the pollution crisis, and water and food scarcity;
— the crisis faced by **Indigenous nations** as they continue to be subjected to harm and disempowerment perpetrated by settler colonialism and corporations;
— multiple **geopolitical** crises, including ongoing genocide, famine, wars, energy security, and nuclear risk;
— the **economic** crises of persistent poverty, extreme inequality, and ballooning sovereign debt
— the **refugee and migrant** crisis;
— the risk of **exponential technological development**, such as artificial intelligence, gene editing, synthetic biology, and novel chemical manufacturing creating unintended catastrophic consequences
— **social** crises, including the anxiety, depression, and loneliness spreading predominantly in high income countries; and
— **health** crises, including pandemics, cancer, and autoimmune diseases.

The authors believe that these are signs that Gaia is not healthy. The Gaia hypothesis, first published by James Lovelock and Lynn Margulis in 1979, postulates that the Earth's surface is maintained in a habitable state by self-regulating feedback mechanisms involving organisms (including humans) tightly coupled with their environment. Through this lens, Gaia is understood as a single, global entity that keeps the conditions on the planet within boundaries that are favorable to life.[40] The polycrisis can then be understood as self-regulatory feedback to humanity – the species currently most responsible for deteriorating conditions for life and also capable of perceiving this feedback in its culture – that urgent change in human-made systems is required.

In recent years, warnings of systemic collapse of various forms (e.g. civilizational, economic, ecological, social, political) have been growing in number and urgency from a diversity of scientists, complex systems modelers, historians, and social

40   The Gaia Hypothesis is based on several observations: The atmosphere is in an extreme state of thermodynamic disequilibrium owing to the activities of life, yet aspects of its composition are remarkably stable. Present conditions at the surface of the Earth are close to optimal for the dominant organisms. Life has persisted for over 3.8 billion years despite increasing solar luminosity and variable exchange of matter with the inner Earth. The Earth system has repeatedly recovered from massive perturbations. (Science Direct: Gaia Hypothesis - an overview)
41   Rowson, Jonathan: Prefixing the World

philosophers.[42] Acknowledging the wide range of definitions for collapse, predicted timelines, and rigor of study, the authors take the general message as credible: a continuation of "business as usual" is very likely to soon trigger dramatic and catastrophic changes in our social, economic, and ecological systems, and the arrival of the polycrisis may signify that this process has already begun. However, we believe it is ethically essential to frame any discussion of collapse within the understanding that this phenomenon has already been, and is currently being, experienced by many human and more-than-human communities as a result of dominant social and economic systems and the worldviews driving them. Some of the ways collapse has already been experience include: genocide, forced migration, slavery, mass slaughter of animals like the buffalo, destruction of primary forest, river damming, decimation of insect populations, coral reef bleaching, political re-education, strategic cultural destruction, institutional racism, structural disadvantage of certain populations (particularly Indigenous and Afro-descendent peoples), water and air pollution, and oil spills among others.

In this book we primarily focus on the ecological crisis and those aspects of the polycrisis most closely linked to it: importantly the continued crisis faced by Indigenous communities, who are the most important stewards of the world's biodiversity and hold the knowledge needed to enable humanity to return to a 'right relationship' with the Earth.[44] However, we do so with the understanding that these aspects of the polycrisis are not separable from others, and with the hope that the proposals we offer hold potential for supporting communities in simultaneously and synergistically addressing the set of challenges they face through pathways of biocultural regeneration, whether within a context of collapse or not.

42 The 1972 Limits to Growth report by The Club of Rome is considered a major starting point of this vast conversation. The report discussed results from complex systems dynamics modeling of 12 scenarios that showed different possible patterns—and environmental outcomes—of world development over two centuries from 1900 to 2100, including a "business as usual" scenario leading to collapse in the first half of the 21st century. See Donella Meadows (2002): A Synopsis: Limits to Growth: The 30-Year Update and The Club of Rome (2022): The Limits to Growth+50 for updated modeling and reflections.

43 Definition by James Sire, referenced in D.C. Wahl: Design for human and planetary health: a transdisciplinary approach to sustainability.

44 See Wildcat and Voth: Indigenous relationality: definitions and methods and Armstrong et al.: Ethnoecological perspectives on environmental stewardship: Tenets and basis of reciprocity in Gitxsan and nɬeʔkepmx (Nlaka'pamux) Territories for thorough explorations of relationality and reciprocity.

1.3 A turning point for the Earth and the financial sector

"The world is a complex, interconnected, finite, ecological - social - psychological - economic system. We treat it as if it were not, as if it were divisible, separable, simple, and infinite. Our persistent, intractable global problems arise directly from this mismatch."

- Donella Meadows

The scale, scope, and severity of the ecological crisis are so significant that it has proven overwhelming to every individual, institution, nation, or coalition of actors that has attempted to address it so far - no matter how bold their aspirations. Over the past 60 years,[45] there have been numerous instances where optimism soared, influential individuals gathered with noble intentions, apparent progress was made - and yet the relentless extraction and destruction of the natural world persists. Recent years, however, have witnessed a consequential shift in the environmental movement. After decades during which policy and funding responsibility for land and water stewardship primarily fell upon the public and non-profit sectors (and Environment Ministries in particular), now economic and financial policymakers, the financial sector, and real sector corporations have become integral participants in the discussion of how to avoid mass extinction.

A key realization is now spreading: the global economy cannot survive the ecological and social destabilization that is starting to be felt, as it is fundamentally nested within and

45 That is, since Rachel Carson published her book, *Silent Spring*, in 1962, which exposed the devastating effects of pesticide use and catalyzed a turning point in the environmental movement.

dependent on larger systems (see Figure 3.). A significant body of research[46] assessing the economic and financial risks associated with destruction of the biosphere makes the case that over the past century, rising incomes and consumption, as well as an increasing population and life expectancy, have made humans a significant force in the dynamics of the Earth's systems.[48] The recognition among economic and financial policymakers, the financial sector, and real sector corporations of the interlinkages between the economy and the Earth marks a shift away from the false, myopic, and ecologically devastating view (still foundational in neoclassical economics) that the economy is separate from the biosphere. The research has paved the way for actors in the financial sector to reevaluate how the sector can become a force for the regeneration of life. This signifies a transformative shift in the human-Earth relationship, one that is currently mediated by the economy in a fundamental way – a change which the authors of this book believe opens a door for a radical reimagination of our financial system and economy so that they work with rather than against life.

46   Some critical papers include: Independent report commissioned by the UK government: The Economics of Biodiversity: The Dasgupta Review; The Coalition of Finance Ministers for Climate Action: An Overview of Nature-Related Risks and Potential Policy Actions for Ministries of Finance: Bending The Curve of Nature Loss; Network for Greening the Financial System: Nature-related Financial Risks: a Conceptual Framework to guide Action by Central Banks and Supervisors; Network for Greening the Financial System: NGFS Recommendations toward the development of scenarios for assessing nature-related economic and financial risks; John Fullerton: Regenerative Capitalism.
47   Britannica: Biosphere
48   So much so that scientists now argue that we have entered a new geological epoch, the Anthropocene (National Geographic Education).

Figure 3. Nested systems view of local and global financial systems

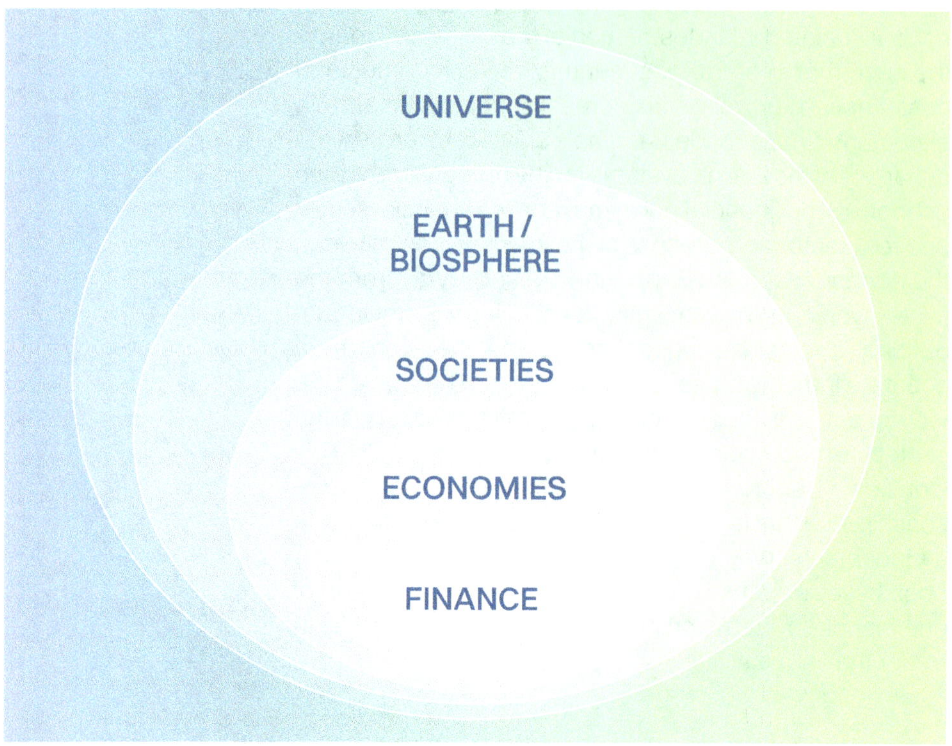

In December 2022, organizations representing more than 80 finance ministries and more than 100 central banks published a statement in the leadup to the Convention on Biological Diversity COP15 in Montreal, indicating that their members should *"work towards ensuring that economic activity and associated financial flows become increasingly aligned with a sustainable, nature-positive future."* The statement cited that, "because environmental degradation often follows a nonlinear pattern – compounding, reaching tipping points, and sometimes resulting in rapid ecological collapse – continual nature loss could have severe and sudden impacts on the economy, and hence on the financial system."[49] Some finance ministries even issued nature-focused strategic policy plans.[50] Additionally, financial institutions and businesses have also improved their understanding of how destruction of the biosphere could directly affect their operations and profitability, even before regulation.[51] Moreover, there is increasing recognition that the structure of the economy is driving the crisis.[52] According to research produced by the Coalition of Finance

49   Coalition of Finance Ministries for Climate Action: Finance Ministries, Central Banks and Supervisors Recognize Nature-Related Risks and Commit to Deepening Their Understanding
50   Ministry of Finance Finland: Strategy on Climate and Nature
51   World Bank: Mobilizing Private Finance for Nature; SwissRe: Biodiversity and Ecosystem Services Index. McKinsey: Nature in the balance: What companies can do to restore natural capital; World Economic Forum: Nature-Positive Industry Sector Transitions. PWC: Managing nature risks: From understanding to action.
52   Independent report commissioned by the UK government: The Economics of Biodiversity: The Dasgupta Review. The Coalition of Finance Ministers for Climate Action: An Overview of Nature-Related Risks and Potential Policy Actions for Ministries of Finance: Bending The Curve of Nature LossJohn Fullerton: Regenerative Capitalism.

Ministers for Climate Action, *"Nature-related risks are not inevitable, but can be reduced by altering the economy and the financial sector's impact on* nature*."* [53]

It is becoming clearer each day that the consequences of continuing on our current economic trajectory are not only unsustainable economically, but include significant existential risks. Humanity must swiftly and dramatically shift how it feeds, clothes, shelters, and transports itself. It must change how it builds its cities and manufactures its goods. It must repair the relationship between people and place. For these changes to be effective, they must be rooted in a worldview shift where we return to seeing and experiencing the Earth as a living, breathing, interconnected organism – of which humans evolved as an integral part – and not a resource to be extracted from.[55] All life on Earth is connected, and so the only two paths forward are mutually assured destruction or mutually assured thriving.[56] Today, we are equipped with an unprecedented array of capabilities and tools to support us in sensing, sensemaking, decentralized governance, coordination, planning, and envisioning. If properly deployed, the incredible technical capacities humanity has built can help us meet the complex challenges we are facing collectively.

53 The Coalition of Finance Ministers for Climate Action: An Overview of Nature-Related Risks and Potential Policy Actions for Ministries of Finance: Bending The Curve of Nature Loss
54 IPBES: nature
55 "Human beings are not exempt from the iron law of species interdependency. We were not inserted as ready-made invasives into an Edenic world. Nor were we intended by providence to rule that world. The biosphere does not belong to us; we belong to it." (E.O. Wilson: *Half Earth*)
56 Future of Good (YouTube): "Mutually assured thriving": Indy Johar on the future of caring for one another #socialimpact

– R. Buckminster Fuller

1.4 Moving beyond closing the "nature finance gap"

As awareness and understanding about the risks of destroying the biosphere and the resulting regulatory pressure increases, actors from across the financial sector are beginning to direct financial capital towards supporting regeneration. The Paris Agreement and the Kunming-Montreal Agreement both set goals to increase private investment in supporting the stewardship and restoration of ecosystems. Throughout the negotiations of these agreements, and now in the implementation process, coalitions of organizations sprung up that are working to scale nature-related investment and ecological credit (eco-credit) markets focused on biodiversity.[57] Ambitious monetary targets have been set for investment and the growth of these markets. Investment funds focused on natural assets are increasing in scale and number.[58] Institutional investors and family offices are also discussing the allocation of a percentage of their portfolio to natural assets.[59] As a result of these shifts, a wave of capital is building, committed to "investing in nature."

While on the surface it might seem promising that more financial resources are allocated toward nature restoration, there is a significant risk that if these resources flow through the existing financial architecture, they could lead

---

57   These include: the Finance for Biodiversity Pledge, the Voluntary Carbon Markets Integrity Initiative (VCMI), the Integrity Council for Voluntary Carbon Markets (ICVCM), the Taskforce on Nature Markets, and the Biodiversity Credit Alliance.
58   Carbon Pulse: Pollination plans blended regenerative agriculture fund worth billions
59   See Nature2 - an emerging coalition of investors committing to allocate 2% of their managed assets to "nature-positive investments."
60   Adapted from input from Regen Foundation.

to further commodification, privatization, financialization, and centralization of natural assets and wealth.[61] This could stem from the often extractive current return requirements of investors and the way that new asset classes become new forms of capital that reinforce existing power and wealth inequities (Pistor, 2020). Financial capital is thus far not being deployed in a way that addresses the structural characteristics of the economy that are driving the ecological crisis.

The authors believe that pushing more financial capital through the existing financial architecture could support the continuation of the paradigm at the heart of planetary destruction. This paradigm is characterized by the separation of humans from the rest of life on Earth; the treatment of the Earth as a resource to be extracted from; the destruction of relational capital between all living beings, including through deepening inequality; and ultimately the loss of function of ecosystems and of the intelligence inherent in those ecosystems. The cumulative effect would be that this capital works against local and global regeneration goals,[63] and may further destabilize social and ecological systems, and financial and economic systems. This clearly runs counter to the objectives of well-intentioned actors who truly want to regenerate life on Earth.

---

61   Carbon reductionism is one of the main issues with nature-related investing to date ('Carbon colonialism' in Africa meets resistance). The authors do not believe that carbon on *its own* is a good proxy for life or the things that matter to communities. Nature-related investments focused solely on maximizing carbon sequestration can bring about unintended ecological and social consequences. While we acknowledge that there are some carbon credit projects that have led to high integrity social and ecological outcomes, we believe there is a need for a broader basket of metrics to be used to ensure these outcomes are realized. Additionally, contemporary nature-related investment is driving a concentration of ownership and the financialization of agricultural land – creating far-reaching social and ecological consequences. "Who Owns the World's Land?", Land Report 100

62   Capital Institute: The Field Guide to a Regenerative Economy

63   Here we are referring to those laid out in the various agreements made under the Rio Conventions (Convention on Biological Diversity (CBD), UN Framework Convention on Climate Change (UNFCCC), and Convention to Combat Desertification (UNCCD)).

64   Much attention has been paid to the nature finance gap identified in the UNEP State of Finance for Nature report – an estimated $4.1 trillion between 2021-2050.

Thus, closing the "nature finance gap" alone is not sufficient.[64] Financial capital for regeneration (see Figure 4.) is certainly lacking. And yet, where and how those resources are spent and who gets to make those decisions is as important as the amount. In particular, how financial resources support the transformation of systems, relationships, and worldviews will determine whether they are successful at addressing the ecological crisis and polycrisis which we collectively face. Finally, there is the critique of money itself – a vast, essential topic which is not within the scope of this book. As a simple introduction to this conversation however, we note that dominant fiat currencies are increasingly being recognized as inherently extractive in their design and issuance processes – particularly for countries in the Global South.[65] Accordingly, we suggest that a comprehensive effort to finance planetary regeneration cannot succeed if wholly dependent upon dominant fiat currencies. The potential to develop and deploy complementary and Nature-based Currencies is discussed in Section 6.2.

Figure 4. From degenerative to regenerative design of an economy[68]

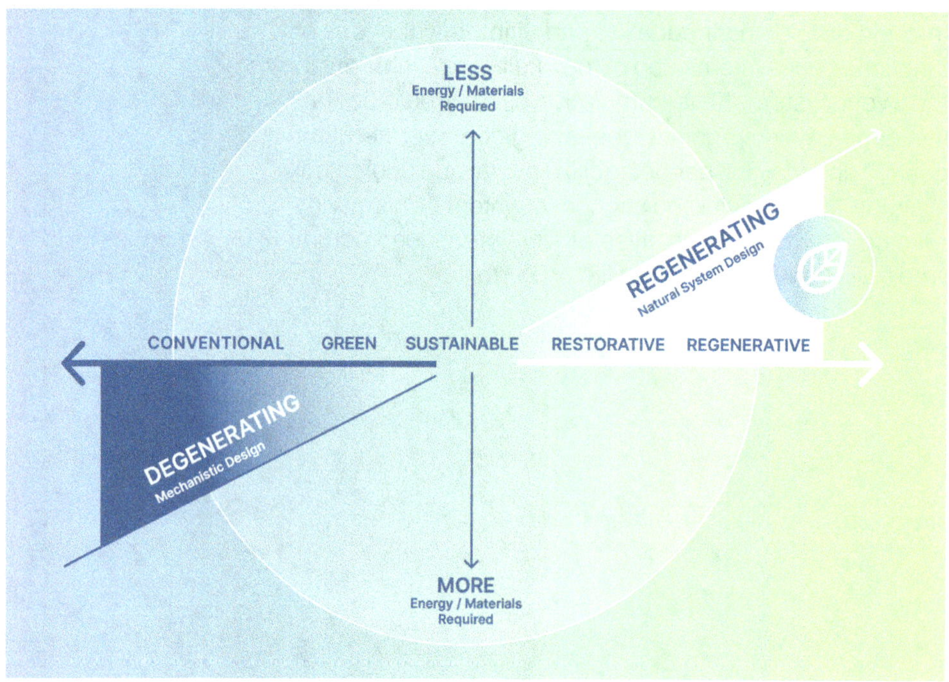

65   Dark Matter Labs: Towards multivalent currencies, bioregional monetary stewardship and a distributed global reserve currency. Part 1 (of 4): What are the issues that make money (and our dominant monetary systems) so problematic?
66   Bernard Lietar: Scientific Evidence of Why Complementary Currencies are Necessary to Financial Stability
67   Inspired by Open Earth Foundation: Nature Based Currencies.
68   Adapted from Bill Reed, Regenesis.

2. The Cascadia Bioregional Financing Facilities

2. The Case for Bioregional Financing Facilities

2.1 Bioregionalism harnesses the intelligence of place

In an attempt to slow and reverse the ecological crisis, and in the absence of sufficient or expedient action by global actors, nation state governments, or the private sector, communities around the world have started to organize living economies, ecological management, and governance systems at the bioregional scale.[69] Daniel Christian Wahl has powerfully articulated the potential for bioregional-scale regeneration to support planetary health.[70] Bioregions are defined by ecological, geographical, and/or cultural boundaries ("hard lines, soft lines, and human

69   Indigenous groups have organized themselves around bioculturally significant territories for at least 50,000 years (including San peoples in Africa and Australian Aboriginals). The modern bioregional movement can be traced to the work of Patrick Geddes (regional survey and Outlook Tower in Edinburgh, 1892) through Lewis Mumford, Leopold Kohr, Fritz Schumacher, and Ray Dasmann to the practical work of Peter Berg and the Planet Drum Foundation in San Francisco (1973-present). The bioregional movement has found expression in regional assemblies, continental congresses, mapping and planning methodologies, political theory, and many other domains.

70   See Wahl (2016) and Bioregional Regeneration for Planetary Health.

lines")[71] as opposed to more arbitrary, jurisdictional ones.[72] The bioregional movement has experienced a powerful resurgence since the late 2010s, with the development of various organizing entities across the world. These include:

— **Individual bioregions**, including Regenerate Cascadia, Ecotrust, and Salmon Nation Trust in the Pacific Northwest, North America; Collaborative for Bioregional Action Learning and Transformation, Casco Bay, Maine, US; Regenerate Barichara, Colombia; Tayside Bioregion and the Bioregional Learning Centre in South Devon, UK
— **Regional networks,** including Bioregional Weaving Labs in Europe, Costa Rica Regenerativa, Colombia Regenerativa, and Regen Places Network in Australia and New Zealand
— **Global networks**, including the Design School for Regenerating Earth, Regenerative Communities Network, Commonland, and Ecosystem Restoration Communities.

"The naming of something that is already going on is the power of bioregionalism."

-Judith Plant

Bioregionalism - A socio-political and ecological philosophy that argues for the organization of human societies based on natural ecological or biocultural regions, or "bioregions." Bioregionalism advocates for the alignment of economic activity, ecological management, and governance with the natural systems and cultures of the region. Bioregions can be seen as the *natural units of place-based regeneration*, enabling the interweaving of life's flows across species, the physical territory, and the cultural meanings of <u>place</u>. Bioregionalism suggests that the invisible and visible regenerative efforts occurring across multiple scales (individual, family, neighborhood, community, organization, ecoregion, global) can be anchored and organized in large, bioculturally coherent landscapes that federate through affinity, solidarity, and reciprocity to fulfill planetary potential.[74] Bioregionalism is deeply rooted in a worldview of fundamental global entanglement and does not seek to establish the division, separation or isolation often inherent to other relocalization efforts, for example, those promoted by nationalists.

Place - where geographic reality and human culture intersect. It is the foundation for culture and economy.[75]

71   Credit to Brandon Letsinger, Regenerate Cascadia.
72   We acknowledge that all boundaries are arbitrary, that in reality there are ecotones between ecosystems, but believe that boundaries informed by ecological and cultural characteristics can be useful in supporting effective organizing, governance, and resource allocation that can drive regeneration.
73   One Earth: What is a bioregion?
74   This is articulated in the vision, mission, and goals of the Regenerative Communities Network.
75   Credit to Capital Institute.

Ecoregion – A relatively large area of land or water that contains a geographically distinct assemblage of plant and animal communities. Ecoregions can generally be understood as encompassing biome subtypes (e.g. a grassland prairie biome can include multiple different grassland ecoregions — tall grass, short grass, etc.).

Ecotone – a transition area between two ecosystems where they meet and integrate. It may be narrow or wide, and it may be local (the zone between a field and forest) or regional (the transition between forest and grassland ecosystems). An ecotone may appear on the ground as a gradual blending of the two ecosystems across a broad area, or it may manifest itself as a sharp boundary line.[82]

Various resources describe and propose boundaries for the world's bio- and ecoregions. The non-profit organization One Earth has developed a map of 185 bioregions and 844 ecoregions based on scientific analysis of ecological characteristics.[77] There are also a range of highly granular watershed maps available.[78] These and other geographic or ecological maps can serve as important inputs into bioregional processes to develop bioregional boundaries that are also culturally meaningful for people in a given place. Maps of Indigenous territories can serve as an important input in developing boundaries to serve modern organizing. Native Land Digital has a global map representing research on historical Indigenous territories.[79] These territories show significant overlap, just like ecotones between ecosystems – providing a critical insight about the lack of any firm boundaries and the need to work with neighbors in bioregional organizing. A set of bioregional "Vision Maps" is available from Sanctuary Earth and ecological history story maps[80] can also serve as helpful inputs. Bioregional maps that serve as interesting examples include the Gulf of Maine to Casco Bay bioregional map and this detailed map of Cascadia. In addition to accounting for the overlap of different data layers, some relevant data points are also dynamic – changing throughout the year and over longer time horizons. Animal migration maps like those used by Salmon Nation (see Case Study 1: Salmon Nation) can serve as an important input to bioregional mapping.[81] A marine bioregional map could be developed around whale migration corridors, for example. Beyond

76   Capital Institute Discovery Dialogue with John Fullerton.
77   See Bioregions: Nature's Map of the Earth which maps 185 bioregions, and 844 ecoregions. This data is also available on a different UX here.
78   Grasshopper Geography maps, Waterway Map, and Data Basin are examples.
79   An important disclaimer Native Land Digital provides on its website: '[We are] representing Indigenous nations and people on their own terms and not trying to be an "arbiter" of truth when it comes to territory claims.' Their map explorer is available at native-land.ca.
80   For example, the one by the LA Landscape History Project.

what we can see, underground life can also serve as a useful input to mapping. The Society for the Protection of the Underground Network (SPUN) is developing maps of underground mycorrhizal fungal networks, which could inform bioregional mapping.

> "While there are few straight lines in nature, there are many definite and powerful edges – various ecotones, watershed divides, climatic zones, fault lines and scarps. Careful attention should be given to such beginnings and endings, for these dramatic turnings in the Earth serve as clear and powerful articulations of diversity."
>
> *-David McCloskey, On Bioregional Boundaries*

There are differing definitions of the scale of bioregions.[83] We believe that organizing, governance, and resource allocation at a scale informed by biocultural and living systems patterns and principles is needed to address the ecological crisis. We do not at this point have a strong opinion on the scale at which this should take place. Ongoing efforts show that working across a small territory (Bioregional Learning Centre focuses on South Devon, UK, approximately 30 km x 50 km in extent) can be effective, as can working across a large territory of greater than 1,000 km in its largest dimension (Cascadia, Pacific Northwest, North America and Amazon Sacred Headwaters Alliance, Ecuador and Peru).

Living system - Living systems, as contrasted with nonliving complex systems - such as the stock market, computer simulations, or car traffic patterns - are characterized by the following set of key features: complexity, self-organization, interdependence, nested hierarchies, dynamic balance, and the emergent properties of cognition, adaptation, and autopoiesis – the capability of a system to produce and maintain itself by producing its own parts.

81   Recent research by the UN Environment Program demonstrates that the world's migratory species of animals are in decline and their extinction risk is increasing.
82   Wikipedia: Ecotone ("ecosystem" has been substituted for "biological community").
83   One Earth: What is a bioregion? 22 ways to define a bioregion; Brandon Letsinger: What is a bioregion?

Using the building blocks of landscapes, minor watersheds, Indigenous territories, ecoregions, major watersheds, and bioregions can be an effective way of organizing and governing fractally.[84] These diverse building blocks may sometimes nest easily within each other, and will often overlap. A novel, interconnected bioregional financing architecture can be designed at all of these scales; the term "bioregional" is used for simplicity throughout this book to denote the importance of reconnecting finance with place-based regeneration.

The size and population of a selected region will have implications for resource mobilization (since funders and investors might in some cases prefer larger regions to achieve sufficient diversification and investment scale), organizing, sensemaking, and governance. ReCommon, for example, which has developed an adaptive bioregional governance framework it calls the "Regenerative Community Land Trust" has decided that ecoregions are the most appropriate scale for it to organize around to raise resources and invest in common land ownership structures. Regenerate Cascadia works across all four layers of building blocks and brings these nested efforts together across a geographic area spanning 75 distinct ecoregions and a 2,500 miles of Pacific coastline (see Case Study 9: Regenerate Cascadia). Ultimately, bioregional regeneration work is highly contextual, and local regenerators are often best positioned to decide on the appropriate scale of organizing in a place.

> "Like the word or concept sustainability before it, bioregion has become too prevalent, powerful, and useful to ignore."
>
> *- Robert L. Thayer Jr., Life Place*

---

84 In the World Bank book, *Decentralization and Biodiversity Conservation* (published in 1996), the Multilateral Development bank lays out, in 10 country case studies and 32 projects analyses, how decentralization of governance (including political, fiscal, administrative, and legislative power) can positively support biodiversity conservation outcomes. "A conclusion from the historical review of country experience is that centralized, top-down conservation is seldom effective, except where large budgets are available for enforcement and the society concerned is willing to accept a rather undemocratic conservation process."

Salmon Nation: Envisioning a Nature State

By Spencer Beebe, Christopher Brookfield, Cheryl Chen, Ian Gill, Edward West

About Salmon Nation

Salmon Nation is two things: a bioregion whose boundaries are defined by the presence of wild Pacific salmon from Central California to the North Slope of Alaska, from the ocean to the mountain tops; and an idea that people can organize themselves within a nature state: a big, diverse, powerful and holistic integration of people and place with thriving local communities, living in deep relationship with the lands and waters that nourish them.

Theory of change

The idea of Salmon Nation is organized around the idea that there are abundant enterprising individuals, particularly in "edge communities," which are outside the centers of power and money, who are actively adapting to climate change and innovating a path towards a more enduring prosperity. The theory of change of Salmon Nation holds that at the "edges" exist the seeds of a new way to live in step with natural systems. Edges are rural and urban, but typically remote from traditional sources of power. Edges are diverse and innovative, and they hold profound stocks of human and natural capital resources. At this intersection of built and natural infrastructure, edges represent vast areas of land and water that can accommodate a bioregional shift toward regenerative practices.

To advance this theory of change, The Salmon Nation Trust (a public benefit LLC) and the Magic Canoe (a non profit organization), and more recently, Salmon Nation Studios, were launched to use whole system design and human networks focused on celebration, storytelling, reciprocity, and the replication and acceleration of what works to support creative individuals in ways that improve social, economic, and natural well-being and unleash regenerative innovation. Together they aim to find, connect, and support a network of entrepreneurs across the bioregion engaged in deep innovation across a full spectrum of initiatives: regenerative agriculture, ecological forestry and fishing, language preservation, tribal sovereignty, watershed protection and restoration, community level health delivery, housing, arts, culture, education, social media, social networks, small business development, and local governance.

The Salmon Nation Trust's main focus is to incubate and spawn bioregional ventures and is lightly governed by high-profile advisors who hold high public trust to maintain mission alignment, integrity and public benefit impact. They are "Trustees" with the ability to call for the Trust's dissolution if there is material mission drift, but without operating control or fiduciary liability. This public-trust based governance and equity structure allows the bioregion as a whole to be the ultimate benefactor of this collaborative. Bioregional ventures the Trust has spawned include The Magic Canoe, a public purpose enterprise designed to celebrate and amplify stories that have the power to inspire tangible, at-scale change in our bioregion; as well as Salmon Nation Studios, which is focused on accelerating collaborative ventures that catalyze the development of local, place-based solutions.

A holistic approach

A holistic strategy is implemented under this collaborative structure, which is framed by three core functions:

1. *Discovery & Storytelling* – Immerse in edge communities, cultivate reciprocity and trust, share, amplify, inspire what works, and surface diverse entrepreneurs of place-based creativity and innovation.

2. *Weaving & Connecting* – Connect, share, inspire, and instigate unlikely collaborations and cross-pollination.

3. *Replication & Acceleration* – Apply human, social, and financial capital to support, scale, and replicate regenerative solutions that are already working in the edges. Enable edges to 'leapfrog' the centers.

2.2 Financial resources are needed to catalyze bioregional regeneration and the transition to a regenerative economy

Despite the immense promise and potential of bioregional-scale organizing, strategic planning, and implementation, these initiatives and the organizations and individuals they work to support are chronically underfunded around the world. Resources that are mobilized still hinge on a financial architecture that is ill-suited to catalyze regeneration efforts. As a result, progress is far too slow and limited in scale given the pace of change required by the polycrisis. Ensuring food and water security as well as disaster resilience, to name only a few key challenges, will all require major investments in *bioregional resilience and regeneration and the transition to a regenerative economy.* In conducting this research, we spoke to pioneering watershed, landscape, and Bioregional Organizing Teams as well as Indigenous community members from around the world, and all of them share the challenge of accessing sufficient investment to support this economic transition.

2.3 Bioregional Financing Facilities – decentralizing financial resource governance and growing the connective tissue between resources and regeneration

"You never change things by fighting the existing reality. To change something, build a new model that makes the existing model obsolete."

– Buckminster Fuller

The current financial architecture has created a historically significant concentration of wealth in the hands of the few. If financial resources (public, private, and philanthropic) are truly to drive biocultural regeneration and the transition to a regenerative economy needed to fend off ecological collapse and deliver wellbeing for all, resource governance will need to be decentralized. This will enable the emergence of economic activity aligned with living systems principles and Indigenous wisdom. Critically, it will allow for those best positioned to deliver regeneration to begin, deepen, or expand their work.

A participatory, transparent, place-based approach is needed to identify those people and projects that must urgently be provided financial resources to enable their work. Current investment decision-makers are not positioned to engage in such a process,[86] and are rarely connected to the places they are investing in. Impactful projects and businesses around the world - providing critical ecological and social value - often struggle to attain sufficient financial resources to support their work. At the same time, investors with minimum investment ticket sizes in the millions of dollars complain of a shortage of investable opportunities.

Additionally, public and philanthropic grant capital often flows to multilateral or regional development banks, multilateral agencies, or large NGOs that have high overhead, burdensome bureaucracy, and may lack close relationships with grassroots efforts. In the case of financial resources reaching Indigenous land and water stewards, there is often a government entity between the organization with the funding and the Indigenous nation or community. This creates problematic power dynamics that prevent the resources from getting to the people on the ground.[87,88]

85   adrienne maree brown: *Emergent Strategy*
86   Reasons from our experience include: Small staff, lack of contextual knowledge and connection to place, transactional lens, lack of deep understanding of local interdependencies, looking at benefits through quantified models, general abstraction of the global financial system, due diligence being expensive and therefore ticket size often needing to be quite large, lack of ability to hold complexity.
87   This is the case with large multilateral funds focused on ecological regeneration including: the Global Environment Facility, the Green Climate Fund, and the Climate Investment Funds.
88   Rights and Resources Initiative: State of Funding for Tenure Rights and Forest Guardianship

There is a lack of connective tissue (trunk and branches in *Figure 5*.) between those that hold and manage the large (and increasingly concentrated)[89] pool of financial resources (leaves of the tree) and the coalitions of actors on the ground (regenerators) carrying out these critical regenerative activities (roots and mycelial network).

Figure 5. Bioregional Financing Facilities: Connecting financial resources and regenerators

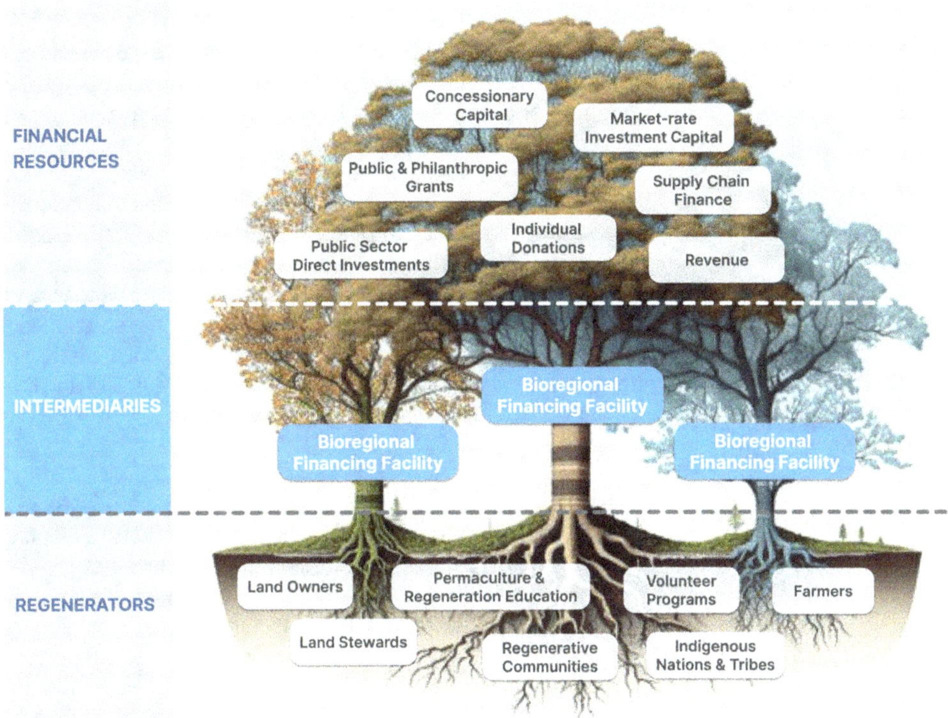

At this critical moment, the authors propose a new layer in the global financial architecture, through the creation of Bioregional Financing Facilities to serve every bioregion on Earth. Bioregional Financing Facilities can drive the decentralization of financial resource governance, the design of project portfolios for systemic change, and the transition to a regenerative economy. They have the potential to become the connective tissue between financial resources and on-the-ground regenerators. They can achieve this

Note: The categories of financial resources and regenerators included here are illustrative, but not comprehensive. Art credit: Cory Brown supported by Midjourney.

89   World Inequality Lab: World Inequality Report 2022, p. 3: "Between 1995 and 2021, the top 1% captured 38% of the global increment in wealth, while the bottom 50% captured a frightening 2%. The share of wealth owned by the global top 0.1% rose from 7% to 11% over that period and global billionaire wealth soared."

by enabling integrated capital raised from a variety of sources to flow to aggregated portfolios of systemically coordinated and supported regenerative projects on the ground. In return, regeneration benefits can flow back to investors in a community-determined, non-extractive way. We believe this infrastructure is needed to put financial systems in service to life.

Objectives of Bioregional Financing Facilities (BFFs)

Drive decentralization of financial resource governance: Move the distribution of financial decision-making authority and management responsibilities away from a centralized or top-down authority and toward local self-determination supported by collective intelligence across scales. This can be accomplished with a group of representatives that is more connected to a particular place and its ethnic or cultural identities and more attuned to the patterns of the living systems in that place. This aims to improve the efficiency, effectiveness, and responsiveness of resource allocation in delivering regeneration and resilience to avert and mitigate further ecological, social, and economic collapse. It also shifts the current unsustainable power imbalance inherent in economic inequality and the abstraction built into the current structure of the global financial system.

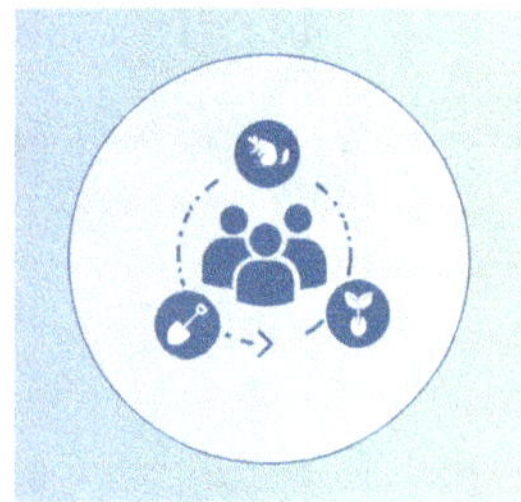

Organize synergistic portfolios of projects: Work with Bioregional Organizing Teams and key bioregional actors to identify and organize synergistic portfolios of projects[90] that create cascading benefits to advance biocultural regeneration and systems change, knowing that isolated approaches to achieving these objectives will not be effective. In addition to supporting projects through the allocation of financial and non-financial resources (such as shared tools and infrastructure), BFFs can serve an important role in promoting the transparent exchange of knowledge and best practices among them. This enables continuous optimization of these portfolios through learning and co-evolution with a systems change lens.

Catalyze the transition to a regenerative economy[92]: A shift from dependence on a globally-embedded, extractive, brittle economy to a more place-based, sovereign, circular, resilient economy that supports the regeneration of cultures and ecologies. Regenerative economies strengthen the relational fabric in context by acknowledging the diverse forms of value that exist. They recognize that value exists within relationships, rather than reducing everything to abstracted 'things' whose entire value can be measured completely in dollars. Such an economy becomes increasingly self-reliant, staying within its ecological boundaries without compromising the ability of other bioregions and future generations to meet their needs.

Regenerative economies will look different in every bioregion, marking a move away from the current monoculture economy that touches almost every corner of the planet, to more biodiverse economies[93] that are driven by community needs and values, and their ecological contexts.[94] Regenerative economies enable people in a place to decide collectively what they value, map those assets in their bioregion, and invest holistically in their regeneration. Bioregional Financing Facilities are a critical membrane allowing communities to effectively resource alternative visions as they rebuild economic sovereignty to address the polycrisis – while avoiding extractive entanglements with the existing global financial architecture.

"A society which practices living-in-place keeps a balance with its region of support through links between human lives, other living things, and the processes of the planet—seasons, weather, water cycles— as revealed by the place itself. It is the opposite of a society which makes a living through short-term destructive exploitation of land and life."

– Peter Berg and Raymond F. Dasmann

While every bioregion will have its own particular investment needs[95] that will inform the design of the facilities it creates, and each facility within a bioregion will have a different structure, there are twelve high-level attributes our

90   A need identified by the UN Decade on Ecosystem Restoration Finance Task Force in its Stocktake Report: Scaling Up Ecosystem Restoration Finance as follows, "Financing restoration at scale often requires a coalition of investors and donors that support a consortium of actors implementing a suite of actions on the ground. It is critical to improve the efficiency and standardization of portfolio management so such financing can be scaled up."

91   Buckminster Fuller Institute.

92   "Regenerative economics is the application of nature's laws and patterns of systemic health, self-organization, self-renewal, and regenerative vitality to socio-economic systems." (Capital Institute)

93   One source that served as inspiration to the authors that explores a range of economic structures beyond capitalism, is the book *Thrive: Fundamentals for a New Economy* by Kees Klomp and Shinta Oosterwaal. Some of the economic structures the book explores include: the Well Being Economy, System Value Economy, Eco-feminist Economy, Indigenous Economy, Sacred Economy, Radical Circular Economy, and others. Other sources of inspiration include: Indigenous Economics: Sustaining People and Their Lands by Ronald Trosper and Hoodie Economics by Jack Manning Bancroft.

94   In these economies financial returns should be informed by what is regenerative in the context of an ecology and culture, not a global benchmark.

95   These will be closely tied to the sequencing of activities, the current level of financialization of an economy, whether the primary activities are rural or urban, whether territory is still governed by Indigenous peoples, the level or investment readiness, etc.

research tells us each facility should work towards, and eventually meet to achieve its dual objectives. These attributes are as follows (for further explanation see Section 4):

1. Aim to align with living systems principles[96] and Indigenous wisdom

2. Serve the realization of the Bioregional Regeneration Strategy

3. Implement an inclusive and participatory governance structure that represents the bioregion

4. Work to shift power imbalances

5. Be transparent and enable empowered participation

6. Leverage an integrated capital structure that embeds regenerative principles

7. Treat growth and returns as a means, not an end

8. Raise capital from purpose-aligned funders/investors

9. Provide aggregation and matchmaking

10. Apply an integrated approach to sensing and MRV

11. Invest in storytelling

12. Engage in partnerships, place-based citizen-stewardship, and the community of practice

96 In a way that recognizes the interconnectedness of everything on Earth (rocks, minerals, water, plants, fungi, animals, air, etc.). Recognition of this interconnectedness is foundational in Indigenous traditions from around the world and is also laid out in Western science in the Gaia Hypothesis.

2.4 Introducing four types of Bioregional Financing Facilities

"The next big thing in finance is a lot of little things." [97]

Built on the objectives and attributes laid out in the previous sub-section, we envision four types of Bioregional Financing Facilities (also depicted in Figure 6. below):

1. The Bioregional Trust

2. The Bioregional Venture Studio

3. The Bioregional Investment Company

4. The Bioregional Bank

Templates of these facilities, details on their design, and steps for implementation are provided in Section 4.

97   Authors' adaptation of a quote from designer Thomas Lommée.

Figure 6. What are Bioregional Financing Facilities?

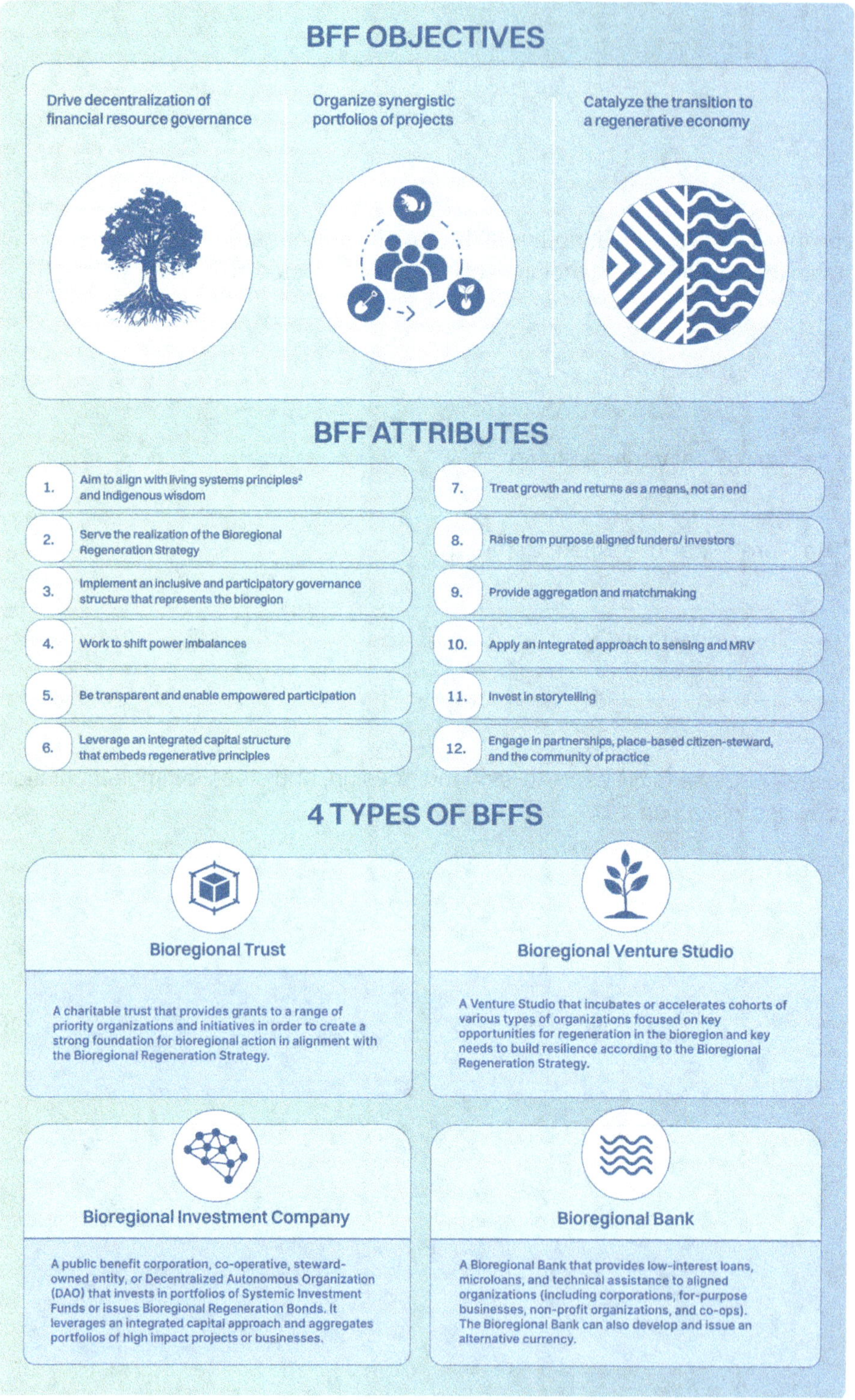

3. The Enabling Environment for Bioregional Financing Facilities

Disclaimer: The work of organizing bioregionally and transitioning to regenerative economies is complex, and the approaches we propose in this book are developed with the understanding that a plurality of approaches are being taken and will emerge in actual implementation. Examples in this book are meant to serve as templates that can inspire and guide action adapted to the context of a given place. We trust that Bioregional Organizing Teams and other key bioregional actors will be guided by what is needed to support economic transition and regeneration in their place, and celebrate the necessary diversity of approaches.

3. The Enabling Environment for Bioregional Financing Facilities

Community organizing, weaving, and activation – The processes of gathering, facilitating connection between, and empowering community towards a shared purpose and vision.

Weaving – The practice of cultivating meaningful relationships, within, between and across socio-ecological systems. It connects people, projects, and places in synergistic and purposeful ways to help cohere fragmented change-making efforts. It seeks to strengthen the socio-ecological fabric and the system's resilience by addressing the vital and relational aspects of trust, common meaning, capacity for learning, and capacity for self-organization.[98, 99]

Bioregional Organizing Team – A team of local stakeholders that initiates a bioregional regeneration process. This team organizes and activates other stakeholders, leads the design of bioregional governance, and catalyzes the design process for the Bioregional Hub(s) and Bioregional Financing Facilities. The team is ideally deeply embedded in local communities and part of the local tapestry of social connections. It connects people, projects, and places in synergistic and purposeful ways, and usually excels in five core Weaving practices:[100]

1. Helping systems see
2. and sense themselves
3. Cultivating trust-based relationships
4. Aligning on a shared purpose and vision
5. Facilitating collective
6. (un)learning
7. Fostering (experimental) action

3.1 Bioregional organizing and value creation

To effectively serve bioregional regeneration, Bioregional Financing Facilities should be designed and implemented once there is already a strong foundation of organizing and activation in the bioregion. This foundation will most likely include a dedicated team in charge of the community organizing, weaving, and activation. See Regenerate Cascadia's case study for an example of a Bioregional Organizing Team facilitating a participatory bioregional regeneration program building on decades of community organizing.

While BFFs could potentially invest in early-stage activities to accelerate their pace, a balance should be struck between speed and trust building – noting that if financial resources come in before a local stakeholders have built trust through practical experiments in coordination and the cultivation of shared identity and purpose in their collective organizing, they could undermine the efficacy of the effort, possibly irreversibly. Critically, the Bioregional Organizing Team will need to have built trust with a wide range of key actors across the bioregion (see *Table 1. below*).

98   Hussain et al.: Socio-Ecological Resilience: 'Weaving' to scale Nature-based Solutions
99   The Weaving Lab: What is Weaving?
100 Bioregional Weaving Labs: Weaving

– Stephen M.R. Covey

In her book *Emergent Strategy: Shaping Worlds, Shaping Change*, adrienne maree brown blends insights from science fiction and living systems to articulate an approach to visionary community organizing and world building, including core principles that can serve Bioregional Organizing Teams:

— Small is good, small is all. (The large is a reflection of the small.)
— Change is constant. (Be like water.)
— There is always enough time for the right work.
— There is a conversation in the room that only these people at this moment can have. Find it.
— Never a failure, always a lesson.
— Trust the People. (If you trust the people, they become trustworthy.)
— Move at the speed of trust.
— Focus on critical connections more than critical mass—build the resilience by building the relationships.
— Less prep, more presence.
— What you pay attention to grows.

In addition to the "emergent strategy" that brown describes as arising from the multiplicity of relatively small actions, a formally articulated Bioregional Regeneration Strategy can provide substantial coherence and guidance to organizing efforts. We, as authors, are agnostic on whether a Bioregional Regeneration Strategy should be developed prior to the creation of a version of the first BFF. However, the governance of this preliminary facility needs to be structured so that when the strategy is developed, the mandate of the facility transitions to raising and allocating financial resources in service to the realization of this strategy document.

Bioregional Regeneration Strategy - A detailed plan and set of processes for how a given bioregion will be regenerated over time, including a guide to the worldviews, values, and principles recommended in approaching the work. The plan should be developed through an open, transparent, participatory process involving a wide range of representatives within the bioregion and could be adopted at a bioregional congress. The strategy is built on a baseline assessment of the current state, including existing regenerative projects and organizations, a comprehensive mapping of key opportunities and threats facing the bioregion, and a systemic analysis of the priority transition areas (e.g. food systems, energy systems, housing, transport). This assessment may be guided by such tools as the Doughnut Economics methodology as introduced in Section 1. The strategy is informed by the history and essence of the place and could span 20-100+ years (or multiple generations) into the future. The Bioregional Regeneration Strategy serves as the basis for ongoing adaptive management in the region, and is itself updated as conditions warrant. Processes to guide Bioregional Organizing Teams on how to develop a Bioregional Regeneration Strategy are already underway.

Table 1. Key Actors

Key actors to be consulted early in the bioregional organizing process[102]

Indigenous peoples[103]

> Local residents, across generations, and community organizers

> Those working on the land, including farmers, foresters, and fishermen, and those with living histories of personal or ancestral relationships to the land - for example agricultural slaves, migrant laborers, refugees, and laborers on ecologically transformative infrastructure projects

> Professionals in the areas of regeneration, resilience, adaptation, or conservation, including biologists, social workers, hydrologists, geologists, teachers, guides, developers, civil engineers

> Informal community groups and citizen associations

> Community weavers, artists, and healers

> Local and regional nonprofits

> Public agencies with decision-making authority in the bioregion, at the local, county, regional, or state level, as well as politicians and policymakers

> Chambers of commerce and local businesses whose future is linked to the health of the bioregion

> Engineers, design professionals including architects, and ecologists

> Educators and academic organizations doing relevant research

> Existing and potential funders or financiers supporting regeneration

Ecological integrity - The ability of an ecosystem to support and maintain ecological processes and a diverse community of organisms.[104]

Supported by the Bioregional Organizing Team, a wider group of local stakeholders embarks on a journey to regenerate ecological integrity in their bioregion. It is important that this type of early engagement includes the effective navigation of relationships and protocols with local Indigenous peoples, assisting in bridging the cultural gap between local Indigenous and non-Indigenous people, and starting to build systems of trust-based co-stewardship.

All regeneration efforts are eventually aligned with the co-created Bioregional Regeneration Strategy and will seek to generate a range of returns across the spectrum of natural, social, and economic or financial returns – as well as the return of inspiration to communities in the bioregion.

102 Adapted from Lawrence Grodeska and the Bay Delta Trust.
103 That may be living there or may have been displaced.
104 IPBES: Ecological Integrity

Table 2. Illustrative regenerative actions and returns (inspired by 4 Returns Framework)[105]

INSPIRATION

Actions:	*Returns:*
> Connecting people to place and ecology > Revitalizing a sense of beauty > Experiencing positive change > Collective visioning through art	> Sense of purpose > Sense of connection to place & ecology, identity, pride, and belonging > Return of hope

ECOLOGICAL

Actions:	*Returns:*
> Rewilding > Restoring water cycles > Wildlife corridors > Ecological conservation > Carbon sequestering and emission reduction > Regenerative agriculture & forestry	> Soil health improvement > Increased biodiversity > Restored water cycles and improved water quality > Resilience against extreme weather > Mitigation of natural hazards > Increased food security and sovereignty

SOCIAL

Actions:	*Returns:*
> Revitalization of spiritual practices, healing rituals and language > Youth engagement and empowerment > Education > Food, music, storytelling, arts & culture > Bioregional and watershed identity > Connecting interrelated social issues within a bioregional lens > Bioregional learning	> Social connections > Human health (physical, mental, spiritual, etc.) > Knowledge > Skills > Safety

ECONOMIC AND FINANCIAL

Actions:	*Returns:*
> Building regenerative food industries > Establishing local, community-owned renewable energy production > Empowering local entrepreneurship > Promoting social entrepreneurship > Establishing ecotourism > Bioregional frameworks and place-based economy > Supporting the transition to relational economies	> Direct & indirect local job creation > Land value uplift > Profit and economic prosperity > Local investment opportunities > Financial return on investment > Lower value-at-risk

105 Commonland: 4 Returns Framework & 4 Returns Platform

3.2 The phases of multi-stakeholder bioregional regeneration

As seen in the pioneering and successful work of both Bioregional Weaving Labs and Regenerate Cascadia, efforts can be organized in 5 phases of Preparation, Mapping and Analysis, Convening and Activation, Co-initiation and Co-creation, and finally Co-evolution. This is, accordingly, a process that organizing teams may want to follow, and is outlined below (also see Table 4 for an overview).

The initial phase of **Preparation** allows the Bioregional Organizing Team to form, clarify roles, and build a shared understanding of the mission – stewarding the regeneration of their bioregion. Often, this team of intrinsically motivated and dedicated individuals is "hosted" by one or more already established backbone[106] organizations that allows the team to use its facilities and provides it with initial resources. The hosting organization is usually a mission-oriented entity that already seeks to drive change in the region in some way.

During the second phase, **Mapping and Analysis**, the organizing team convenes local Indigenous peoples and residents alongside subject matter experts to share their unique knowledge of place in order to better understand the current state of the region and the small watersheds and landscapes within it. This phase comprises a combination of participatory processes such as place mapping and high-level mapping of biophysical, social, and economic systems; assets and opportunities; and risks, needs, or challenges (see *Table 3.*). These become powerful tools for analysis and decision making, and enable the development of a shared and coherent story of place that can be built on in later phases. Particular attention should be given to stocks and flows of natural assets (including potential uplift).[107] The 4 Losses and 4 Returns[108] approach can be used in this process. Asset mapping is another tool which may be used – a systematic process by which Bioregional

---

106 Healthcare Value Hub: What are backbone organizations?
107 There are a variety of tools Bioregional Organizing Teams can use to assess historic, current, and potential future biophysical and economic values of natural assets including those offered by: Cultivo, Landbanking Group, and Credit Nature.
108 Commonland: The 4 Losses and 4 Returns

Organizing Teams can catalog key services, benefits, and resources within the bioregion, aligned with the Bioregional Regeneration Strategy. These would include natural assets, individuals' skill sets, organizational resources, physical space, institutions, associations, and elements of the local economy.[109] Using a similar methodology, the team can map key ecological, social, and economic risks specific to the particular bioregion – for example, mining sites that require reclamation, oil or gas wells leaking methane, or a dam that is contributing to ongoing ecological destruction.

In the Mapping and Analysis phase, the organizing team will also seek to understand potential levers for systemic change, and to establish a high-level Theory of Change[112]. Key stakeholders and their relationships will be mapped, the boundaries of the bioregion may begin to be defined (see Section 2.1), and an overview of already established change initiatives, both incremental and systemic, will be created. Finally, an initial mapping of potential investment sources for the organizing team and for bioregional interventions more broadly can be a useful step during this phase.

In the third phase, **Convening and Activation**, the organizing team facilitates multiple forums and activities, deliberately including a wide range of stakeholder groups in collective and highly participatory processes to drive deep biocultural regeneration as outlined above. Integrating community art, ritual, ceremony, and conviviality into this activation phase enables networks of trust to form, from which a shared vision for the landscape is co-created for example, in the form of a manifesto (see BWL South East Ireland case study). This joint vision serves as the foundation for the subsequent development of a long-term Bioregional Regeneration Strategy, such as the BIORE-GIONAL PLAN 2030 of the Amazon Sacred Headwaters Alliance. This 'living blueprint' to protect 86 million acres of bio-culturally diverse tropical rainforests was developed through a three-and-a-half year participatory process. 30 Indigenous nations in Ecuador and Peru drew on their Indigenous stewardship visions and practices, and the principles of "Buen Vivir" (an Indigenous approach to collective well-being), to identify "solution pathways".[113]

When it is time to move into the fourth phase of **Co-initiation and Co-creation**, the organizing team may want to establish or empower the establishment of one or several stand-alone Bioregional Hubs, as outlined in Section 3.3, that can help enhance local capacity and prepare projects for potential investments. A key focus in this phase is placed on aligning existing initiatives with the Bioregional Regeneration Strategy, and amplifying their impact in accordance with the strategy. Simultaneously, the engagement of activated stakeholders may lead to the inception of new projects and initiatives. Drawing inspiration from successful models elsewhere, proven solutions can be adapted to suit the unique context of the bioregion. It is in this phase that we also suggest properly setting up BFFs, as detailed in Section 4.

---

109   Rural Health Innovation Hub: Clear Impact Asset Mapping Toolkit
110   Regenesis Group: Story of Place
111   Credit to Lawrence Grodeska of the Bay Delta Trust
112   Wikipedia: Theory of Change
113   The bioregional plan seeks to address five shared bioregional objectives: improving living conditions, advancing Indigenous rights and territorial governance, stopping deforestation and degradation, conserving forests and restoring degraded areas, and stopping the advancement of extractive industries (Amazon Sacred Headwaters)

Table 3. Bioregional asset and risk mapping

Bioregional Assets[111]	Bioregional Risks
> *Human Capital:* Indigenous communities historically living in the bioregion (incl. tribes, communities, languages, sites of importance, historical settlement patterns, etc.) and Individuals & other potential allies (incl. local heroes, power brokers, community leaders, activists, tradition- bearers, regeneration/ resilience/adaptation/ conservation professionals, artists, writers, musicians) > *Cultural Capital:* Recurring events (incl. fairs and festivals, parades, public holidays) and history & traditions (incl. memorable events, cultural traditions, historic building sites) > *Institutional Capital:* Non-profit institutions, higher educational institutions, local public institutions, citizen associations, private institutions > *Related Projects, Programs & Services:* Any existing initiatives in alignment with bioregional regeneration. > *Natural Assets:* Waterways, national parks/forests, state parks, community/ regional parks, greenways/linear parks, urban parks, community gardens, other public spaces, material feedstocks, composting facilities, etc. > *Infrastructure:* Water treatment facilities, water utilities and associated infrastructure, electrical grid, composting facilities, universities, hospitals, public transportation, agriculture, cities, etc. > *Datasets*: Resident demographics, resident attitudes and attributes, GIS layers (water, soil, flora, land use, etc.), MRV	> *Natural Hazards:* Risks related to natural disasters such as floods, earthquakes, wildfires, hurricanes, tsunamis, and landslides. > *Ecological:* Risks to ecological systems and ecosystem services, such as disruptions to food webs, loss of keystone species, invasive species, soil erosion, and habitat fragmentation. > *Climate Change:* Risks associated with climate change, including rising temperatures, changing precipitation patterns, sea-level rise, extreme weather events, and their impacts on ecosystems and communities. > *Socio-economic:* Risks related to socio-economic factors, including poverty, inequality, food insecurity, access to clean water and sanitation, economic vulnerabilities, demographic shifts, and social conflicts. > *Health:* Risks to public health, including infectious diseases, air and water pollution-related illnesses, vector-borne diseases, and other health impacts associated with ecological degradation. > *Infrastructure:* Risks to critical infrastructure such as transportation networks, energy systems, water supply systems, and communication networks as well as from legacy infrastructure such as abandoned oil and gas wells or mines. > *Governance and Institutional:* Risks related to governance structures, institutional capacities, policy gaps, regulatory frameworks, and governance failures that may exacerbate ecological and socio-economic risks.

Note: This table is not comprehensive.

This includes the meticulous identification of a decentralized governance structure that empowers citizens to become decision-makers in financial resource allocation and the recruitment of a skilled management team. To broaden the scope of the bioregional regeneration process and to democratize agency, additional stakeholders are invited to engage, while efforts are made to explore and adapt cutting-edge bioregional governance systems. A concerted communication strategy can be implemented to share learnings and efforts with the wider public, and channels may be established for effective communication with neighboring bioregions, fostering collaboration and knowledge exchange.

Throughout all phases, it is important to understand this process as **Co-evolution**: a continuous cycle of adaptive iterations. Learnings need to be integrated on an ongoing basis and actions adapted to emergent developments[114] in complex undertakings such as bioregional regeneration through a bottom-up multi-stakeholder approach. Mutual exchange of learnings and insights with regeneration teams of other bioregions can inform the process and create a strong tapestry of bioregional work around the world.

While these phases can be initiated in a linear fashion, they can also be referenced nonlinearly through an ecosystem approach, particularly for bioregions with an extensive history of organizing. For example, Mapping & Analysis and Co-evolution may happen throughout all phases, supporting iterative sense-making and learning for robust Co-initiation and Co-creation activities. See Regenerate Cascadia's case study as an example of a large bioregion with extensive bioregional organizing history engaging these phases nonlinearly.

The Bioregional Weaving Labs in Europe provide an example of a network of organizations championing bioregional regeneration that follow most of the process as described above. A more detailed case study with a spotlight on the bioregion in the South East of Ireland, is provided below (see Case Study 2).

114 More on working with emergence in adrienne marie brown's book *Emergent Strategy.*

Table 4. Recap: The phases of multi-stakeholder bioregional regeneration[115]

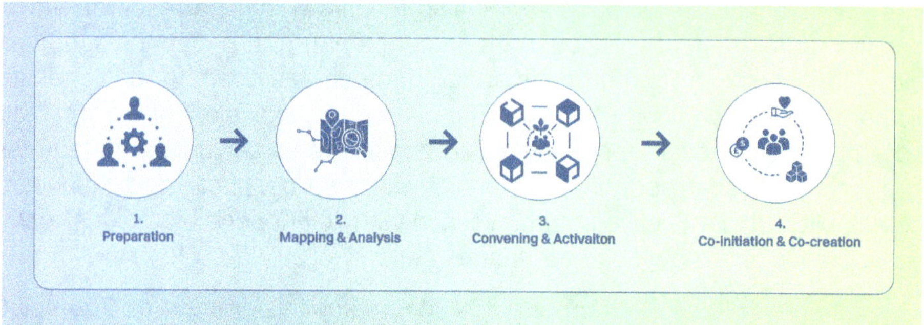

Phase	Activities	Actors

1. Preparation	> Formation of organizing team with strong connections to place and well-established network across the bioregion
	  > Clarification of roles
	  > Shared understanding of mission
		"Hosting" organization(s) that initiate or support the organizing team

2. Mapping & Analysis	> Stakeholder interviews & workshops to learn about and build on potential previous mapping exercises and analyses > High-level mapping and analysis of physical, biological, social, cultural, and economic systems; assets and opportunities; and risks, needs, or challenges > High-level system change analysis and Theory of Change > Mapping of key stakeholders & relationships > Definition of bioregional boundaries > Mapping of past and current bioregional interventions (incremental & systemic) > Mapping of investment sources for the organizing team and for bioregional interventions	Organizing team + subject matter experts (incl. Indigenous peoples)

115 Credits to the teams of Bioregional Weaving Labs and Regenerate Cascadia.

3. Convening & Activation	> Engaging and building trust among a critical mass of stakeholders > Coherence-building activities to establish a shared bioregional context and narrative for diverse stakeholders to align within > Defining joint landscape vision (e.g. manifesto) > Defining Bioregional Regeneration Strategy based on outputs from Mapping & Analysis and Convening activities	Organizing team + special facilitators
4. Co-initiation & Co-creation	> Setup of Bioregional Hub (Section 3.3) to build capacity and get projects ready to receive grants or investment > Alignment of existing projects with Bioregional Regeneration Strategy + scaling their impact > Setup of new projects & initiatives by activated stakeholders > Adapting proven solutions from elsewhere > Setup of Bioregional Financing Facilities (Section 4.2), identification of governance board and support with hiring management team > Inviting additional stakeholders into overall Bioregional Regeneration process > Exploring and adapting new Bioregional Governance Systems that support consistent representation/collaboration across all scales of the bioregion > Communicating efforts to the wider public > Creating channels of communication with neighboring bioregions	Organizing team + activated stakeholders + subject matter experts
5. Co-evolution [throughout all phases]	> Continuously integrating learnings and evolving the interventions based on emergent developments > Continuous co-learning and exchange with multi stakeholders within the bioregion and externally with other bioregional regeneration teams	Coordinated by organizing team

The Bioregional Weaving Lab in South East Ireland – An Example of a Multi-stakeholder Process for Bioregional Regeneration

By Sarah Prosser & Karin Müller

About Bioregional Weaving Labs

A Bioregional Weaving Lab (BWL) is a geographically grounded, multi-stakeholder partnership process that connects place, people, and projects to regenerate bioregions. It builds capacity and supports local Changemakers and their communities, including regenerative farmers, social entrepreneurs, leaders in public institutions, corporate leaders, NGOs, students, educators etc., in coordinating collective action for the required change on a systemic level. The idea is that an inclusive process leads to more local ownership and better implementation of more resilient and effective strategies to accelerate the uptake and scaling of regenerative practices – like agro-ecology, agroforestry, seagrass restoration, and other Nature-based Solutions.

The BWL approach combines the emerging leadership practice of 'Weaving', with a Theory U-inspired lab process and a holistic impact framework to generate 4 Returns in the bioregions (natural, social, and financial returns, and the return of inspiration). Each BWL is led by one or a small team of dedicated 'Weavers', often hosted by strong local partner organizations, and supported by the international BWL Backbone Team. All the bioregional weaving teams across Europe are participating in the overarching BWL Learning Network with regular online sessions and an annual Learning Summit to catalyze peer-to-peer learning. Apart from the Learning Network, the BWL collective is building a growing portfolio of systemic, regenerative innovations and practices from all over the world – including from Ashoka Fellows – that are community-based, replicable and scalable, and can inspire and support the bioregions in their regenerative landscape development.

The Bioregional Weaving Labs (BWL) Collective is a growing international alliance that currently consists of 30+ organizations, including Ashoka and Commonland, working together to mobilize one million Changemakers to restore, protect and regenerate one million hectares of land and sea in Europe by 2030. The Collective is representing hundreds of practitioners in the field, like farmers and nature conservationists, and has the ambition to grow into an international movement of regenerative Changemakers.

Since January 2022, the Bioregional Weaving Labs Collective has activated

25 Weavers facilitating 8 BWLs in 8 countries in Europe: Ireland, Germany, The Netherlands, Austria, Romania, France, Spain, and Poland.

BWL South East Ireland

The BWL in South East Ireland, was one of the first ones to be established and has since facilitated a series of place-based trust-building activities as well as regular multi-stakeholder workshops with farmers, local institutions and social innovators in the bioregion. The workshops are designed to look at systemic and mindset changes needed for landscape transformation through collective action, and have proven to be a space where isolated initiatives find strength in numbers and a sense of belonging.

The South East of Ireland is dominated by intensive agricultural practices, mostly dairy and beef, supplying a major export market, with smaller areas of upland features along the northern edge of the bioregion, and a craggy coastline to the south facing out to the Celtic Sea and the Atlantic beyond. The effects of extractive business practices and broken food systems are becoming increasingly visible in this superficially green and thriving corner of Europe. Water quality is poor in many of the rivers, dairy farming has reached a point where the carrying capacity of the land and soil is exceeded, and communities are detached from nature, and each other, due to urban growth and shifts in social connections in rural settings. There is an increasing awareness of the fragility of the situation and the harmful effects of such systems. There is also an increasing determination to do something that will restore and regenerate the region, but there is little access to knowledge or demonstrations of how to make such a major change.

An early initiative in the work of the Irish BWL was to give local stakeholders ownership of their own vision for the future of their food systems - and the changes that will be needed in local natural and social structures to get there. They did this by co-writing this powerful manifesto that now guides the direction and content of the BWL work in Ireland.

The multiple activities and initiatives led by the BWL in South East Ireland represent both the tangible and intangible aspects of transformative change. The weaving staff support local projects with micro catalyst grants, and by creating shared language and sharing tools that facilitate systemic and collective change. Events have included landscape walks and artistic interventions, as well as formal workshops and seminars. Over the course of 18 months, ten concepts have emerged as being both innovative and potentially collectively impactful in their ability to achieve the shared vision in the manifesto and contribute to the overall mission of the European BWL collective. The concepts range from new kinds of regenerative farming to rural hubs, from upland sustainability through generations to unleashing the social capital of the third age[116], and from a mission-driven geopark to stiching nature corridors together across the bioregion.

In addition, the BWL in South East Ireland is involved in a 'deep demonstration' partnership with the Irish government to test landscape approaches to the future of sustainable dairy. These activities and approaches mean that the BWL is now in a position to i) establish a new entity – the Bioregional Weaving Alliance – designed to support learning and initiatives leading to bioregional regeneration, restoration and protection, especially in the South East, and ii) offer a portfolio of emerging concepts for holistic investment.

An emerging portfolio of regeneration projects

The portfolio of concepts can be thought of as a collection of systemic innovations that together can trigger a bioregional transition to local regenerative economies as well as thriving landscapes and communities, in line with the manifesto and overall BWL mission. The portfolio was developed through residential and local workshops – including at the evocative localities of Dromana House on the Blackwater river and the Coastguard Cultural Centre overlooking Tramore Bay. A major conference was held to consider innovative landscape and community financing using the portfolio and the support platform of the BWL and its BWL catalyst funds as a case study.

Currently the 10 concepts are in the process of being matured and developed to become fundable and investable as an integrated portfolio of critical interventions for the bioregion. The concepts are interdependent and entangled, and the local team believes that only when viewed as a whole can investment and finance flows expect to address unexpected externalities, risks beyond linear value chains, and the potential of holistic aggregated returns. The hope is that investment in such an emergent portfolio will catalyze large-scale positive change for communities and for the landscape – and generate inspiration, social, natural, and financial capital.

Both the weaving team and local stakeholders are determined to find new ways of holistically financing the regeneration of their bioregion through a support structure and emergent portfolio that is built on local knowledge and bottom-up decision-making and inclusive, equitable governance structures.

116 Referring to the lives of those who are retired but not facing any disability stereotypically associated with the "old." (Radtke et al.: Aging, Identity, and Women: Constructing the Third Age)

3.3 Bioregional Hubs

As early as 1983, legendary systems thinker Donella Meadows envisioned "[...] *a number of centers where information and models about resources and the environment are housed."* She said, *"There would need to be many of these centers, all over the world, each one responsible for a discrete bioregion. They would contain people with excellent minds and tools, but they would not be walled off, as scientific centers so often are, either from the lives of ordinary people or from the realities of political processes. The people in these centers would be at home with farmers, miners, planners, and heads of state and they would be able both to listen to, and talk to, all of them."* [117]

Meadows was outlining the capabilities of an institution that would function as a place-based knowledge broker and capacity builder to catalyze collaborative action toward what we now call regenerative economies. She called these institutions Bioregional Learning Centers (BLCs). Today, there are dozens of such centers[118] established around the world – like BLC South Devon, UK (see Case Study 3: The Bioregional Learning Center in South Devon) and BLC Barichara, Colombia. Organizers from around the world gather regularly to share insights and strategies from BLCs in digital learning forums like the Design School for Regenerating Earth's 'Birthing BLCs' program. These centers typically focus on education, research, and skill-building related to the specific ecological, cultural, and social aspects of a bioregion. They offer various programs, workshops, seminars, and courses that focus on topics such as ecology, permaculture, sustainable living practices, Indigenous knowledge, and local history. The primary goal is to provide opportunities for individuals and communities to deepen their understanding of the unique characteristics and challenges of their bioregion, while equipping them with the knowledge and skills necessary for regenerative living and stewardship of place.

Building on and extending the concept of Bioregional Learning Centers, we suggest the development of Bioregional Hubs. A Bioregional Hub can be designed as part of a process of more comprehensive bioregional organizing, or

117 Meadows: History of the ideas underlying the Ballaton Group
118 Joe Brewer: What is a Bioregional Learning Center?

it can be a node that initiates the organizing. Each hub could provide the critical technical, place-based, and grassroots work needed for BFFs to effectively support the transition to regenerative bioregional economies. One bioregion may have multiple hubs, each supporting a specific community, or with a focus on a certain geography or aspect of the bioregional system. Critical roles that Bioregional Hubs can perform to support the development of BFFs include:

1. ***Stewarding the implementation of the Bioregional Regeneration Strategy***

   In order for a genuinely bottom-up transition to a regenerative economy to succeed across a bioregion, local stakeholders have to align on a vision and unifying strategy that guides the various projects. The Bioregional Regeneration Strategy is built on a baseline assessment of the current state, a comprehensive mapping of key opportunities and threats facing the bioregion, and a systemic analysis of the significant transition areas that are apparent in the local context (e.g. food systems, energy systems, housing, transport). This process may be guided by tools like the Doughnut Economics methodology introduced in Section 1.

2. ***Listening, ongoing and comprehensive systems mapping & research***

   Bioregional Hubs are well-positioned to organize listening sessions to tap into what regenerators want to focus on in the short, medium, and long-term. In many cases, this can and should be based upon positive regenerative land use activities already under way in the Bioregion. These activities are often underfunded, and may represent existing "shovel ready" projects. Additionally, Hubs can carry out ongoing, contextual systems mapping exercises to identify which systems the local community wants to work on shifting first, and map a strategy for doing so. Hubs can also conduct research programs informed by listening sessions and the systems mapping.[119]

---

119 This mapping can highlight interdependencies between systems and can include an assessment of dynamics such as feedback loops, tipping points, and leverage points.

3. *Capacity building & upskilling*

New skills and capabilities will be required across sectors to mitigate the compounding effects of ecological collapse, and for the regenerative transition of economies and societies. Bioregional Hubs can provide the institutional framework for the necessary upskilling and capacity building. In addition, they can curate programming and education for community members of the bioregion as well, strengthening climate resilience and community weaving.[120] Bioregional Hubs can ensure that Traditional Ecological Knowledge (TEK) and Indigenous wisdom[122] are integrated with cutting-edge scientific insights and that wisdom and knowledge are paired to inform regenerative action across the bioregion. When dominant culture and economic forces orient to TEK and Indigenous wisdom as *tools to be used* for some form of gain in power, status, or wealth, this can lead to the cooptation of ideas and the erosion of sacred meaning. To guard against this, access to and the sharing of TEK and Indigenous wisdom must be navigated with deep care in alignment with local practice and guidance from Indigenous leadership. This knowledge will likely need to have strongly held membranes around who accesses which components and in what way.[123] These exchanges should be built on a foundation and recognition of Indigenous sovereignty. In some cases, it may be possible to co-locate Bioregional Hubs and Indigenous Knowledge Systems Labs[124], which can support Indigenous co-design. This function of Bioregional Hubs will enable the devel-

Traditional Ecological Knowledge (TEK) – The ongoing accumulation of knowledge, practice, and belief about relationships between living beings in a specific ecosystem that is acquired by Indigenous people over hundreds or thousands of years through direct contact with the environment, handed down through generations, and used in life-sustaining ways. It encompasses the world view of a people, which includes ecology, spirituality, human and animal relationships, and more.[121]

120 The hosting and facilitation of trainings and gatherings can be an important revenue stream for Bioregional Hubs. Bioregional hubs may also serve as a maker space or co-working space – other potential sources of revenue.
121 U.S. National Park Service: Traditional Ecological Knowledge
122 In *Social Forestry: Tending the Land as a People of Place*, Tomi Hazel Vaarde differentiates between TEK and Indigenous Ecological Knowledge (IEK), with TEK being defined as "a collection of stories and procedures that holds wisdom and pertinence for Place-based culture." Vaarde notes that "some TEK survives in epics that have been moved through migration, yet still contain resonance in a newly settled Place." This differs from IEK which is based on an unbroken tradition of land stewardship held by a specific lineage of people in a particular place, usually involving regular ritual or ceremonial practices over millennia. In this book, we use the term 'Indigenous wisdom' as a more general term that certainly includes IEK, but is not limited to the category of ecology. We suggest that a thorough understanding of the term IEK would not consider ecology as something separate from other aspects of existence, wisdom, or fields of study, however we use the more general term to limit the risk that readers confine their interpretation within a separate category, something the Western mind has been trained to do.
123 Practice of the R Values is critical here. (see Page 70)
124 The initial Indigenous Knowledge Systems Lab is based at Deakin University, Australia. Dozens of additional Labs are under exploration.

opment of projects and organizations that BFFs can invest in, as well as increasing their likelihood of success, thus de-risking investments.

4. ***Identification and incubation/acceleration of regenerative business cases***

Being deeply embedded in a local bioregional context, Bioregional Hubs will play a critical role in both identifying and supporting regenerative business cases or projects that are aligned with the Bioregional Regeneration Strategy. Both structured and needs-based programs can support the formation of regenerative projects and organizations, and incubate and accelerate them. Drawing on their embeddedness in communities and ecosystems, Bioregional Hubs will also play a critical role in organizing synergistic portfolios of existing and new projects and organizations that BFFs can then invest in. All of this, again, will be informed by the land use and systems mapping capabilities that Bioregional Hubs can provide. This function supports the development of approaches to catalyzing the economic transition.[125]

5. ***Transparent and real-time progress tracking & data collection***

Bioregional Hubs have the potential to aggregate Monitoring, Reporting, and Verification (MRV), by providing transparent, real-time progress tracking against the Bioregional Regeneration Strategy and agreed-upon evaluation metrics. MRV can help with effective financial capital deployment and optimization of impact. While we recommend that comprehensive bioregional MRV is managed under the Bioregional Trust (see Section 4), it is possible that Bioregional Hubs feed into data aggregation. By playing a critical role in identifying localized metrics, evaluating effective monitoring tools, and calibration to ensure accuracy, Hubs might act as important partners to a BFF by distributing work among practitioners and collecting aggregate MRV information to track results. Additionally, MRV technology could be tested at a Hub site – another potential source of revenue for Hubs.

125 Including the building blocks of technological, legal, financial, governance, and other innovation.

6. ***Curating interfaces with global networks of Bioregional Hubs & Learning Centers***

As part of an international network, individual Bioregional Hubs can ensure that local experiences are shared beyond the boundaries of the bioregion, catalyzing action around the world. Simultaneously, Hubs can draw on the data, knowledge, and wisdom in the global network to inform ongoing regenerative action and, as a result, financial resource governance. Coordination between Hubs can help to establish and share frameworks, optimize operations, channel opportunities, and inform data assessment, best practices, and other activities.

The Bioregional Learning Center in South Devon – Modeling Bioregional Hubs

By Isabel Carlisle

About Bioregional Learning Center South Devon

Bioregional Learning Center South Devon was founded in 2017 by three designers, ecologists and climate activists as a systemic response to the systemic impacts of climate change. The Center works creatively and collaboratively in and at the intersections of economy, ecology, learning, arts and culture and the gaps in between. While the bioregion it covers is South Devon, its projects operate at scales that range from the whole of the South West, to Devon and down to the Dart catchment, or just a stretch of the river.

Bringing a bioregion into being

The Center's aim is to create a resilient region that functions as a learning landscape by making collaboration possible and giving civil society a leading role alongside landowners, experts, NGOs, and policy-makers. Because it has received only a small amount of unrestricted core funding, the evolution of the Center has been mainly through funded projects in which it has honed its way of working. These projects represent the steps for bringing a bioregion into being, and are the core functions that any Bioregional Learning Center would need to perform.

1. Develop a story of place - This regenerative design process enabled the Center to understand the bioregion it serves, how it functions, and where its edges are. The character of a place is revealed by overlaying different lenses, all the way from deep geological time, through social and political history, to land use and human culture. The pattern that is revealed points to where the fuzzy boundaries of this island of coherence lie, and how it relates to its immediately surrounding places and the bigger region or nation. See: Story of Place for NW Plymouth.

2. Reveal the systems within the region - Humans have always lived in webs of life-support systems – both ecosystems and human systems – that meet humanity's basic needs. Today these systems are typically managed by public utility companies and large-scale businesses, and regulated by local authorities and the state. By mapping for vitality in its bioregion, getting out on the land and meeting people, the Center organizing team developed an understanding of local systems and could determine how best to support and connect innovators. See: Learning Journey for Climate Resilience.

3. Intervene and demonstrate - Through leading or participating in projects in our bioregion Center members look for creative ways to intervene in systems such as the drinking water system. In a move towards common pool resource management[126] they make sure to bring in the voice of civil society, as well as experts, using data, design, the arts, and dialogue to bridge the gap between academia, policy makers, and people on the ground. The Center acts as a trusted neutral player, with its learning center as a backbone organization. See: Voices of the Dart.

4. Launch a multi-sector design process - The Center grasped the opportunity to start a big region-wide conversation in establishing the Devon Doughnut Collective. Over a year of fortnightly Zoom meetings, the collective put together an ecological and economic assessment of Devon, with twin-track indicators and pathways to action for both policy-makers and civil society. The Center hosted the project as an action learning endeavor, bringing key change-makers from all sectors into the same space to create an interactive Doughnut, available on a dedicated website. See: The Devon Doughnut.

5. Widen reach and impact - The Center is currently embarking on the first steps to a climate adaptation strategy for the region, with funding from the regional government. In this first year, Center members plan to take elected councilors, government staff, community climate groups, and some members of the UK adaptation community of practice on a 5-day learning journey around the region, to widen the conversation, look at the risks and challenges, and visit the places and people already making strides towards adaptation. The second part of this programme will see the launch of a touring exhibition on climate challenges and adaptation. In future years the Center will set up demonstrator projects and a learning network for exchanging information locally. All of these activities aim to provide capacity building and the upskilling of relevant communities and actors.

6. Document and showcase your learning region - the center continually converts practice into resources to showcase the work, interpret it, and share it, as seen on the website. Center members act as ambassadors for the region on public platforms, and take part in international bioregional conversations. Data, measuring, and working with experts increasingly takes place in a 'backroom' for the bioregion, while polycentric governance grows out of building a network of generative relationships and trust.

Growing a funding ecosystem

BLC is now focusing on designing and prototyping a 'funding ecosystem' in South Devon that can build community and ecological wealth through a linked suite of

---

126 See Elinor Ostrom's 8 Principles for Managing a Commons (Ostrom, 1990).

philanthropic and investment vehicles that can be replicated elsewhere without the need for philanthropic funding. The outcome will not only be a quantifiable return on investment expressed through multiple value gain: the Bioregion is also being skilled up in climate literacy; enhancing the ability of citizens to collect, interpret and share data; and enabling their participation in the governance of the natural systems of the bioregion - water, soil, biodiversity, air, and marine habitats.

The Bioregional funding eco-system will resource, through innovative financial instruments, projects that shift the needle on regenerating systems and the regeneration activators that are leading them. The Center is setting out to prove that there is cascading value, and a return on investment, from working in a joined-up bioregional way. The overall impact of all this interlocking action on a whole bioregion has not yet been modeled. Nor has it been placed into a landscape-wide climate adaptation and resilience plan. The Center believes that the time has come to do that and make the model publicly available as part of growing climate literacy.

4. Designing, Building, and Implementing Bioregional Financing Facilities

4. Designing, Building, and Implementing Bioregional Financing Facilities

"Finance should be in service to the real economy, which should be in service to life."

– Kate Raworth

Once a Bioregional Organizing Team (see *Figure 7.*) has brought together key bioregional actors to develop a Bioregional Regeneration Strategy as part of the Co-initiation & Co-creation phase (see Section 3.2), Bioregional Financing Facilities can be set up[127] to fund and finance the realization of the vision laid out in the strategy.[128] BFFs do this by working hand in hand with the Bioregional Organizing Team and Bioregional Hub to enable the decentralization of financial resource governance, the design of synergistic project portfolios, and the transition to a regenerative economy. Whereas Bioregional Hubs work to bring together and empower a bioregional regeneration network by facilitating regenerative flow of all capital types, BFFs focus specifically – but not exclusively – on facilitating the regenerative flow of financial capital. With this focus, and a staff with relevant expertise, BFFs can facilitate interaction with existing legal, economic, and political systems, and intermediate in ways that a Bioregional Organizing Team or Bioregional Hub may not be designed or resourced for.

127 Or evolved from existing, aligned institutions.
128 Please note (as stated in Section 3) that if a Bioregional Financing Facility is set up before the strategy is agreed upon, that it needs to be able to incorporate the strategy into its governance process once the strategy is created.

Figure 7. Moving from organizing to economic transition and regeneration

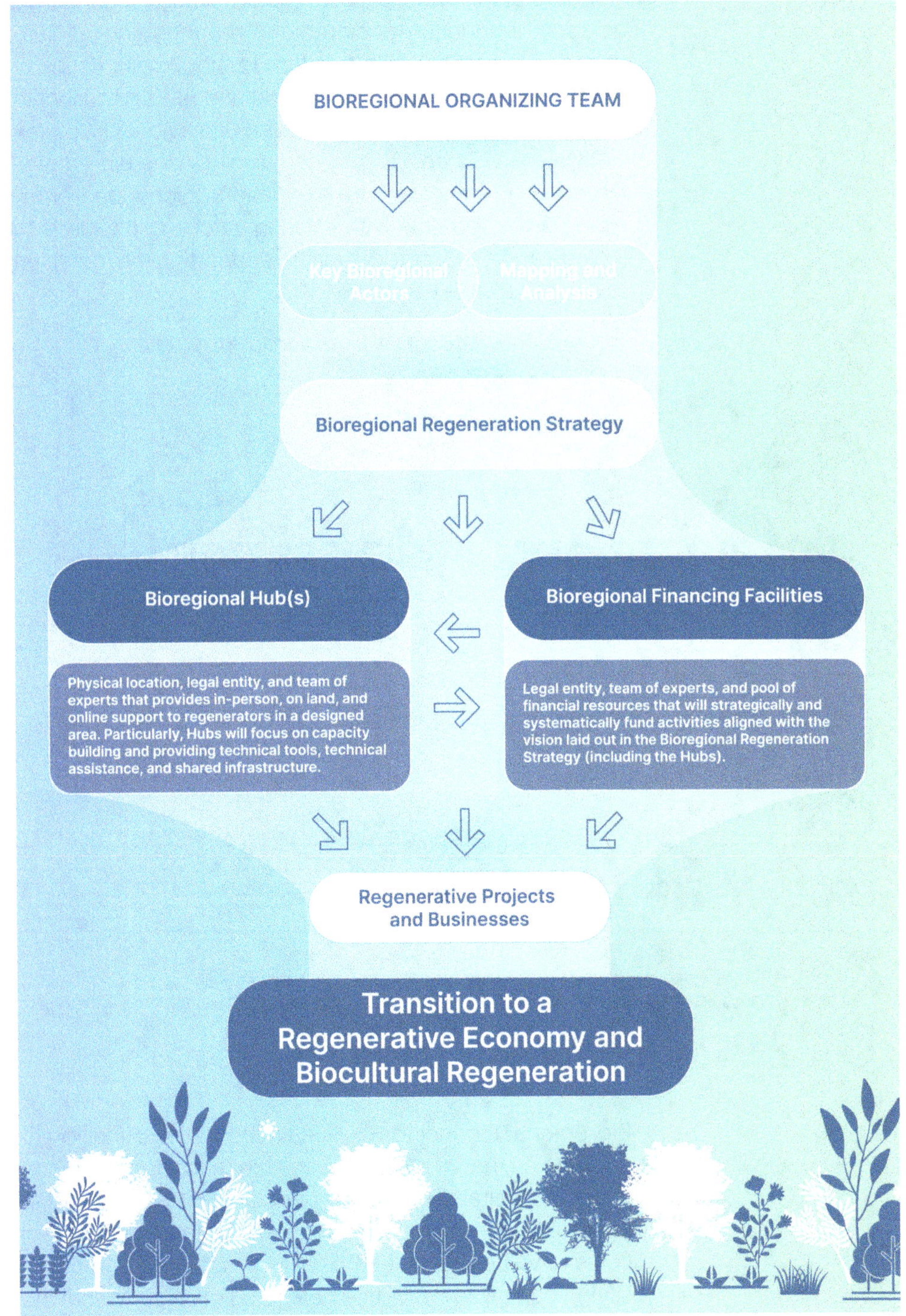
BIOREGIONAL ORGANIZING TEAM
Key Bioregional Actors
Mapping and Analysis
Bioregional Regeneration Strategy
Bioregional Hub(s)
Physical location, legal entity, and team of experts that provides in-person, on land, and online support to regenerators in a designed area. Particularly, Hubs will focus on capacity building and providing technical tools, technical assistance, and shared infrastructure.
Bioregional Financing Facilities
Legal entity, team of experts, and pool of financial resources that will strategically and systematically fund activities aligned with the vision laid out in the Bioregional Regeneration Strategy (including the Hubs).
Regenerative Projects and Businesses
Transition to a Regenerative Economy and Biocultural Regeneration

Together, the Bioregional Organizing Team, Bioregional Hub, and BFFs form the three legs of a stool that can serve as a solid foundation for bioregional regeneration (as illustrated in *Figure 8.*).[129] In addition to funding portfolios of regenerative projects and organizations, BFFs can allocate financial resources to one or more Bioregional Hubs (as illustrated in *Figure 9.*). They can also fund the Bioregional Organizing Team to ensure foundational bioregional organizing work deepens with existing actors, and widens to include additional actors that are supporting the transition to a regenerative economy.

Figure 8. The three legs of bioregional regeneration

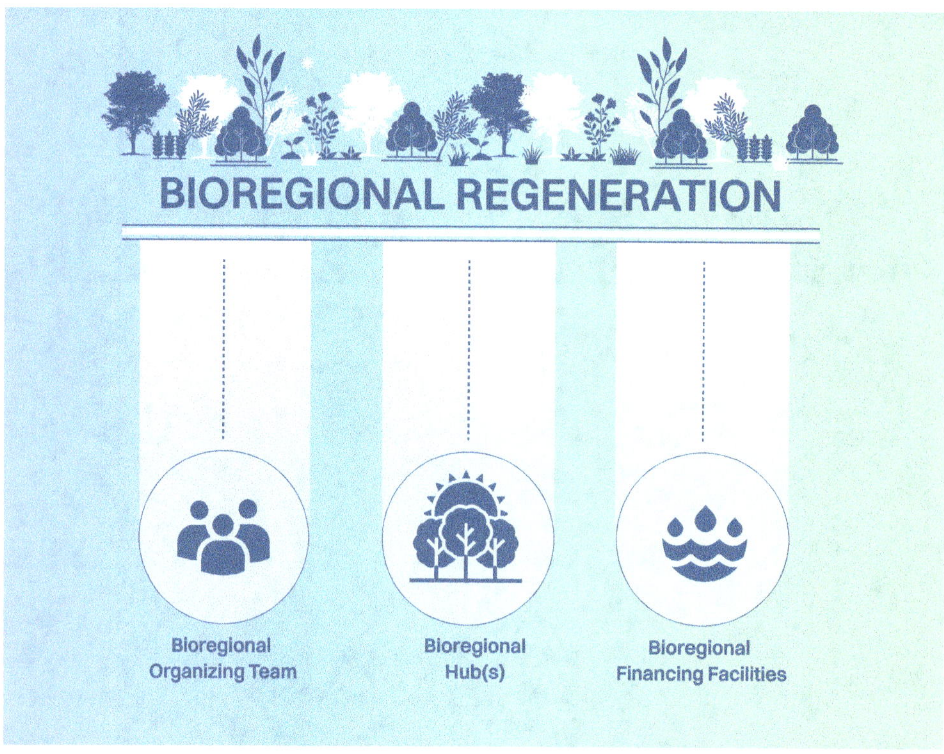

Bioregional Financing Facilities support the transition to economies that are less, rather than more dependent on financial capital overall and financial capital from outside the region, and where financial flows better align with real flows of value. However, this aim of localizing and diversifying capital flow must be navigated carefully within the global historical context in which centuries of colonialism

129 Noting that their role is to realize synergies and build networks between the many critical actors in a bioregion.

and neocolonialism have extracted diverse forms of wealth from certain bioregions and transferred it to others. In places that have grown rich from this extraction, not only will capital diversification be made easier by the excess material and financial capital present, but capital localization efforts made without sincere engagement in decolonial processes of reconciliation, reparation, and healing are likely to further deepen inequality and injustice. In extracted contexts, the need for outside financial capital may be more pressing, and the regenerative impact of financial capital may be greater. Thus, BFFs may offer appropriate infrastructure for forming relationships of solidarity, rebalancing, and reciprocity between diverse regions with shared history.[130] For example, BFFs might enable Indigenous communities to receive and manage Overseas Development Assistance (ODA) from Global North countries to support Indigenous stewardship and the realization of the targets set in the Global Biodiversity Framework.[131]

BFFs will work on creating regenerative flows at multiple levels – at the organizational level and at various levels in nested systems. This includes supporting the development of the enabling environment conditions needed for regenerative organizations to succeed – deepening and expanding markets for regenerative activities; creating regenerating pools of funding to support management of common assets and public goods; raising aligned investment capital; leveraging derisking approaches; and creating cutting edge, integrated MRV strategies.

130 Contribution from Tyler Wakefield.
131 Target 19a of the Global Biodiversity Framework is laid out as follows: "Increasing total biodiversity related international financial resources from developed countries, including official development assistance, and from countries that voluntarily assume obligations of developed country Parties, to developing countries, in particular the least developed countries and small island developing States, as well as countries with economies in transition, to at least $20 billion per year by 2025, and to at least $30 billion per year by 2030."
132 Elinor Ostrom: *Governing the Commons: The Evolution of Institutions for Collective Action*
133 Wikipedia: Public good (economics).

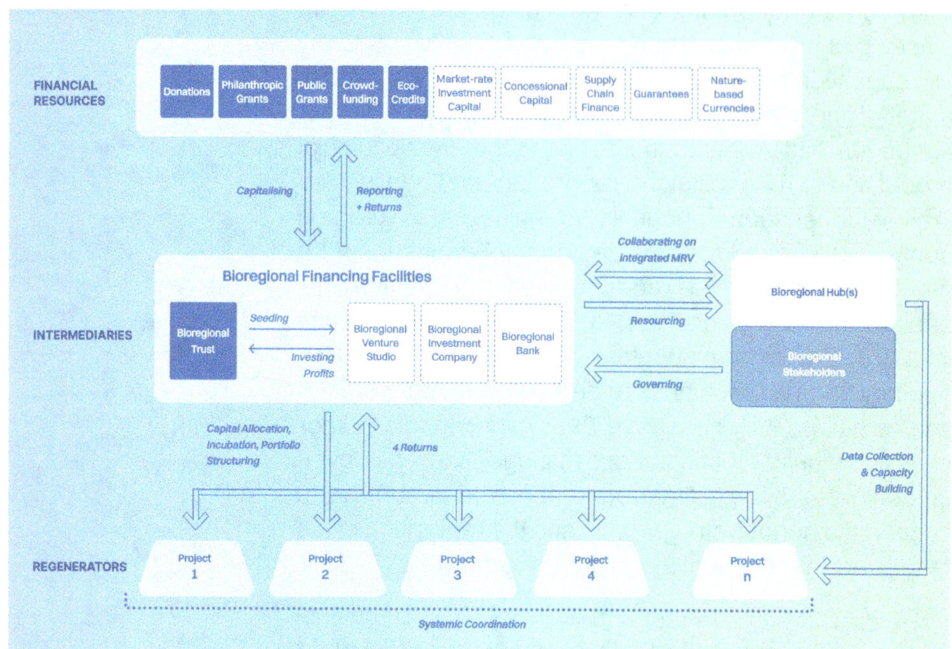

As described in Figure 5 (Section 2), BFFs have the potential to become the connective tissue between various sources of financial capital and grassroots regenerative actors, large land and water projects, and tools and technologies supporting these actors and the economic transition. BFFs can bring much needed financial capital into the mycelial network of bioregional regenerators and bring the integrated benefits of regeneration (we use the 4 Returns framework) to financial capital providers, land and water stewards, and all of the life in the bioregion.

It is up to the Bioregional Organizing Team to decide on the appropriate time to begin the design and implementation of Bioregional Financing Facilities in their bioregion. The team may need to call in specialized expertise[134] to support them in this work.

---

134 A network of consultants working on landscape, watershed, and bioregional-level finance is coming together to support bioregions in this work and will be invited to join the forthcoming BioFi Community of Practice.

4.1 Attributes of Bioregional Financing Facilities

As Bioregional Financing Facilities are designed to serve each unique Bioregional Regeneration Strategy, their structures will vary. Diverse, decentralized organizations can support increased systemic resilience, and improve the effectiveness of BFFs as connective tissue.[135] Therefore, we do not seek to be overly prescriptive on how BFFs should be designed. Instead we lay out twelve high-level attributes our research tells us each facility should work towards, and eventually meet in order to effectively support the realization of the BFF objectives. We then introduce templates for BFFs that can serve as a starting place in design.

Attributes of Bioregional Financing Facilities:

1. **Aim to align with living systems principles and Indigenous wisdom** – BFFs are not meant to be designed as machines to be used for moving money between investors and regenerative activities; they are *themselves meant to serve as regenerative activity*. This is a purpose inseparable from the objective of catalyzing regenerative economies; thus BFFs should work to embody living systems patterns and principles[136] in their organizational design and culture. The BFF, its relationships, the organizations it invests in, the local economy, the global economy, and the broader social and Earth systems they are nested in are all living systems; accordingly, BFFs should foster conditions for health at every level and develop methods for evaluating health in relationship to investment. Finally, BFFs should work to understand contextually-sound Indigenous worldviews, values, and ways of knowing or being that can offer trustworthy guidance on investment and put them into practice. We recommend the "R Values" described in the box below as a place to start. These will naturally support BFFs to invest in ways that recognize the interconnectedness of everything on Earth, as laid out in the Gaia Hypothesis,

R Values – Jan Hania (Tuwharetoa, Raukawa-ki-te Tonga, Te Atiawa of Aotearoa/New Zealand and the Principal of Strategy Development for Biome Trust) uplifts the "R values" of relationality, reciprocity, responsibility, respect, reverence, regeneration, redistribution, and reconnection – noting that language must be contextualized and place-based.[137] The authors also uplift re-membering, restorying, rewilding, and rematriation.

135 Nunes: *Neither Vertical Nor Horizontal*
136 More about this in the Capital Institute's 8 Principles for a Regenerative Economy and the Biomimicry Institute's 6 Life's Principles.
137 The Regeneration Will Be Funded (Podcast): Jan Hania

and in understanding their work as *nature investing in nature* – rather than humans investing in something separate called nature.

> "Nature is a totally efficient, self-regenerating system. If we discover the laws that govern this system and live synergistically within them, sustainability will follow and humankind will be a success."
>
> *– Buckminster Fuller*

2. **Serve the realization of the Bioregional Regeneration Strategy** – Every bioregion will need to develop, adaptively manage, and update as conditions warrant, a long-term (20-100+ year or multigenerational) Bioregional Regeneration Strategy as the guiding document for all bioregional organizing, capacity building, economic development, land use planning, and capital allocation. Every Bioregional Financing Facility that is established sets the Bioregional Regeneration Strategy as its guiding document and raises and deploys financial capital in service to realizing the vision laid out.[138] This attribute makes BFFs unique, in that it focuses their capital on large-scale ecological and social regeneration and the realization of cascading benefits through systems change. In practice, this means that BFFs will need to prioritize bioregional regeneration activities and objectives in order to identify which BFFs to set up and in what sequence. From there, the strategy of each BFF should be crafted, with both the short and long term aspects of the broader Strategy as its objectives. BFFs can create tests to determine whether a given investment supports the transition to the regenerative economy,[139] including healing and reconciliation, or whether it is further entrenching the economy of the bioregion in increasingly fragile global supply chains and systems built on extraction and destruction.

---

138 Alternatively, a Facility creates a legal structure that enables the Strategy to become its guiding document once it is developed if the Bioregional Financing Facility is set up first.
139 Based on the bioregion's vision for the regenerative economy.

3. **Implement an inclusive and participatory governance structure that represents the bioregion** – It is critical that each BFF has a governance structure that is broadly representative of and based on the input of the people living and working in the bioregion, the people that have historically stewarded land in the bioregion if they have been misplaced, and the more than human life in that place. This structure should include management, a board, an investment committee, and participatory processes that feed into its decisions and operations. The role of the Bioregional Organizing Team to organize and activate key bioregional actors is important. Through this trust-building process, the early scaffolding of contextually-sound governance structures and practices can be built, and appropriate bioregional representatives to serve in BFF governance can be identified. The board should be ethnically and culturally representative of bioregional residents and their interests. BFFs should pay special attention to ensure Indigenous groups and communities that have faced structural violence and exploitation are represented in the places where they reside. We also recommend the inclusion of more than human life on BFF boards[140] to ensure that the financial capital raised is not used to narrowly serve human interests, but is allocated to benefit all of the life in the bioregion. Additionally, a process should be established to have regular input from both youth and elders. We also recommend that governance boards rotate periodically in order to bring new energy and ideas to BFFs. A bioregion may decide to hold a town hall, citizens assembly, or election to select board members at regular intervals (more about governance in Section 4.5).

4. **Work to shift power imbalances** – By serving as connective tissue, Bioregional Financing Facilities help address the power imbalances often inherent in funder-fundee or investor-investee relationships. BFFs should work to address the power imbalance between those controlling large amounts of financial capital today and those struggling to resource the implementation of their regenerative projects. This includes imbalances across bioregions, such as those in places that have grown materially rich from colonial extraction and those in places that have been extracted from. It also includes imbalances within bioregions, such as those created by economic, racial, religious, and gender discrimination and violence. The transition to a regenerative economy should lead to a more equitable society where well being for all is prioritized.

BFFs are designed to empower local land, water, and neighborhood stewards to implement the strategies they believe are most effective in their place – recognizing the value of local knowledge in delivering the 4 Returns. One practical way they do this is by working together with Bioregional Hubs to reduce the burden of applying for grants or securing investment capital, and the reporting requirements that come if a project or organization is success-

---

140 The rights of nature movement has made progress, particularly since the inclusion of nature's rights in Ecuador's revised constitution (ratified in 2008), to gain legal recognition of the rights of life other than humans to exist. The Earth Law Center, in particular, has been working to elect oceans, rivers, animals, etc. to corporate boards. These entities are represented by a human proxy that votes on their behalf.

ful in raising capital. Additionally, BFFs can support a shift in the power imbalance between humans and the more-than-human world, and promote greater harmony in the relationships between all life on the planet. At every level, BFFs should work towards restoring 'right relationship' – rooted in the principles of reciprocity and mutualism found in both biology and Indigenous wisdom.[141]

5. **Be transparent and enable empowered participation** – It is critical that Bioregional Financing Facilities meet a high threshold for transparency in capital raising and allocation, to ensure the trust building critical to bioregional regeneration. To the extent possible, BFFs should seek to make documents about capital raising and allocation public, and publish decision criteria about which projects are selected and why. The affiliations of the board, investment committee, and management of BFFs should be disclosed, so conflicts of interest can be observed and addressed as appropriate. Web3 technologies, including blockchain and smart contracts, can support traceability of capital flows. Such robust capital allocation tracking can hopefully enable grant and investment resources that have been wary of funding or financing Indigenous peoples and local communities directly to do so. Transparency will be critical for BFFs to be able to receive ODA, for instance. It can help to move some of the resources stuck in organizations with high overhead and burdensome bureaucracy to the ground where regeneration is happening.

Web3 – In contrast to the current internet era (Web2) characterized by centralized platforms and services where user data is controlled by a few large corporations, Web3 represents an emerging internet that is decentralized, enabled by blockchain technology, where users have greater control over their data, identities, and interactions through peer-to-peer networks and protocols.

Additionally, BFFs should aim to empower everyone in the bioregion to negotiate for their own needs and

141 Inspired by the Capital Institute's 8 Principles for a Regenerative Economy.

contribute their unique gifts towards bioregional regeneration. Through rights of nature and kinship-informed approaches, the conditions for health for the more-than-human life in the bioregion can also be taken into consideration. Beyond implementing a representative governance structure, BFFs might host citizens assemblies or town hall meetings at regular intervals to hear about urgent investment needs directly from community members before making grant or investment decisions. This approach can enable wisdom, innovation, and insights from the edges to inform systems change.[143] A participatory approach could also be applied to grant allocation, including voting on projects (more about this in Section 6) or a prize model (such as the Edge Prize or the Wellbeing Protocol).

6. **Leverage an integrated capital structure that embeds regenerative principles** - BFFs may apply an integrated capital structure that aims to leverage grant capital to mobilize investment capital, large grants (to create BFFs, Bioregional Tithing programs, and eco-credits) to mobilize an even larger sum through many small donations or eco-credit purchases, and local capital to mobilize capital from outside of the bioregion.[144] BFFs aim to (i) rapidly scale up the amount of financial capital flowing to bioregional regeneration; (ii) diversify the types of capital used to meet varied financing needs and risk profiles, in an integrated capital structure; and (iii) strengthen local value flows. The primary objective of the integrated capital structure is not to guarantee investor returns, for which blended finance transactions are often criticized, but to strategically de-risk, change risk perception, fund synergistic portfolios of projects to drive systems change, fund common assets, and stimulate and build markets aligned with regeneration.

Importantly, Bioregional Financing Facilities can enable investors to allocate capital to portfolios of smaller, high impact, synergistic projects driving systems change, increasingly referred to as 'sys-

142 Global Alliance for the Rights of Nature: What are the Rights of Nature?
143 Inspired by the Capital Institute's 8 Principles for a Regenerative Economy
144 Demonstrating that local investors with a deeper understanding of bioregional dynamics and influence in the bioregion can help to reduce perceived risk by external investors and enable them to co-invest.

temic investing',[145] and to do so at scale. Investors can invest in a range of Bioregional Financing Facilities in target geographies, benefitting from both diversification and the 4 Returns these portfolios will achieve. For investors or companies that want to support innovation, the Venture Studio (more details in Section 4.2) can provide exposure to innovation from the edges of the system and from the resurgence of Indigenous knowledge systems – both of which will be critical in building resilience in the years to come.

Potential motivations for investing in bioregional action for philanthropists, investors, corporations, governments, or citizens are wide-ranging (and are explored in detail in Section 4.3). BFFs enable capital holders to invest collaboratively with like-minded funders and financiers. These facilities are designed to support and strengthen relationships, including among funders and financiers and between funders and financiers and the people, places, and changes unfolding in the bioregion. BFFs aim to ensure high levels of credibility and to speak the language of finance in order to establish a solid base of investor confidence. By bridging community-led governance together with current financial industry standards, these facilities also function as important interfaces between local initiatives and external investment – for example, from global capital markets – catalyzing their co-evolution.

7. **Treat growth and returns as a means, not an end** – The cycles of growth and decay are integral to living systems. BFFs are designed to support the transition to a regenerative economy that is rooted in this natural law, and does not mistake growth and returns for ends in themselves. There can be no infinite growth of a material system within a closed environment of finite materials without bringing about its collapse.[146] To this end, BFFs recognize that growth should not be the purpose of a healthy economy or organization and financial returns cannot be the purpose of an investment.[147] Financial models, term sheets, risk assessment approaches, and broader economic transition plans should reflect holistic objectives, deriving from the Bioregional Regeneration Strategy and the goals of regenerative organizations. When determining what level of returns an ecosystem and the people stewarding it can healthfully produce, we recommend BFF leadership apply the principle of the Honorable Harvest[148] in their local social, economic, and ecological context.

145 See the work of the TransCap Initiative.
146 It should be noted that economic growth is the driving force behind the economic policies of most nation states on Earth, and in 2020, Helmut Haberl et al concluded in A systematic review of the evidence on decoupling of GDP, resource use and GHG emissions, part II: synthesizing the insights, that "large rapid absolute reductions of resource use and GHG emissions cannot be achieved through observed decoupling rates."
147 Returns and liquidity can still act as a constraint for investment (inspired by work of the Capital Institute).
148 More about this in Robin Wall Kimmerer's book *Braiding Sweetgrass*.

– Robin Wall-Kimmerer

8. **Raise from purpose-aligned funders or investors** – It will be important to attract capital providers of all types who believe in the importance of realizing the Bioregional Regeneration Strategy and are willing to try new, more relational models for assessing and mitigating risk[149] – such as social credit scores, trust circles, aggregation, and integrated MRV.[150] Many bioregions have socio-economic conditions that limit access to capital for certain communities based on conventional systems of assessing and mitigating risk.[151] BFFs should seek to engage with capital providers who wish to support the decentralization of financial resource governance and the economic transition of the bioregion, and are interested in all 4 Returns. Potential motivations and incentives for various categories of capital providers are laid out in Section 4.3. The realization of bioregional regeneration strategies and success of regenerative organizations will depend upon the flexibility offered by purpose-aligned funders to address the specific barriers to deploying capital within each bioregion and the communities of which they are woven. Growing or deepening the relationship of funders and investors with the bioregion will be key to developing alignment.

9. **Provide aggregation and matchmaking** – Bioregional Financing Facilities will bundle a range of projects and organizations in investment portfolios for systemic change to facilitate streamlined access to investment for small bioregional initiatives, and present an attractive proposition to major funders and investors seeking diversified, impactful, and aligned portfolios focused on bioregional regeneration.[152] This way, Bioregional Financing Facilities effectively bridge the systemic gap between the modest financing demands of in-

---

149 The efficacy of such models has been demonstrated in microlending by the Grameen Bank, BRAC, etc. Additionally there are interesting pilots taking place using social risk metrics to finance on-reservation Native American housing in the US (Flower Hill Institute).

150 Such aligned capital providers may initially account for a small percentage of capital pools, but the push of global efforts to stabilize planetary systems and the pull of BFFs establishing strong track records of bioregional regeneration should increase this percentage rapidly by the late 2020s. In addition, significant pools of purpose-aligned funding should become available through forthcoming loss and damage and reparations payments.

151 In Indian Country in the US, for example, some of the factors contributing to this risk perception include: tribal sovereign powers, inalienability of tribal land, lack of trust and historically poor relationships with colonial financial institutions (credit to Atherton Phleger, Flower Hill Institute).

152 When developing portfolios for impact investors, BFFs can focus on a specific asset class to fit into the investor's capital allocation framework.

dividual projects and the substantial capital required for meaningful impact at scale. The aggregation and matchmaking function also importantly reduces the burden on projects and organizations to engage with the bureaucracy inherent in government, philanthropy, and impact investment, associated with accessing capital and reporting on its use. In their role as connective tissue , BFFs are able to interface with projects and capital providers, speaking the language of both, and meeting the needs of each to help bring them together.

Due to the unique role networks of local support can play in the success of these projects, BFFs may also assist in advancing alternative forms of project selection and underwriting.

10. **Apply an integrated approach to sensing and MRV** - BFFs should develop MRV strategies that leverage modern technology and Traditional Ecological Knowledge (TEK)[153] and Indigenous wisdom, quantitative and qualitative data, and sophisticated modeling and on-the-ground verification by citizen scientists.[154] Together with Bioregional Hubs, there is potential for BFFs in a bioregion to develop a comprehensive MRV strategy and to share the overhead cost of a platform to host this information.[155] This platform should include project or site-specific data and overall bioregional health data to effectively enable tracking of the systemic impact of investments. The platform should be managed as a commons and can enable accountability beyond just the projects BFFs invest in. Technologies such as eDNA analysis, bioacoustics, remote sensing, and life-centered AI[156] can support improved sensing, which can serve BFFs and bioregional citizens in better sensemaking when applied in an integrated framework with TEK, Indigenous wisdom, and citizen science.

There are several ecological MRV platforms available that bring many datasets into one place, that a bioregion might opt to use, together with bottom-up metrics.[157] Building on attributes 7 and 9, an important efficiency of BFFs is that they aggregate MRV, reducing the burden of reporting and due diligence on individual projects and investors. These tools have the ability to meet on-the-ground projects where they are—through workflows, automation, and locally designed interfaces that interoperate with existing tools. This, combined with

153 See differentiation between TEK, Indigenous Ecological Knowledge,and Indigenous wisdom in section 3 (Vaarde 2023).

154 Examples of direct compensation mechanisms for Indigenous communities for species monitoring/tracking include Biocultural Jaguar Credits issued on Regen Registry and the Biodiversity Credits issued by Savimbo.

155 An entity like the developing Nature Tech Collective could possibly support BFFs in this area.

156 Active Inference technology might be particularly relevant here since it is based on the cognitive processes of humans and other species, embedded in particular geospatial settings, and inherently trackable and traceable (Designing Ecosystems of Intelligence from First Principles, Karl Friston et al.) . The essay The Gaia Attractor by Rafael Kaufmann proposes a planetary AI co-pilot network to address the metacrisis. James Lovelock proposed something similar in his last book, Novacene, while Timothy M. Lenton and Bruno Latour's influential article Gaia 2.0 suggested that humans could add some level of self-awareness to Earth's self-regulation (Science, 2018).

157 The Nature Tech Collective has published a Nature FinTech Sector Map that maps organizations with offerings in the following areas: monetization, modeling, and measurement and monitoring.

their ease of use, can play a critical transitional role in meeting legacy reporting requirements while supporting the emergence of self-determined practices, processes, and outcomes.[158] These bioregional MRV or sensing platforms can leverage the falling costs of sensing technologies[159] and become embodied intelligence systems, as laid out in Bruno Latour's article, Gaia 2.0. In addition to supporting community members in their ongoing sensemaking and reducing external reporting burdens, community-centered MRV tools and resources, such as those offered through Open Future Coalition's Open Impact platform, provide pathways to generating local economic returns through training and compensation for peer-to-peer impact validation.

> "It's not about Western knowledge and systems or their Indigenous alternatives being dominant. This moment calls for bridging and co-design for the thriving of all of life."
>
> *– Tyson Yunkaporta*

11. **Invest in storytelling**[160] – Putting finance in service to life requires new, compelling stories of value, identity, and place. Extractive finance is built upon millenia of stories that are deeply embedded in our culture.[161] Both new and ancient stories are essential when we are reassessing what we value and reorienting our culture and resources toward that. For people on the ground, the practicalities, benefits, and beauty of a thriving bioregion can be directly experienced. However, when communicating both the tangible local impact (e.g. the 4 Returns[162]) and the more intangible global effects of a distributed bioregional movement to non-local investors, robust storytelling is needed. BFFs can treat investment as a form of storytelling itself: breathing life into stories of action waiting to be told. BFFs can act with the understanding that the ways investments are rationalized, structured, and accounted for tell additional stories. Through capital raising, capital allocation, and broader marketing and communications, it is critical that BFFs nurture and enhance the foundation of stories around bioregional history, identity, and shared vision told and developed during the initial phases of bioregional organizing (see Section 3). Lastly, BFFs can invest in catalytic art and storytelling that enables the scaling of a grassroots movement and an economic transition that is only possible through inspiration.

---

158 Informed by Open Future Coalition's experience working with grassroots impact efforts globally to reduce the burden of existing reporting requirements while bridging towards community-driven quantitative and qualitative metrics.

159 For example, we have access to higher resolution, more up to date remote sensing data than ever before. The launch costs for satellites have fallen 95 percent (with another massive reduction expected in the coming years) thanks to reuse, improved engineering, and increased volumes.

160 Inspired by thoughts shared by filmmaker Louis Fox and writer Tyler Wakefield.

161 Yuval Noah Harari illustrates the role of these stories well in his book *Sapiens: A Brief History of Humankind.*

162 See '4 Returns' Framework in Section 3.

– Toni Cade Bambara

12. **Engage in partnerships, place-based citizen-stewardship, and the community of practice** - BFFs are embedded in place and in local partnerships. To achieve their objectives, BFFs must be built on a strong relational foundation. They are set up by the people of a particular place to serve the vision of the Bioregional Regeneration Strategy. While they will have their own governance boards, management, and investment committees, the facilities should have close relationships and overlap with Bioregional Organizing Teams and Bioregional Hubs. Regular meetings between entities and ongoing, live feedback are important to ensure the success of the co-evolution process laid out in Table 4. The shared MRV platform can support cooperative sensing and sensemaking among these actors. There is potential for a range of MRV-related partnerships including with Indigenous communities, academia, companies, NGOs

Additionally, BFF leadership should understand that their work or "practice" cannot be limited to the context of fundraising and making investment decisions. Sincere engagement with, and better investment in, biocultural regeneration requires living in relationship to place as a place-based citizen-steward, engaging in intentional learning and unlearning opportunities, and tending community through involvement in offerings from Bioregional Hubs and local partners. These may include land-based service projects, educational or healing courses and workshops, and Indigenous and nature-based ceremony and ritual. The Bioregional Trust could also fund some of these activities. Finally, BFF leadership are encouraged to engage in the soon-to-be-launched BioFi (Bioregional Finance) Community of Practice stewarded by the BioFi Project. This online

Living in relationship to place - Having an intentional, embodied, and perhaps spiritual connection and responsibility to specific lands, ecology, and place-based culture. In contrast, many people in modern culture may experience a "placelessness" – a disconnection from geographic roots due to factors like globalization, technological change, and dominant culture that considers humans as separate from nature.

163 More info about this to come at biofi.earth.

community, hosted on Hylo, will support BFFs in sharing tools, insights, and best practices at all levels of practice.[163] The BioFi Community of Practice will also be a place where practitioners playing various roles can meet each other to form collaborative partnerships – for example, a Bioregional Organizing Team can find expertise to support their bioregion in designing and implementing a BFF.

4.2 Setup of Bioregional Financing Facilities:

A phased approach

Four Bioregional Financing Facilities, templates of which are laid out in Table 5 below, have the potential to support the economic transition and regeneration of bioregions around the world. Each BFF will invest in portfolios of synergistic projects or organizations that create cascading benefits. We recommend that the Bioregional Financing Facilities are implemented in two to three phases, beginning with a Bioregional Trust – a facility that will be capitalized initially with philanthropic and/or public grant capital, but could also raise resources through the development of a Bioregional Tithing, an eco-credit, or a tax program (more details on the latter in Table 5 below). The Bioregional Trust can also serve as a Common Asset Trust – holding the rights to manage key ecosystems in the bioregion as a commons. In their 2021 paper, Robert Costanza et al. lay out how forests, watersheds, mountains, and other parts of the biosphere can be held in a trust that charges those who take from the commons and compensate those that regenerate it.[164,165] The Bioregional Trust can support better management of common assets within the bioregion and "recommoning."

164 While BFFs do not yet have taxation authority, there are precedents for such authority being devolved to place-based governance entities – including utility districts and urban renewal districts.
165 Costanza et al.: Common Assets Trusts to Effectively Steward Natural Capital at Multiple Scales
166 The Sogorea Te' Land Trust received a $20 million Shuumi Land Tax contribution in early 2024 - the single largest known cash gift to a Native land trust in history.

Following the Trust (and still in Phase 1), we suggest the setup of a Bioregional Venture Studio. Fundamentally, the purpose of a Venture Studio is to take an ecosystemic view of a bioregion: understanding the resources (i.e. what is abundant, what can grow, what can be harvested, and what can be manufactured); the skills, capacity, and expertise (of the residents, organizations, and initiatives); and the broader world conditions (what is in demand, how technology is changing, and how the climate is changing), in order to identify critical projects, initiatives, and companies that are required to achieve the Bioregional Regeneration Strategy. A Venture Studio can simultaneously or sequentially incubate cohorts of entrepreneurs, creating synergistic organizations that, together, push key levers for systems change in a bioregion. Through identifying key opportunities for a cohort to drive bioregional regeneration and resilience and facilitating their co-learning and development, the Venture Studio enables organizations to create change greater than the sum of their parts. This will involve supporting the discovery of various approaches to catalyzing the economic transition[167] and aligned market development. The Venture Studio can support a range of different regenerative organizations with diverse legal structures, such as Indigenous economic entities, perpetual purpose trusts, Decentralized Autonomous Organizations (DAOs), Natural Asset Companies (NACs), commons management organizations, co-operatives, self-sovereign ownership, and multi-species governance. While Venture Studios are often for-profit ventures, investing their own capital for equity stakes or revenue shares in the businesses they incubate and launch, the Bioregional Venture Studio may additionally or alternatively be funded with grants. These grants might come from the private sector in exchange for access to dealflow, or more traditional philanthropic or government sources.

Once the bioregion reaches a more advanced stage of organizing, activation, and strategy, where markets for regeneration are forming and projects and businesses are ready to take investment, the Bioregional Organizing Team or Bioregional Trust governance team can help to launch a Bioregional Investment Company. This facility develops *Systemic Investment Funds and Bioregional Regeneration Bonds*, which help to scale up the financing of synergistic portfolios of projects (see Section 4.4) through aggregation and matchmaking. An initial Systemic Investment Fund might focus on a wide variety of businesses. Subsequent funds might be dedicated to specific components of the economic transition – like transitioning the food system or energy system in the bioregion. Asset class frameworks used by targeted investors should be taken into account in the portfolio design process.

---

167 Including the building blocks of technological, legal, financial, governance, and other innovation.

The *Bioregional Bank* can be set up in phase 2 or 3, and either before or after the Bioregional Investment Company. The Bioregional Bank will lend specifically to organizations providing goods and services aligned with the Bioregional Regeneration Strategy. It can also provide advisory services. For bioregions that are interested in developing and issuing complementary currencies,[168] including nature-based currencies, the Bioregional Bank can lead this process, supporting a shift in perceptions of value in the bioregion. For example, if the Bioregional Bank issues a currency that is backed by the health of the salmon population or of a key river flowing through the bioregion, those entities become the basis of the value of the currency – attaching currency value to natural assets on which all the life in the bioregion depends (see Section 6 for more details on complementary and Nature-based Currencies). Bioregional Banks can be set up as Community Development Financial Institutions (CDFIs) or the national equivalent, leveraging federal or other guarantees to underwrite loans to small businesses and even non-profits, which are often deemed too risky to lend to (according to traditional credit risk models, which do not accurately account for systemic risk or the 4 Returns).

The activities for BFFs included in the templates below are options, illustrative of the range of activities a given facility can support. It is critical that these templates are applied and adapted by Bioregional Organizing Teams to serve the economic transition and regeneration that is emergent in a given place. Each facility is designed to be flexible and modular: some bioregions might choose to combine multiple functions into one facility. In addition, existing aligned financial vehicles like CDFIs, charitable trusts, land trusts, Perpetual Purpose Trusts, landscape and biodiversity-focused private equity funds,[169] could be

168 "Complementary currencies facilitate transactions that otherwise wouldn't occur, linking otherwise unused resources to unmet needs, and encouraging diversity and interconnections that otherwise wouldn't exist," writes co-designer of the Euro, Bernard Lietar, in his 2011 essay Scientific Evidence of Why Complementary Currencies are Necessary to Financial Stability.
169 The consortium 1000 Landscapes for 1 Billion People has identified a range of innovations for integrated finance on large landscapes and created a five-step process called Integrated Landscape Management (ILM), designed to identify landscape project portfolios with synergistic co-benefits. Its open source technology platform Terraso helps local leaders and landscape partners practice ILM.

adapted to become BFFs or operate in partnership with them. Regardless of the functions established and precise legal structures incorporated, we encourage any treatment of ownership be infused with the essence of steward-ownership. One BFF the authors believe is needed, but is not within the scope of this book is a Bioregional Insurance Company.[170]

170 The BioFi Project will be conducting further research on this.
171 Purpose Economy: What's steward-ownership?

PHASE 1

1. Bioregional Trust

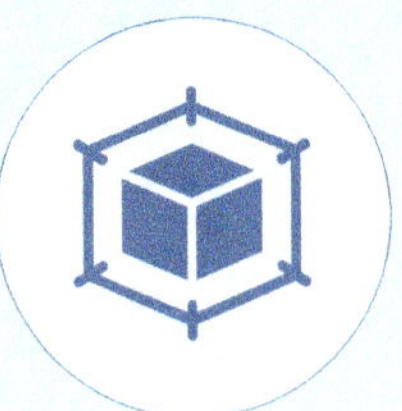

2. Bioregional Venture Studio

1. Bioregional Trust	2. Bioregional Venture Studio
A trust that acts as a catalytic grant fund – providing grants to a range of priority organizations and initiatives in order to create a strong foundation for bioregional action. It can also set up and manage bioregional eco-credit programs, Common Asset Trusts, and Ecological Institutions. **Capital Raising** > Philanthropic and public grant capital (could be sub-national, national, or multilateral), as well as individual donations (including through crowdfunding) > Bioregional Tithing program[172] **Capital Allocation** > Provides grants to fund key processes laid out in steps 2-5 of the Multi-stakeholder Bioregional Regeneration (Table 4) > Provides grants to priority projects or organizations aligned with the Bioregional Regeneration Strategy > Provides grants to Bioregional Hubs and Bioregional Organizing Teams > Funds the development of a bioregional MRV platform (to be developed together with a Bioregional Hub) > Sets up the Bioregional Venture Studio, Bioregional Investment Company and Bioregional Bank **Both Capital Raising and Allocation** > Works with citizen groups to develop, bundle, and sell bioregional scale eco-credits (including to companies operating in the bioregion) > Sets up Common Asset Trusts – holding the rights to manage key ecosystems in the bioregion as commons > Sets up Ecological Institutions – supporting greater sovereignty and economic legibility of bodies of nature	A non-profit, public benefit corporation, co-operative, steward-owned entity, or DAO that supports the development of a cohort of synergistic regenerative organizations to drive systems change. These organizations provide dealflow for the Investment Company. **Capital Raising** > Philanthropic grants > Public sector grants (could be sub-national, national, or multilateral) > Supply chain finance > Concessional capital **Capital Allocation** > Invests in and incubates cohorts of early-stage organizations that work together to change a specific system and generate cascading benefits

172 Credit to Edward West of Applied Alchemy.

3. Bioregional Investment Company

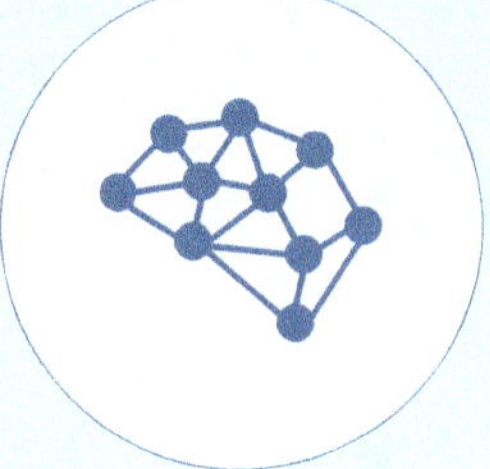

4. Bioregional Bank

A public benefit corporation, co-operative, steward-owned entity, or DAO that develops a portfolio of Systemic Investment Funds and Bioregional Regeneration Bonds. It leverages an integrated capital approach, aggregates portfolios of high impact projects or businesses.

Capital Raising
- Market-rate investment capital
- Concessional capital
- Philanthropic grants
- Public sector grants (could be sub-national, national, or multilateral)
- Supply chain finance

Capital Allocation
Systemic Investment Funds
- Invests in diversified portfolios of projects & businesses designed to create systemic impact

Bioregional Regeneration Bonds
- Same objectives as the funds, but through a fixed income security

A bank that provides low-interest loans, microloans, lines of credit, and technical assistance to aligned organizations. It can also provide retail banking services to individuals and can develop and issue a complementary or nature-based currency.

Capital Raising
- Concessional capital
- Public sector grants (could be sub-national, national, or multilateral)
- Philanthropic grants
- Guarantees
- Deposits

Capital Allocation
- Provides low interest loans to aligned organizations
- Provides technical assistance

Currency Creation
- Develops and issues complementary or nature-based currency

Note: Phase 2 can be split into phases 2 and 3, as deemed appropriate in a given bioregion.

Below we describe each type of Bioregional Financing Facility including some options for the legal structure each could take. Some of these elements are demonstrated in case studies at the end of the section or in Section 5.

Description	A trust that acts as a catalytic grant fund. It provides grants to a range of synergistic projects and organizations with cascading benefits in order to create a strong foundation for bioregional action.
Legal structure	We recommend a non-profit charitable trust or perpetual purpose trust structure. An Indigenous nation, tribe, or consortium of nations and tribes might have an alternative legal structure they choose to use. The Trust could also be an initiative of an existing non-profit organization or start as a Donor Advised Fund (DAF), or equivalent.
Building trust	The Bioregional Trust is the first Bioregional Financing Facility we recommend setting up. We use "trust" to describe both a form of social capital and a financial vehicle. These two aspects of "trust" must be deeply interwoven in the design and implementation of this BFF. The financial capital that flows into this facility should be carefully allocated to support the repair and strengthening of relational trust in the bioregion.
Creating a strong foundation for bioregional action	The Trust will be responsible for investing in the foundational elements of bioregional organizing and activation. It can fund any of the activities in stages 2 through 5 of the multi-stakeholder bioregional regeneration, Table 4 (Mapping and Analysis, Convening and Activation, Co-initiation and Co-creation, and Co-evolution) – including possibly supporting Bioregional Organizing teams. Together with the Bioregional Hub(s), the Trust will be responsible for mapping which systems within the bioregion to focus on transitioning first and strategically allocating grants to support whole ecosystems of organizations that can drive that transition. The Trust can also serve as a fiscal sponsor to projects in the bioregion that do their own fundraising.
Capacity building	If there are not one or more Bioregional Hubs already in place, this is one of the initial activities we recommend the Trust to fund. As noted in **Section 3**, the Hubs will support projects and organizations in the bioregion to prepare for investment. Trusts can also make grants to projects and organizations directly to help them get to the stage where they are operating regenerative business models[173] or to prepare them for investment.
Capacity raising	The Trust receives philanthropic and public grant capital, as well as individual donations. It may introduce a Bioregional Tithing program. It is important to note that the public grant capital can be sub-national, national, or multilateral, and the Trust may need to meet certain criteria to receive these grants. The Trust can play an important role in ensuring that large pools of public capital (e.g. from loss and damages, reparations, climate, and ecological restoration funds) meant to be invested in global public goods or common assets are efficiently used and that they reach on-the-ground regenerators.

173 Does not require that an organization is profitable, but that it is regenerating itself in terms of its funding/financing structure in alignment with the purpose and life cycle of the organization. This approach acknowledges regenerative organizations might have a death date at which they choose to end their operations.

Capital allocation	It provides grants to fund key processes of multi-stakeholder bioregional regeneration (including what is often referred to "the spaces in between" – organizing, convening, relationship building, art, learning & integration, etc.) and to priority projects and organizations aligned with the Bioregional Regeneration Strategy. As mentioned above, grants can be allocated through a participatory budgeting process including voting as part of a prize model (such as the Edge Prize – see **case study**), through Quadratic Voting (such as in the Golden Bay bioregion – see **case study**), or Quadratic Funding (see **Section 6** for examples). The Trust can also set up and/or seed the Bioregional Venture Studio, Bioregional Investment Company and Bioregional Bank.
Eco-credits:[174] **both capital raising and allocation**	The Trust can work with key bioregional actors to develop, bundle, and sell eco-credits (including, importantly, to companies operating in the bioregion or companies that have historically contributed to extraction or destruction in that bioregion). A platform like the **Regen Marketplace** (see the **Regen Network case study**) can enable the development of a methodology aligned with the priority regeneration activities in a given bioregion. This methodology should be developed through a participatory, transparent process. Once the methodology is agreed upon and approved by the platform of choice, the Trust can support regenerators from across the bioregion to engage in designated activities. As discussed above, the integrated MRV capabilities of the Trust will enable it to track credit delivery, and bundle and issue credits accordingly. Proceeds will then flow to regenerators – perhaps with the Trust taking a small fee to cover its services. We see this as an effective approach to scaling up strategic, decentralized action quickly to drive regeneration. This tool could be used to drive long-term outcomes like watershed restoration or species recovery, but could also be used to drive rapid fire risk mitigation activities in advance of the fire season in a bioregion, for example. An important part of this process will be cultivating relationships with potential eco-credit buyers – noting that there is not yet strong demand for eco-credits beyond ICROA-certified carbon credits, which do not take into account a holistic composition of biocultural factors. The potential for eco-credits to connect corporations operating in a bioregion with regenerators stewarding that bioregion is significant. We believe that the voluntary carbon market is ripe for disruption, and that a bottom-up, bioregional, approach to credit development could be catalytic in driving financial resources to regeneration. We have already seen a regulated carbon market prioritize credits aligned with a locally developed methodology – in the case of Querétaro, Mexico[175] and the role that the **Sierra Gorda Reserve** played in shaping the legislation.

174 Attestations about ecological state which prove regeneration is occurring, has occurred, or will occur. It is our recommendation that eco-credits are based on community-developed and governed definitions of regeneration, which are rooted in context and include a composition of ecological factors (rather a single parameter, such as carbon) (adapted from input from Regen Foundation). A reflection from Gregory Landau of Regen Network on the term eco-credit here: To Credit, or Not to Credit.

175 More details available here: UNDP Equator Initiative Case Studies: GRUPO ECOLÓGICO SIERRA GORDA.

Common Asset Trusts: both capital raising and allocation	The Bioregional Trust can serve as a Common Asset Trust – holding the rights to manage key ecosystems in the bioregion as commons. In their 2021 paper, Robert Costanza et al. lay out how forests, watersheds, mountains, and other parts of the biosphere can be held in a trust that charges fees to those who take from the commons and compensates those that regenerate it.[176] The Bioregional Trust is well suited to support "recommoning" – the transition of land from private ownership to commons management. It can also support more effective management of common assets by leveraging the bioregional MRV platform to track use or degradation, as well as regeneration. Eco-credits can support the compensation for the regeneration of common assets. Legal structures aligned with the rights of nature and self-sovereign nature could be applied in a Common Asset Trust structure.[177]
Ecological Institutions: both capital raising and allocation	Recent innovations in rights of nature have created legal legibility for ecosystems and more-than-human species. Innovation in the Web3 space has paved the way for economic legibility to be layered on top of this legal layer – enabling bodies of nature to have their own blockchain addresses. A Bioregional Trust could set up an Ecological Institution with a blockchain address for a watershed or buffalo herd and could raise capital into a wallet at that address to be allocated to improve the health of that body of nature (more about this in the **Regen Network Case Study**). People will be elected as proxies or guardians for the body of nature to determine how capital should be allocated. Technological tools and Indigenous wisdom will both have an important role in supporting sensing of ecosystem health and resulting capital allocation decisions. This can change from a fully automated Ecological Institution that acts based on data inputs about ecosystem or species health to a "Convivial Ecological Institution" that relied more on human sensing of an ecosystem and its inhabitants.[178]
Examples of similar entities	> **Salmon Nation Trust** – a Public Benefit LLC created to "discover, connect, and fund regenerative entrepreneurs and the emergence of a vibrant Nature State" in the Salmon Nation bioregion (see **Case Study** 1). > **Sea Coast Trust** – a permanent funding mechanism created to provide access to capital for Indigenous-led conservation projects that place local communities at the center of efforts to achieve a healthy environment (see Case Study 5: Spruce Root Trust). > **Reimagine Appalachia** – an NGO leading strategic coordination of funding, through creating a funders network, to support regeneration across the region of Appalachia.

176 While BFFs do not yet have taxation authority, there are precedents for such authority being devolved to place-based governance entities – including utility districts and urban renewal districts.

177 More about this from the Earth Law Center, the Center for Democratic and Environmental Rights, and Sacred Contract.

178 Regen Foundation: Ecological Institutions Protocols to Grow Autonomous and Convivial Ecological Actors

BIOREGIONAL VENTURE STUDIO

Description	It takes an ecosystemic view of a bioregion to identify critical projects, initiatives, and businesses that are required to achieve the Bioregional Regeneration Strategy. It then supports the synergistic, coordinated development of one or multiple cohorts of regenerative organizations to drive systems change. These organizations provide investment dealflow for the Bioregional Investment Company.
Legal structure	A non-profit, public benefit corporation, co-operative, steward-owned entity, perpetual purpose trust, or DAO. The Venture Studio could also start as a Donor Advised Fund (DAF) or equivalent.
Innovation	Through identifying key opportunities for a cohort to drive bioregional regeneration and resilience and facilitating their co-learning and development, the Venture Studio enables organizations to create change greater than the sum of their parts. This will involve supporting the discovery of various approaches to catalyzing the economic transition and aligned market development. It can incubate or accelerate organizations of various types of legal structures including Indigenous economic entities, perpetual purpose trusts, Decentralized Autonomous Organizations (DAOs), Natural Asset Companies (NACs), commons management organizations, co-operatives, self-sovereign ownership, and multi-species governance organizations. It can support entrepreneurs in applying legal structures that support worker ownership, rights of nature, and expansion of the commons. The Studio can connect buyers engaging in the supply shed[179] with entrepreneurs who can help address their business challenges – particularly related to the risks associated with ecological degradation and climate change.
Capital raising	Possibilities for funding the Venture Studio include philanthropic or public grants, grants from corporations wanting to make investments in supply shed resilience and to develop future dealflow,[180] founders' equity, studio-level equity, revenue sharing agreements, or option pools.
Capacity allocation	The Bioregional Venture Studio will invest in and incubate or accelerate cohorts of early-stage organizations focused on key opportunities for bioregional regeneration and resilience. It will support innovation that can drive economic transition and catalyze new markets. Each cohort will focus on shifting a particular system and will work to build an ecosystem of actors that can work synergistically to drive that change – rooted in coordinated, strategic action.

179 We use this term rather than "supply chain", noting that materials do not flow in a linear process, but rather more like a watershed.

180 This investment could come from the sustainability, R&D, operations, or even the marketing budget within a corporation.

Examples of similar entities	> **Hawaiʻi Investment Ready Initiative** – an accelerator program for social enterprises in Hawaiʻi, supporting thematic, systems-based cohorts of enterprises with access to investment capital, mentorship, and resources (see **case study** below). > **ProjectTogether** – an open social innovation accelerator catalyzing thematic cohorts of innovators and connecting them to other changemakers (public & private) in Germany. > **Fresh Ventures** – a Dutch venture studio focused on accelerating a circular and regenerative food system in the country. It incubates cohorts of entrepreneurs to develop organizations that work together to shift this system. > **The Nature-based Climate Solutions Accelerator** – a US-based accelerator program that brings cohorts of municipal & community allies through a series of modules designed to grow community capacity to implement "equity-centered, nature-based climate solutions to some of the most pressing climate change challenges facing communities."

Table 8. BFF 3 – The Bioregional Investment Company

BIOREGIONAL INVESTMENT COMPANY	
Description	An organization that develops a portfolio of Systemic Investment Funds – leveraging an integrated capital approach and aggregating portfolios of synergistic, high-impact projects or businesses with cascading benefits.
Legal structure	It can take various forms, including a public benefit corporation (where the majority of shares might be owned by the Bioregional Trust or another affiliated non-profit, this could also function as a holding company), co-operative, steward-owned entity, revolving fund, evergreen fund, perpetual purpose trust, Indigenous economic entity, or a Decentralized Autonomous Organization (DAO). These structures can involve an "exit to community" structure where the community purchases the assets after a set time period. It is important that this company is legally mandated to serve the thriving of all life in the bioregion and is majority owned by people working towards that goal, and perhaps by the more-than-human life there as well. Beyond this, there is a lot of potential for innovation and prototyping with this BFF. As compared to the others, it possibly has the most significant potential to raise financial resources and create a shift in how those resources are owned and governed.
Systemic Investment Funds	
Legal structure	GP-LP structure or DAO with a capped return structure where the fund owns equity in projects or businesses, which it may buy, hold, resell to another investor, resell to the community, or gradually sell back to the founders through profit-sharing. A percentage of profits should flow into the Trust, future funds, and/or the Venture Studio. This model recognizes that any organization in the bioregion turning a profit is benefitting from the commons, and is designed to invest in collective assets on an ongoing basis. Long-term equity will play an important role in building new infrastructure (built, social, or IT) or a new market.

Innovation	As with the overall Bioregional Investment Company, there is significant room for innovation in how these funds are structured – including from fund to fund. For innovative approaches, tools, and templates that these facilities could leverage, explore **Section 6**.
Governance	The management of the Investment Company and a representative from the Trust should serve as the GPs and should represent the interests of the bioregion. The GPs will be tasked with deploying financial resources in service to the Bioregional Regeneration Strategy.
Capital raising	Systemic Investment Funds can raise market-rate investment capital, concessional capital, or supply chain finance. The GPs will develop the term sheet for each fund based on market analysis and financial modeling to determine the returns priority investee projects or businesses can likely generate.[181] Therefore, target returns will stem directly from those projects and businesses aligned with the Bioregional Regeneration Strategy. The primary objective of the integrated capital structure is not to guarantee investor returns, for which blended finance transactions are often criticized, but to strategically de-risk, change risk perception, fund common goods that projects or organizations may generate, and stimulate and build markets aligned with regeneration as a result. Large investors might choose to invest in a range of different funds in neighboring bioregions, around the world, or focused on a particular sector or thematic vertical. By creating an opportunity for investors to gain exposure to portfolios of diversified, yet connected, high impact, regenerative projects, Systemic Investment Funds are filling an existing gap in the impact investing market. For further details on our current thinking regarding systemic portfolios, see **Section 4.4**.
Capital allocation	Invests in diversified portfolios of projects and businesses designed to create systemic impact. Requires consultation of a local expert group (e.g. from Bioregional Hubs) to define interdependencies and leverage points in portfolios (see the case study below on the **Hawai'i Investment Ready Initiative**). These funds will apply financial and systems analytics that enable them to move beyond the widely applied modern portfolio theory, which is a theory of speculation based on backward-looking data that suggests investors have no way to address systemic risks. This is not reflective of the real social, ecological, economic, and financial risks we are facing as the polycrisis unfolds, and disregards the leverage that lies in systemic capital allocation.

181 This Regenerative Term Sheet developed by the Regenerative Investing Institute can serve as a starting place for BFF management teams.

| Examples of similar entities | While we have not yet seen Systemic Investment Funds operational the way we describe them here, some existing initiatives demonstrate certain elements of it, including:
> **AquaSpark** – an open-ended investment fund building a synergistic demonstration portfolio of companies across the aquaculture value chain to take pressure off the oceans.
> **TransCap and Centre for Public Impact: Urban Climate Finance** – a proposal for a systemic funding architecture bringing systemic investing to the challenge of funding urban transformation. |
| | > **Seed Commons** – a network of 30 "locally-rooted, non-extractive loan funds" across the US. Seed Commons takes in investment as a single fund, then onlends to local funds who lend to marginalized communities.
> **The Ujima Fund** – "a democratic investment vehicle" that lends to small businesses and real estate and infrastructure projects led by members of Boston's working-class Black, Indigenous, and other communities of color. The Fund uses a participatory budgeting process in combination with traditional underwriting to "put economic development decisions in the hands of community members." |

Bioregional Regeneration Bonds

Legal structure	A series of privately issued fixed income instruments that fund portfolios of qualifying regeneration activities in a bioregion. The bonds are issued by the Bioregional Investment Company and could be structured similarly to municipal bonds.[182]
Governance	The Bioregional Investment Company will set the terms for the bond. These will be based on the portfolio of priority projects identified through the Bioregional Regeneration Strategy, public consultations, and market analysis. The management of the Bioregional Investment Company will oversee relationships with investee projects and investors. If there is cooperation with municipal or sub-national authorities, the management will also oversee these relationships.
Capital raising	The bonds can be structured similarly to municipal bonds and tap into the sizable, tax-advantaged municipal bond market, which includes institutional investors. They can raise market-rate investment capital or concessional capital. It is also possible for Central Banks to purchase these bonds to address the myriad economic and financial risks emanating from destruction of the biosphere. These bonds can leverage innovative structures, for example by linking to bioregional regeneration targets in a structure known as a "sustainability-linked bond." If regeneration targets are met, the borrower pays a lower interest rate. This enables the sharing of the financial value of risk reduction that comes with regeneration.[183] The MRV platform BFFs build will be an important enabler to setting and monitoring such targets.

182 A similar bond could also be issued by a municipal or sub-national authority.

183 The World Bank has developed a Feasibility-AmBitiousness (FAB) Matrix for sovereign sustainability-linked bond criteria, which can be used to guide bioregional target setting.

Capital allocation	The Bioregional Investment Company will identify and allocate capital to a portfolio of synergistic projects that together drive a particular part of the economic transition or address an ecological need in the bioregion. The bond will be purchased by return seeking investors, so the underlying assets should generate a financial return. For common asset projects, such as large-scale infrastructure or ecosystem regeneration projects, it is possible for the Bioregional Investment Company to work with local authorities to collect taxes to pay for both the principal and interest on the bond.
Examples of similar entities	> **DC Water Green Bond** – an Environmental Impact Bond issued by the DC Water and Sewer Authority in 2016. The funds raised paid for green infrastructure to support stormwater management across the city. The payout on the bond was linked to the ecological performance of the underlying projects. If the projects outperform the target, the investors receive a premium on the base rate and if the targets are missed, the investors will receive a discount on the base rate, and in some cases could lose some of the loan principal.[184] > **Forest Resilience Bond** – an ecological outcomes-linked bond issued by non-profit conservation finance organization Blue Forest that raises capital from private investors and then aggregates diverse beneficiaries to pay for outcomes for improved forest management in Northern California.

184 A case study on this bond is available in the World Bank report Mobilizing Private Finance for Nature on page 49.

Hawai'i Investment Ready Initiative – An Intermediary for Investing in a Resilient Economy for All Hawai'i

About the Hawai'i Investment Ready Initiative

In the heart of the Pacific, Hawai'i grapples with the delicate balance between economic prosperity and ecological preservation, especially considering its vulnerability to climate change and the fragility of its ecosystems. Against this backdrop, the "Hawai'i Investment Ready" (HIR) initiative has emerged – charting a pioneering course in bioregional financing. HIR is a collaborative effort between government agencies, environmental organizations, and private investors, that seeks to redefine the relationship between economic development and ecological well-being.

HIR was established in 2013 as the first Indigenous-led social enterprise accelerator program in the United States. It has supported businesses spanning diverse sectors, including renewable energy, eco-tourism, sustainable agriculture, and marine conservation. Community engagement is integral to the ethos of HIR, and the selection process of businesses to support ensures that local voices inform decision-making, fostering a sense of shared responsibility for economic and ecological outcomes.

Growing a more resilient economy

In 2017, HIR started pioneering the field of impact investing in Hawai'i, spearheading efforts to educate funders and investors on this approach to financing social enterprises. Through the impact investments that HIR catalyzed by linking impact investors with viable and promising impact ventures, it has played a pivotal role in diversifying Hawai'i's economy, reducing dependence on traditional industries and fostering a more resilient economic landscape. Green jobs have been created across various sectors and skills development programs were developed to equip the local workforce for emerging opportunities in the green economy.

The onset of the COVID-19 pandemic in 2020 spurred another significant shift within HIR. Needing to address the compounding challenges posed by climate breakdown, the organization decided to advance from merely supporting incremental improvements within individual enterprises to catalyzing transformational shifts across entire systems. It became evident that the escalating complexity of these challenges demanded equally intricate solutions.

The new holistic Theory of Change became:

> "When we accelerate the coordination and collaboration of
> capital to seed and scale systemic solutions, we are investing in
> Hawai'i's economic transformation."

In 2022, HIR launched its first prototype in shifting systems, focused on the vertical of Hawai'i's food systems. This endeavor commenced with a redesign of its social enterprise accelerator program to take a systems change approach. Transforming Hawai'i's Food Systems Together conducted an exhaustive systems mapping exercise, meticulously identifying interdependencies, feedback loops, and potential leverage points. HIR leveraged this work in the redesign of its approach. It became clear that various interventions would require a coordinated investment approach between different types of capital, however, an accompanying 'Hawai'i Capital Scan' report revealed that financial resources remained siloed with limited collaboration taking place between diverse capital holders. Consequently, HIR initiated conversations with food system investors within its network and helped them solve the problems of a) managing risks, b) creating leverage, and c) placing the best bets in this complex investment environment by initiating collaboration and de-siloing the capital stack. As a side effect, this also helped to level power hierarchies between investors and investees in the face of a shared purpose.

Catalyzing regenerative investments

Emerging as a strategic intermediary, HIR discerns the optimal deployment of funds to effectively drive systemic change. By identifying where different types of capital could be best utilized within the capital stack, HIR significantly enhanced its value proposition for all stakeholders involved. The next step for HIR is to track the investment portfolios against a set of systemic metrics and to effectively fund the health of entire ecosystems.

Co-initiated by HIR, the 'Āina Aloha Economy Fund is Hawai'i's first catalytic capital fund integrating HIR's program expertise and research with the work of 'Āina Aloha Economic Futures, a partnering initiative around which 2,600+ community members and organizations have coalesced to develop a vision for Hawai'i's economic future. Offering adaptable, patient, and risk-tolerant debt capital, the Fund addresses the critical capital gap between initial grants or startup funding and commercial capital. It helps to smooth over the capital stack allowing investors' capital to work better together. This strategic approach provides a necessary runway for systems entrepreneurs, particularly those focused on Native-led and sustainable foodways, to implement their strategies for fostering a more equitable and regenerative island economy. In addition to financial support, the Fund is committed to enhancing the success of these enterprises by offering ongoing technical assistance and help to navigate resources and other financial providers.

Beyond catalyzing funds and investment across the capital stack, HIR has recognized the important role of policy and advocacy work in order to win a supportive enabling environment for bioregional investments. It is thus actively collaborating with other institutions to facilitate conversations between funders, entrepreneurs, and policymakers.

As an intermediary at the intersection of systems change and capital allocation, HIR currently operates on catalytic grant capital from philanthropy, distinct from the investments made in for-profit ventures and not-for-profit projects within its cohorts. HIR aims to transform Hawai'i's systems (such as food & agriculture, housing & real estate, etc.) and to serve as an example of how a non-profit can catalyze the transition to a regenerative economy. In its own words, HIR describes this ambition as "*becoming a fractal of what could happen in a more holistic global financial system.*"

Table 9. BFF 4 – The Bioregional Bank

BIOREGIONAL BANK	
Description	A Bioregional Bank that provides low-interest loans, microloans, lines of credit, and technical assistance to aligned organizations (including corporations, for-purpose businesses, non-profit organizations, and co-ops). The Bioregional Bank can also provide retail banking services to individuals and can develop and issue a complementary or nature-based currency.
Legal structure	We recommend the Bioregional Bank is set up as a bank, public bank, Community Development Financial Institution (CDFI), non-profit,[185] a publicly-owned entity (owned by the bioregion), or a credit union (with partial ownership by the Bioregional Trust and investors) under the relevant national jurisdiction.
Leveraging debt financing to enable economic transformation	As a bioregion transitions to a regenerative economy, it might eventually wish to have its own bank. One initial option would be to establish this Bioregional Bank as a CDFI. The long track record of CDFIs and all of the hard work of their champions provide a roadmap for the path that Bioregional Banks could take. There are many examples of CDFIs supporting the development of 4 Returns, and indeed, the mission of CDFIs is aligned with many of the attributes of BFFs. CDFIs have successfully leveraged public capital or attained public guarantees to mobilize private investment,[186] based on a model that empowers the CDFI to use flexible underwriting criteria to assess loan applications, enabling the use of relational information and local knowledge to guide risk assessment/management and capital allocation.
Difference from traditional CDFIs	A Bioregional Bank has two main differences from a conventional CDFI: (i) It takes a systemic approach to lending, aligned with achieving the vision of the Bioregional Regeneration Strategy and (ii) it may issue a complementary currency. Its capitalization structure may also reflect a bioregional focus.

185 There are multiple types of CDFIs including banks, credit unions, loan funds, and venture capital funds.
186 CDFIs leverage an estimated $12 of private capital for every $1 of public investment (CDFI Coalition).

Capital raising	Bioregional Banks can raise philanthropic grants, public grants,[187] concessionary investment capital, and investment capital via deposits from individuals or organizations. Importantly, Bioregional Banks, like their CDFI counterparts, will seek to leverage guarantees. Some impact investors invest in portfolios of CDFIs and could do the same with Bioregional Banks. Organizations like the **Native CDFI Network**[188] could be helpful to partners as they assist Bioregional Banks in raising capital.
Capital allocation	Bioregional Banks can provide low interest loans or revolving lines of credit to aligned organizations. They will also be able to offer technical assistance.
Currency development	For bioregions that are interested in developing a complementary currency (including nature-based, energy-based, or community currencies), the Bioregional Banks can design and issue this currency to support a more contextual, relational, and dynamic approach to valuation and value flow within the bioregion (see more about this in **Section 6.2**). Such a currency can incentivize biocultural regeneration. By creating its own currency, a bioregion can also create more economic sovereignty and resilience – possibly moving towards managing its own values-aligned monetary policy.[189] Complementary currencies have been shown to reduce dependence on external capital over time.[190]

187 In addition to the US CDFI Fund, several states in the US have introduced funds dedicated to capitalizing CDFIs. Other governments have similar lending programs or can consider creating a national or multiple subnational funds to capitalize BCDFIs.

188 Organizations like this have a track record that enables them to qualify for federal funding. The Native CDFI Network was recently selected to receive a Clean Communities Investment Accelerator (CCIA) award of $400M from the Greenhouse Gas Reduction Fund. This award will enable the Native CDFI Network to support 63 community lenders across Indian Country to fund 'renewable energy, energy-efficient upgrades, and sustainability projects that will enhance well-being and create employment opportunities for Native people.'

189 Many communities around the world wish to move away from the use of currencies that hinge on an infinite growth paradigm.

190 More about this in research on the Grassroots Economics Foundation's Community Inclusion Currency (CIC) implemented in Kenya.

Examples of similar entities	> CDFIs are mission-driven financial institutions dedicated to serving marginalized communities. As of 2022, more than 1,300 certified CDFIs across the United States held nearly $247 billion in total assets (**Federal Reserve Bank of San Francisco**). Their primary goal is to promote economic development, increase access to capital, and address financial gaps in areas where traditional financial institutions may not adequately serve. CDFIs originated in the United States, but similar entities exist in other countries under different names and structures. Microfinance institutions, development finance institutions, cooperative banks, credit unions, mutual organizations and social investment funds can serve a similar purpose.
	> **Spruce Root** (see **Case Study 5**) – an Indigenous-led CDFI in Alaska that supports Indigenous-owned businesses through providing low interest loans and technical assistance.
	> **Walden Mutual Bank** – a local bank that invests deposits in food systems change in New England and New York through offering strategically designed loans to support regenerative farming.
	> **Beneficial State Bank** – a CDFI based in Oakland, CA that focuses on uplifting low-to-moderate communities (particularly in the San Francisco Bay Area). 79% of its lending portfolio in 2022 supported sectors that "positively impact local communities and the planet."
	> **Triodos Bank** – A Netherlands based bank that only lends to organizations "in the real economy working to bring about positive and lasting change." The bank does not lend to "any organization that puts profit before people and planet."

Spruce Root – An Indigenous-led CDFI Catalyzing a Regenerative Economy

By: Alana Peterson, Kalah Duncan, and India Rose Matharu-Daley

Spruce Root

Founded in 2012, Spruce Root is a CDFI based in Juneau, AK, that works to empower Alaskan Natives, Indigenous peoples, rural populations and communities across Southeast Alaska through equitable economic development. Spruce Root serves 23 communities from Yakutat in the north to Hydaburg in the south.

Spruce Root's core programs encompass small business lending, comprehensive business education, and personalized coaching services.These initiatives are aimed at building organizational capacity, enabling locally-driven enterprises to strengthen Southeast Alaska's economy, promote inclusivity, generate quality employment opportunities, and foster community well-being. In addition to entrepreneurial support, Spruce Root provides technical assistance and facilitation services to support regenerative collaboration between public, private, and Indigenous stakeholders.

Spruce Root was founded with $500,000 in seed funding from the Sealaska Corporation, one of a dozen regional Alaska Native corporations created in 1971 by the Alaska Native Claims Settlement Act (ANCSA). Owned by more than 26,000 Tlingít, Haida, and Tsimshian shareholders, Sealaska's mission is to strengthen its people, culture, and homelands by creating economic prosperity and protecting the environment. Sealaska owns and manages 362,000 acres of land on behalf of its Indigenous constituents, and dominated the timber industry in the region until 2021, when it renounced commercial logging (Resneck *et al.*, 2023). Now, Sealaska has set aside 176,000 acres of Tongass rainforest for carbon sequestration in partnership with The Nature Conservancy (*Woocheen*, no date). The seed funding for Spruce Root came from sales of the resulting carbon credits.

Spruce Root's business development programs

Spruce Root's small business lending program targets entrepreneurs who may not have access to affordable capital through traditional financing channels. However, the program remains open to considering applicants who contribute to economic development and community well-being in the region. Before potential borrowers apply for a loan, Spruce Root provides business and career coaching, and supports them after the loan is issued. The loans can fund startup capital, working capital, business expansion, and more. Between 2012 and 2022, Spruce Root deployed

$1.2 million in loan capital and, in 2022, it issued loans to four Alaska small businesses totaling $350,000. In 2023 new loans deployed amounted to just under $900,000.

Outside the small business lending program, Spruce Root offers business coaching to other stakeholders. For example, in 2022, Spruce Root provided business basics training to Tlingit and Haida citizens, and partnered with Sealaska Heritage Institute on developing a business curriculum for Alaska Native artists.

Spruce Root also organizes workshops and competitions for Southeast Alaska entrepreneurs. Its Path to Prosperity business development competition supports local businesses that have positive social, economic, and ecological impact and promote the regenerative use of the region's resources. In 2022, the competition attracted 23 applications from eight communities. The 12 finalists attended an in-person Business Boot Camp, and received 26+ hours of training and technical assistance from 14 mentors.

In addition, Spruce Root supports Southeast Alaska communities through strategic planning and workforce development. In 2022, it finalized and took part in implementing a five-year strategic plan for the Sitka Tribe of Alaska and began to facilitate an update of the comprehensive community plan for Yakutat in partnership with the local government. Spruce Root also provided one-on-one careers coaching for 10 people from multiple sectors, and led various workshops and training across the region for youth employment and leadership.led an internship program for young people at Sealaska, and collaborated with the Sitka Tribe of Alaska on a youth employment program. For more information see Spruce Root 2022 Annual Report.

Sustainable Southeast Partnership (SSP)

The Sustainable Southeast Partnership (SSP), a program of Spruce Root and Sealaska, is a regional network based on a collective impact model. The SSP aims to foster collaborative, community-driven initiatives that address complex social, ecological, and economic challenges in the region in accordance with Indigenous values. Any individual, organization, business, or government can join, and the network includes Tribal governments, Native corporations and entities, community-minded organizations, state and federal agencies, local businesses, and more.

The SSP appoints community catalysts hosted by village-level entities to conduct community assessments of energy, food, and natural resource and economic sustainability. The community catalysts identify projects, which range from food security and energy independence to habitat restoration and more, and work with regional catalysts on project design, implementation, and monitoring. Regional catalysts also work to influence the policy environment and develop economic cooperatives and social support networks, and organize workshops and training.

Spruce Root is the fiscal sponsor of the Seacoast Trust, a permanent funding mechanism created to provide access to capital for Indigenous-led conservation projects that place local communities at the center of efforts to achieve a healthy environment. The Seacoast Trust guiding principles include respecting community voices, upholding Indigenous governance and leadership, and valuing the integrity of all knowledge systems, including those anchored in 10,000 plus years of Indigenous history, traditions, and stewardship.

The Seacoast Trust will fund the work of the Sustainable Southeast Partnership. Projects slated for funding by the trust include Native forest partnerships, healthy salmon habitat, Indigenous Guardians programs, youth leadership opportunities, food sovereignty, climate migration, regenerative economies, and reduced carbon footprints (*Seacoast Trust Annual Report, 2023*). The Trust provides grants for work programs, loans for small Tribal businesses, Southeast Tribal Land Purchases, and local infrastructure projects, and exchange-traded and impact fund, as well as network coordination and capacity building. Along with Spruce Root, the Seacoast Trust also funds the work of the Sustainable Southeast Partnership.

In 2022, the Seacoast Trust reached an initial $20M funding goal with the help of Sealaska, The Nature Conservancy, and the Rasmuson, Hewlett, Edgerton, Chorus, and Wilburforce foundations *(The Nature Conservancy, 2021)*. The goal of the trust is to reach $100M in order to fully fund the work of Sustainable Southeast Partnership in perpetuity.

4.3 Capitalization of Bioregional Financing Facilities

As shown in Table 5, we recommend a phased approach to setting up Bioregional Financing Facilities, starting with Bioregional Trusts. In *Table 10.*, below, we lay out the types of capital that can be mobilized to capitalize BFFs, the expected returns, examples of aligned activities, and the potential investment rationale behind it. *Table 10.* is meant to serve as inspiration. The rationale for investing in bioregional regeneration is emergent, and will be developed through prototypes in many places and critically, through telling new stories about value and about the relationship between financial capital, the entities that hold it, and bioregions.

One near-term, high-impact way BFFs can support the flow of financial resources at scale to regeneration is through being set up to receive the $20 billion in ODA countries in the Global North have pledged to provide to countries in the Global South by 2025 (under Target 19), in support of achieving the ecological and social targets set in the Global Biodiversity Framework. BFFs could also support capital allocation of Brazil's $600 million Amazon Fund (Reuters 2024). Bioregional Trusts designed to receive and allocate this funding can be built in key biodiversity areas and Indigenous territories. Allocating funds through BFFs can reduce overhead costs, bureaucracy, time lags, and corruption and can also help to address problematic power dynamics often at play between governments and multilaterals and the grassroots efforts they are seeking to resource.

Table 10. Capitalizing Bioregional Financing Facilities

Type of Financial Capital	Aligned returns (from Four Returns Framework)	Examples of aligned activities	Investment rationale
Public grant capital (Overseas Development Assistance – ODA or multilateral funding)	Inspiration, ecological, social, and economic	Regeneration activities aligned with ODA objectives – particularly achievement of the goals set out in various agreements made under the Rio Conventions (Convention on Biological Diversity (CBD), UN Framework Convention on Climate Change (UNFCCC), and Convention to Combat Desertification (UNCCD)). It is possible for such grants to fund a range of multi-stakeholder bioregional regeneration activities (see *Table*	Multilateral and national authorities have resources allocated to various regeneration activities to support the provision of common assets and public goods. As explained in section 1, the authors believe that the achievement of the targets set in the various agreements made under the Rio Convention (particularly the Global Biodiversity Framework) can only be achieved through more efficiently directing resources to grassroots regenerative efforts – importantly to Indigenous communities which protect 80% of the world's biodiversity.[192] Currently a large percentage of ODA flows through multilateral entities, then to national entities, then possibly to sub-national entities before the remainder eventually reaches grassroots organizations and communities. In the case of financial resources reaching Indigenous land and water stewards, there is often a nation state government between the organization with the funding and the Indigenous nation or community. This creates problematic power dynamics that prevent the resources from getting to the people on the ground.[193,194]

192 In the World Bank book, *Decentralization and Biodiversity Conservation* (published in 1996), the Multilateral Development bank lays out, in 10 country case studies and 32 projects analyses, how decentralization of governance (including political, fiscal, administrative, and legislative power) can positively support biodiversity conservation outcomes.
193 Rights and Resources Initiative: State of Funding for Tenure Rights and Forest Guardianship
194 This is the case with large multilateral funds focused on ecological regeneration including: the Global Environment Facility, the Green Climate Fund, and the Climate Investment Funds.

| Public grant capital (domestic) | Inspiration, ecological, social, and economic | 4), large projects, an aggregated portfolio of smaller projects, the Venture Studio, or the seeding of the Bioregional Investment Company or Bioregional Bank. Bioregional organizing teams can work together with relevant authorities to design proposals and manage projects. Regeneration activities aligned with public programs (or that have a case to develop a public program) in a given political jurisdiction. It is possible for such grants to fund a range of multi-stakeholder bioregional regeneration activities (see Table 4), large projects, an aggregated portfolio of smaller projects, the Venture Studio, or to seed the Bioregional Investment Company or Bioregional Bank. Bioregional organizing teams can work together with sub-national or national authorities to design proposals and manage projects. | BFFs can be designed to efficiently and transparently receive and allocate ODA – reducing the overhead costs associated with bureaucracy and more effectively channeling it to synergistic portfolios of projects.

National and sub-national authorities have resources allocated to various regeneration activities to support the provision of common assets and public goods. It is increasingly common to see national and sub-national grant programs mandated to allocate financial capital to communities, but communities[195] are often not organized to apply for or receive these funds.[196]

In this case, the BFFs can play an important connective tissue role – including through providing communities access to tools and processes they need to make decisions about how to regenerate their place[197] and facilitating the submission of organized proposals to public grant programs. BFFs can receive and manage these funds in a transparent and responsive way, overcoming challenges with getting grants to communities who do not have sufficient administrative capacity. |

195 An example is the US Inflation Reduction Act (passed in 2022) that allocated $3 billion in environmental and climate justice block grants and $1.3 billion in neighborhood access and equity grant programs to promote community resilience and access to safe, affordable transportation. An additional $40B was allocated for environmental justice.

196 One program seeking to address this, that is still highly centralized, is the EPA- and DOE-supported Environmental Justice Thriving Communities Technical Assistance Center. BFFs could work together with this Center to improve its efficacy.

197 One such tool is the Accelerate Resilience Los Angeles (ARLA) Living Infrastructure Field Kit (developed by Spherical Studios), which enables communities to engage in the infrastructure design process from the start to ensure their vision is at the center of restoration activities in the Los Angeles River basin in order to deliver health and vitality for the people and more than human life there.

Philanthropic grant capital	Inspiration, ecological, social, and economic	A range of multi-stakeholder bioregional regeneration activities (see Table 4), large priority projects or organizations or a portfolio of small ones, the Venture Studio, or to seed the Investment Company or Bioregional Bank. This funding might also be allocated through a participatory budgeting approach to encourage broader participation in resource allocation. Some of these examples include but are not limited to participatory, trust-based, and power-sharing philanthropy. Delivering capital through a co-aligned process with the grantees, where the grantees are the decision-makers and the trusted distributors.	Philanthropists are seeking to support coordination among grantees, and BFFs provide them a way to invest in catalyzing a coordinated group of actors – leveraging participatory resource allocation. The trust-based philanthropy movement seeks to move funding decisions down to the grassroots level.[198] Additionally, Community Foundations in countries like the US, Canada, and Colombia have shown interest in aligning with bioregional priorities.[199]

198 See the work of Regenerosity or Kinship Earth on "flow funding" (pioneered by Marion Rockefeller Weber) from large donors to multiple projects on the ground through trusted regional intermediaries.

199 Deeper analysis of why philanthropists might donate to institutions with the attributes of BFFs is laid out in Lynn Murphy and Alnoor Ladha's book *Post Capitalist Philanthropy*. The 6 Principles of Trust-Based Philanthropy are also relevant.

Donor-Advised Funds (DAFs)[200]	Inspiration, ecological, social, and economic	Same as above.	As of 2022, there was an estimated $230B in more than 1.2 million DAFs in the US.[201] These funds have already been contributed for public interest purposes and could be quickly mobilized to support BFFs, perhaps starting with DAFs held by Community Foundations that already have a place-based mandate. All BFFs are strong candidates for DAF donations for mission aligned donors. Additionally, the financial capital in DAFs can be invested in Systemic Investment Funds before a donation is made. It should also be noted that there is no requirement that DAFs are invested in return-generating investments.
Individual donations (crowdfunding, Bioregional Tithing, access fees for public lands or lands held as commons, etc.)	Inspiration, ecological, social, and economic	Same as above.	Individuals will have various incentives for donating to a given bioregion. Some of these incentives include: residency; land stewardship; exposure to ecological risks in the bioregion; benefitting from common assets in the bioregion; benefitting from historical or ongoing activities contributing to extraction/degradation; and having an ancestral, cultural, or spiritual connection to a place.
Revenue generated through an Earth fee[202]	Inspiration, ecological, social, and economic	Same as above.	Policymakers, regulators, and companies may choose to pursue this low-friction way to aggregate capital that is relatively inconsequential to the consumer (1 cent on a $10 purchase), but over time could generate significant pooled funding. Companies participating are also able to receive recognition for the positive impact that results.

200 A donor-advised fund is a charitable account, whereby donors make irrevocable, tax-deductible contributions to a charitable sponsor. Donors give up legal control of these donated assets to the DAF sponsor, but retain advisory privileges that allow them to recommend how those funds are distributed to the nonprofits of their choosing and can also recommend how funds in the account are invested (The Foundation Review).

201 In the US, there is currently no spend-down requirement on these DAFs. A problem that could be addressed to increase the flow of funding to regeneration. (National Philanthropic Trust: 2023 DAF Report)

202 An 'Earth fee' is a voluntary transaction fee built into transactions (including financial transactions), such as point-of-sale POS systems, in-app purchases, or other opt-in methods for collecting a small fractional fee based on revenue (e.g. 10 basis points). See Karl Burkart's TED Talk: If nature could draw a map of the world.

| Market-rate investment capital | Inspiration, ecological, social, and economic/financial | Projects or businesses that are expected to generate a financial return, including activities in the following categories: regenerative agriculture, regenerative forestry, eco-tourism, circular economy, regenerative built environment, water purification and efficiency, eco-credits. | Investors are increasingly seeking to realize returns beyond the strictly financial. There is a growing pool of "impact-first investors."[203] Because of the catalytic nature of BFFs – particularly their focus on driving the transition to a regenerative economy and serving as connective tissue – BFFs offer investors inspiration, social, ecological, and economic returns at a potentially significantly higher rate,and with greater upside potential, than what they have access to through alternatives. By investing in BFFs, investors also help to build resilient business ecosystems, and thus, investment markets of the future. |
| **Concession-ary invest-ment capital** | Inspiration, ecological, social, and economic/financial | Same as above, but able to invest in more innovative organizations or projects that might be perceived as higher risk (especially through conventional risk-assessment tools). | Same as above. |

203 Social Finance estimated the annual dealflow of global impact-first investments to be approximately $24 billion.

Insurance company balance sheets	Inspiration, ecological, social, and economic/ financial	Projects or businesses that are expected to generate a financial return and reduce risks to assets that the insurance companies are providing policies for. This includes activities in the following categories: regenerative agriculture, regenerative forestry, eco-tourism, circular economy, regenerative built environment, water purification and efficiency, eco-credits.	Insurance companies are increasingly realizing the risks to their business ecological destruction poses.[204] Investing in regeneration through a systemic, bioregional approach can help insurance companies navigate the risks they are exposed to through their policies and underwriting. If they are able to develop risk-return models that take the value of systemic risk reduction into account, there is potential for them to fund common assets.
Central bank balance sheets	Inspiration, ecological, social, and economic/ financial	Through Bioregional Regeneration Bonds, central banks can invest in activities that support ecosystem recovery and mitigate broader economic and financial risks.	These bonds could be an avenue for Central Banks to support bioregional regeneration and address the myriad economic and financial risks emanating from destruction of the biosphere, which Central Banks are tasked with managing (NGFS, 2023 – both). These bonds can link returns to bioregional regeneration targets in a structure known as a "sustainability-linked bond," enabling the sharing of the financial value of risk reduction that comes with regeneration.[205]

204 The World Bank: Insuring Nature's Survival: The Role of Insurance in Meeting the Financial Need to Preserve Biodiversity
205 The World Bank has developed a 'Feasibility-AmBitiousness (FAB) Matrix' for sovereign sustainability-linked bond criteria, which can be used to guide bioregional target setting.

Supply chain finance	Inspiration, ecological, social, and economic/ financial	Projects or businesses contributing to supply chain resilience, directly or indirectly. Projects or businesses regenerating lands and waters that have historically been extracted from or degraded by the company.	Business operational, reputational, or legal risks posed by the ecological crisis or social instability. Also regulatory or public pressure for reporting on impacts and dependencies on nature, including through reporting frameworks like the Taskforce on Nature-related Financial Disclosures (TNFD).
Revenue through eco-credits (more on this topic in Case Study 6: Regen Network and Eco-credits)	Inspiration, ecological, social, and economic/ financial	Projects contributing to land or water stewardship that fit the criteria for one or more locally developed eco-credit methodologies or a global methodology that accurately reflects ecological value in the bioregion.	Companies increasingly see the need to support locally-defined ecological regeneration as opposed to purchasing credits that have been developed through a top-down approach that is not reflective of the tenets of effective stewardship in a given place.

As the wave of return-seeking capital committing to investing in nature grows (as explained in Section 1), we believe that the owners and managers of financial capital will increasingly see the imperative to drive decentralization of financial resource governance and catalyze the transition to a regenerative economy.

BFFs provide a pathway for even multinational corporations – that often seem to operate everywhere and nowhere at the same time – to come back into relationship with the very real places and people they are dependent on and are in turn impacting. BFFs enable them to move towards healing and reciprocity through how they invest.

We have identified a range of return seeking funds under development that we believe embody criteria that align with what Bioregional Financing Facilities can offer. More such funds are being launched all the time. Pollination and the Green Climate Fund have recently launched a fund that aims to raise billions of dollars to fund the transition of the agricultural system to regenerative practices. The fund plans to finance smallholder farmers via local financial institutions – a role that BFFs are well suited to play.[206] Additionally, there is potential for DAF investment (which does not necessarily require a return), as well as DAF donations, to flow into BFFs. We believe that it is important that capital holders build their capacity to understand bioregional, systemic approaches to regeneration so that they are better equipped to assess and engage with this new category of investment.

206 Carbon Pulse: Pollination plans blended regenerative agriculture fund worth billions

While it is unlikely to be tapped to capitalize Bioregional Financing Facilities directly, *public direct investment* can also play an important role in funding bioregional regeneration. National and sub-national authorities have resources allocated to various regeneration activities to support the provision of common assets. In contrast to the public grant capital, outlined above, public direct investment often involves projects of significant scale. Examples of projects where this form of capital could be tapped include: dam removal and restoration, fire risk mitigation activities on public lands, and coastal flood risk mitigation projects on public land.

Tax revenue and *subsidies* are important sources of funding, which can be raised by sub-national or national authorities to support regenerative activities. BFFs can work closely with these authorities to ensure alignment between economic fiscal policy and Bioregional Regeneration Strategies.[207] Taxes and subsidies will play an important role in funding common assets. One possible structure for this is the Common Asset Trust model. In this model, certain assets are held in common and anyone who degrades them must pay in, where individuals or organizations regenerating them receive compensation commensurate with their contributions. Place-based taxation districts like utility districts, urban renewal districts, municipalities, and counties provide precedents for both voluntary (e.g. Shuumi Land Tax on Ohlone territory) and legislatively-authorized bioregional taxation.

Generally, we want to highlight that capitalization is needed both from outside the bioregion and from within. While further dependencies on external financial capital should be avoided, it will not be possible to mobilize the needed amounts from within every bioregion – particularly in colonized contexts that have been subject to centuries of wealth extraction.[208] At the same time, it is important that both financial and real economic value flows remain rooted in the community, bringing significant economic benefits through local circulation while also fostering a sense of ownership and commitment among local stakeholders (more about the Local Multiplier Effect in **Section 4.5**). In this way, external capital can be transitionary – helping to build endogenous capacity.

Ultimately, mobilizing citizens and local businesses to become active investors, as well as customers, clients, and advocates, should support a healthy local economy that benefits both local and external stakeholders. Complementary currencies can also play a key role here.[209]

207 More about environmental fiscal reform in Section 3.1 of An Overview of Nature-Related Risks and Potential Policy Actions for Ministries of Finance: Bending The Curve of Nature Loss.

208 According to the UN International Panel on Climate Change: "Vulnerability of ecosystems and people to climate change differs substantially among and within regions (very high confidence), driven by patterns of intersecting socio-economic development, unsustainable ocean and land use, inequity, marginalization, historical and ongoing patterns of inequity such as colonialism, and governance (high confidence)."

209 More about this in research on the Grassroots Economics Foundation's Community Inclusion Currency (CIC) implemented in Kenya.

4.4 Systemic Investment Portfolios for Bioregional Regeneration

Bioregional Financing Facilities strive to address the inherent limitations of existing sustainability and regeneration financing mechanisms. Even where individual financing solutions are agreed upon today (e.g. a local bank issuing a loan on concessionary terms to a social enterprise from the region), these merely focus on a single project or intervention at a time, systematically disregarding the interconnected nature of real life. From a systems perspective, catalyzing individual projects in such an uncoordinated manner seldom has a meaningful impact on overall transitions, and is unlikely to tip entire systems on relevant time scales. This is one of the reasons why current approaches in impact investing and venture philanthropy have not delivered the system-wide impact they promised to catalyze. Often, individual project success is stalled by systemic barriers that could be removed through policy change, market creation, or connectivity between different silos of work.

Bioregional Financing Facilities seek to establish a financial architecture that recognizes the complexity inherent to systemic transformation and the fundamental interconnectedness of interventions. We recommend that they build on the emerging concept of systemic investing as an evolution of impact investing.[210]

Table 11. Traditional Impact Investing vs. Systemic Investing (Daggers et al. 2023)

	Traditional Impact Investing	**Systemic Investing**
Impact Frame	Improve a metric	Transform a system
Source of Impact	Individual companies/projects	Portfolio effects
Unit of Analysis / Transaction	Single asset	Strategic portfolio
Impact Metrics	Static gains/reductions	Systems dynamics
Funding Paradigm	Single instrument	Funding architecture
Nature of the World	Predictive, linear, atomized	Uncertain, complex, systemic

Bioregional Financing Facilities can help to build synergistic and systemic investment portfolios that create cascading benefits, which enable mutually reinforcing and positive feedback loops of systemic value generation across projects. Projects bundled in a systemic portfolio (see *Figure 10. below*) enhance each other's regenerative impact and financial performance alike. In addition to viable business cases, investments in such synergistic and systemic portfolios will likely include investments

210 For further information on possible investment strategies under the systemic investing paradigm, see Alban Yau: How Can Impact Investors Enable Systems Change? Exploring the Theory and Practice of an Emerging Field.

in a series of interventions with low or no direct profitability that remove significant obstacles for other projects to become successful in both impact and financial terms. These projects receive financing because of their positive contribution to the overall success of the portfolio. For example, simultaneously financing a set of farms to transition to regenerative practices, an urban education program on healthy diets, and a sustainable transportation system by bundling them in a systemic investment portfolio, helps the projects succeed and strengthens the investment case. In this case, the education program creates demand for healthy produce from regenerative farms, and a sustainable supply chain benefits from increased transport volume from rural areas to urban centers. At the same time, investors benefit from higher expected overall profitability as projects mutually enhance their value proposition.

The current investment paradigm, built on Modern Portfolio Theory, aims to minimize correlation between assets and to maximize diversification to reduce investment risk. This is based on the myth that investors cannot impact systemic risks through their capital allocation decisions.[211] This assumption is becoming increasingly hard to justify in the age of the polycrisis and as assessments of how investment portfolios are contributing to specific risks increase in their robustness and specificity.

In contrast, bioregional investment portfolios intentionally seek to create a harmonious interplay among diverse assets, leveraging spillover effects and fostering mutual reinforcement. By setting the investment strategy to meticulously select and align assets that complement one another, the portfolio generates synergistic effects across the bioregional economy. This mimics how resource flows are structured in living systems, and allows the combined regenerative impact to far exceed the sum of its individual components.

How this works on a bioregional transition or bioregional economy level can be compared to how Venture Capital and Private Equity investments, for example, do not only invest in the production and sales teams of a given company but also recognize the indirect contribution of, for example, the accounting and human resources departments as necessary overheads that require resourcing. At the bioregional scale, such "overheads" might include activism and policy work, systems mapping, multi-stakeholder convening and facilitation work, conflict mediation, and the services provided by Bioregional Hubs more broadly (see Section 3.2).

Through such an ecosystem-based investment approach at the bioregional scale, individual interventions add up to meaningful, directional, and catalyzed transitions. Even innovation gaps can be clearly identified, labeled, and signaled to the public to spur new project development and business creation.

While traditionally, investors or other financial intermediaries would pick projects for their portfolios, new governance mechanisms in the BFFs could ensure that bioregional investment portfolios are built through decentralized decision-making and in alignment with the Bioregional Regeneration Strategy.

---

211 In their 2023 book *Moving Beyond Modern Portfolio Theory: Investing That Matters*, Lukomnik and Hawley debunk this myth.

Bioregional investment portfolios can either cover a series of place-based assets across regeneration themes, or a range of thematic assets across various geographies (see image below). This allows both investors with place-based intentions or restrictions and investors with thematically restricted investment foci to participate in bioregional regeneration finance. Investing in different types of portfolios can also help with diversification and investment risk mitigation.

Figure 10: Possible composition of both place-based and thematic bioregional investment portfolios.

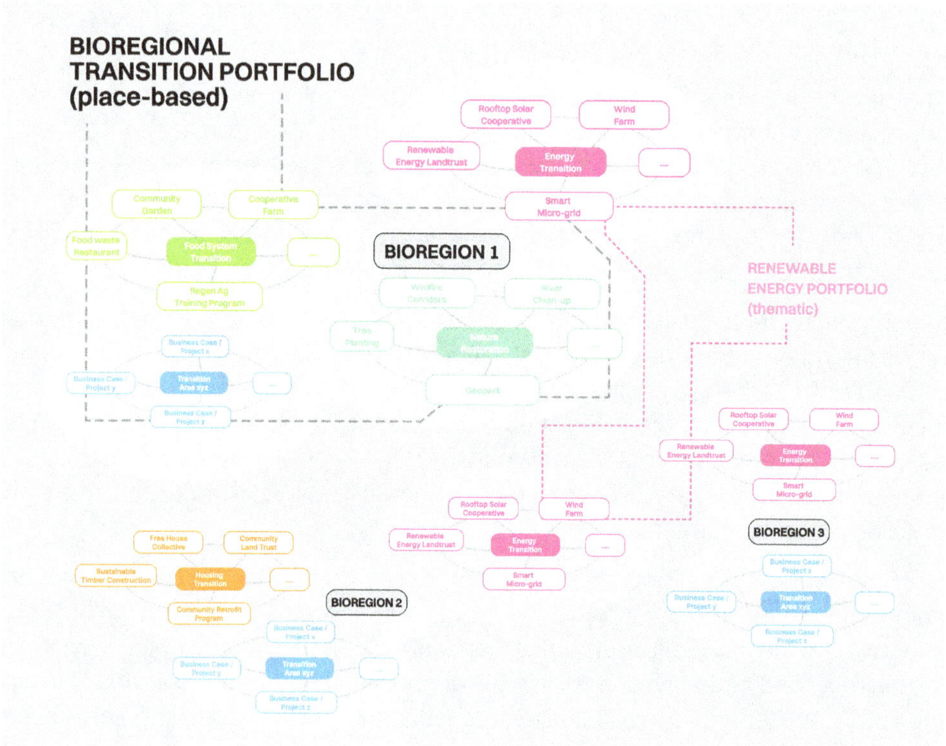

Note: This diagram is indicative only. (Inspired by Hannant et al. 2022.)

4.5 Shifting theories of value and ownership

As shown above, BFFs serve the realization of the Bioregional Regeneration Strategy. Their task is to determine how financial resources can best be deployed to support the transition to regenerative economies. This purpose, embedded in the BFF structure, enables them to support a shift in theory of value in the bioregion. Over time, BFFs can also enable a shift in value for the external actors the bioregion engages with. In *The Value of Everything*, Mariana Mazzucato directs us to look at who defines value, creates value, and reaps the rewards of that value.[212] BFFs can enable value – identified through participatory processes including participatory budgeting – to translate into the bioregional economy, its neighboring economies, and the global economy. Additionally, BFFs support the transition to a more local economy – enabling a greater percentage of the value created by the people there to stay there. The "Local Multiplier Effect"[213] shows that money spent in the local economy circulates more often in that place than money spent at non-local businesses (AIBA). Moving from an individual to a shared ownership model, or even self-sovereignty of living systems, can support a paradigm-level shift to catalyze the transition to regenerative economies.

The concepts of property and ownership often imply notions of dominion and control, leading us to view elements of the natural world, such as animals, land, and minerals, as commodities.[214] In regenerative economies, timber is not worth more than an intact forest and a whale's life is not interchangeable with 23,500 barrels of oil.[215] There is value in their respective existence separate from the value they provide to humans. BFFs can support the repair of relationships between humans and the rest of life in a way that recognizes the intrinsic value of the more-than-human world. Enabling the legibility of this value is something that other financial instruments and institutions have largely failed to do thus far. The monoculturization[216] of value has been reinforced by abstract, decontextualized economic metrics including GDP that take a uniform approach to assessing value. It has also been bolstered by new markets like decentralized finance, with metrics such as "Total Value Locked" that fall into the trap of Goodhart's law, where the measure becomes the target. This collapses dimensionality, as such measures fail to account for real value creation or ecological well being, and do not account for much needed circulation in our value flows.[217] There are promising models like Bhutan's Gross Domestic Happiness (GDH) and metrics oriented towards dynamism and circulation like Total Value Flowed that BFFs can iterate on and contextualize bioregionally.

212 Mazzucato: *The Value of Everything*
213 A term developed by economist John Maynard Keynes in his 1936 book The General Theory of Employment, Interest and Money.
214 Dark Matter Labs: Life Ennobling Economics
215 Buller: *The Value of a Whale*
216 An allusion to the dominant industrial agriculture practice of monoculture, in which biodiversity is destroyed in order to plant an entire field with a single species of crop that can be managed with machinery and inputs so as to maximize short-term production
217 Total Value Flowed is suggested as a potential metric for regenerative (ecological) economics in the book *MycoFi: Mycelial Design Patterns for Web3 & Beyond* by Jeff Emmett & Jessica Zartler.

Pilots of mechanisms through which BFFs can support the legibility of varying dimensions of value – including giving mountains and rivers their own blockchain addresses and wallets – are underway (see more in the Regen Network case study). Indigenous ways of relating to the more-than-human world, particularly through a kinship lens, are beginning to spread. Additionally, shifting technological capacities can support this legibility, as laid out in Gaia 2.0. Finally, the development of complementary or Nature-based Currencies can play a critical role in shifting the local economy to align with what people in a bioregion value.

5. BFF
Gover
and
Alloc

5. BFF Governance and Capital Allocation

The governance structure of BFFs underpins their ability to decentralize financial resource governance, organize synergistic portfolios, and catalyze the transition to a regenerative economy. In this section, we offer high-level guidance regarding several key considerations and aims for governance, and offer various approaches and tools that we hope will be helpful. However, a full exploration of governance is not within the scope of this book.

At their core, financial institutions –BFFs and otherwise – are humans coming together to make decisions about how to raise and allocate resources and build systems to execute those decisions. In other words, they are ultimately about governance, and governance is challenging for all types of organizations. Adding further difficulty, BFFs represent an intentional attempt to encode an institution with worldviews, values, logic, and context that are fundamentally distinct from those of existing financial institutions. The beliefs, assumptions, and habits of governance resulting from education, socialization, and participation in modern institutions can be expected to cause friction where attempts are made to govern resource raising and allocation towards genuine regeneration, free from externalities. While humbled by the magnitude of this challenge, we also believe that the ancient and modern wisdom needed to support this purpose is alive and accessible. Through experiments in creating BFFs around the world, the collective intelligence of place can be harnessed to inform and support an entire network of BFFs - allowing common patterns of trustworthy governance structures to emerge.

5.1 Key consideration: What are the values?

The governance structure (frameworks, processes, and participants) is what encodes values held by individuals or a group into an institution. BFF attribute #3 (Section 4.1) offers the highest level guidance: "Implement an inclusive, participatory governance structure that represents the bioregion." While inclusivity, participation, and representation are values that can be understood very broadly, each Bioregional Regeneration Strategy should work to clarify specific, place-based understandings of these and other values that are to be upheld in any aspect of the work, especially BFF governance. We recommend that the "R Values" that many Indigenous communities center in their governance (Section 4.1) also play a key role in governance design.[218] In particular, we highlight that given the complexity and delicacy of governance, BFFs can only succeed if built on a solid relational foundation that creates a culture of trust.

5.2 Key consideration: Who participates?

The Bioregional Organizing Team will organize and activate key bioregional actors, and identify appropriate bioregional representatives to serve in BFF governance. There are pros and cons in taking a more democratic approach, so BFFs may want to consider an approach of progressive decentralization, where a Bioregional Organizing Team might decide to pursue something more open after a given BFF has a solid foundation. A participatory process to identify trusted actors in the ecosystem (including through leveraging Web3 technologies) can play a role. To sincerely "represent the bioregion", the management, board, investment committee, and participatory processes that feed into the capital allocation should be representative of the people living and working in the bioregion, and the people that have historically stewarded land in the bioregion (if they have been misplaced). We strongly recommend that the

218 For example: relationality, reciprocity, responsibility, respect, reverence, regeneration, redistribution, and reconnection

board be ethnically and culturally representative of bioregional residents and, particularly, that Indigenous groups are represented in the places where they reside.[219] This is important, as Indigenous representatives will bring wisdom from centuries of regenerative land stewardship, relational worldviews focused on kinship, and life-centered theories of value. Additionally, a process should be established to receive regular input from both youth and elders. Additional processes might be established to ensure other underrepresented groups have a voice – including low-income, previously incarcerated, otherly-abled, LGBTQIA+ people, ethnic minorities, refugees, and others. This diversity will be beneficial for cultivating the collective intelligence needed to effectively drive financial capital to regeneration. We strongly recommend that governance boards rotate periodically in order to bring new energy and ideas to BFFs. For the board in particular, a town hall or election could be held to select members.

We also recommend the inclusion of representatives for more-than-human life on BFF boards to ensure that the financial capital raised is not used to narrowly serve human interests, but is allocated to serve all of the life in the bioregion. There is a growing body of work around rights of nature and how nature can be given jurisdictional rights. Species and geological or hydrological features (e.g. rivers and mountains) are also being placed on boards through human proxies and even own assets (more about this in the case study on Regen Network).[220]

Technical expertise and relationships with key stakeholders will also be important enablers for effective BFF governance. BFF management teams must be bridge builders – understanding economics, finance, systems change, as well as having a connection to local context, risks, and opportunities. Team members are likely to be transdisciplinary experts who can perceive and act transcontextually, navigate diverse theories of value, and oversee an integrated approach to data management. The BFF management team should be adept at using software tools – including the latest nature MRV, community engagement,

219 Indigenous Commons, a group of diverse Indigenous representatives working to get more capital governed by Indigenous groups, has developed a set of principles for capital management based on wisdom from a range of Indigenous traditions around the world.
220 Earth Law Center has a public library of rights of nature templates of laws, resolutions, letters and other legal instruments that can be used to support representative governance of BFFs.
221 The International Bateson Institute: Warm Data Labs.

and participatory budgeting software. Governance representatives should also be long-term thinkers, as they will be making investment decisions that should align with a 20-100+ year or multigenerational Bioregional Regeneration Strategy. Selecting the right people for these positions is critical in ensuring that BFFs can effectively serve as connective tissue.

Another consideration for BFF governance is the interplay between public and expert forums. Public forums should be a place for free expression and, therefore, not dominated by experts, while expert forums[222] should provide latitude for experts to exchange specialized knowledge without having to conform to popular opinion or to cultivate a following. BFF governance processes should support this balance, and the integration of voices from both the public and experts can help ensure that decisions are data-driven, account for stakeholder needs, and are democratically legitimate.[223]

5.3 Key consideration: What frameworks, processes, and tools?

A wide range of frameworks can be applied to support the implementation of an "inclusive, participatory governance structure that represents the bioregion." We offer no prescriptions here, besides strongly recommending study of place-based Indigenous governance frameworks and commons management frameworks – including Elinor Ostrom's 8 Principles for Managing a Commons. However, several frameworks that may be useful in establishing a governance structure include:

— Prosocial, a scientific framework (built upon Ostrom's foundational research) and guided process for designing governance structures that support cooperative behavior
— Sociocracy and Holacracy, two similar systems that support self-governance and decentralization[224]
— Traditional hierarchical structures with checks & balances (e.g. wisdom/elder councils, purpose guardians/trustees)

Regarding processes, each BFF will need systems in place to enable transparency and responsiveness around capital raising and allocation. To the extent possible, BFFs should seek to make documents about these processeses public. Decision criteria about which projects are selected and why should be published. Tools such as Open Collective, "a fundraising + legal status + money management platform for grassroots groups," can support these efforts in their early stages. The affiliations of

---

222 More information on this in Block Science: Arbitrum Expert Service Provider Network Program Development.
223 Credit to Jessica Zartler, Block Science.
224 "Holacracy is one form of sociocracy. While sociocracy leaves a lot of room for many parameters to be set by the individual organization, Holacracy comes with a lot of pre-set parameters." (Sociocracy For All: Sociocracy and Holacracy: Sameness and differences).

the board, investment committee, and management of BFFs should be disclosed, so conflicts of interest can be identified and addressed as appropriate. Additionally, BFFs should be responsive to the requests and recommendations of the public. BFFs should enable empowered participation – recognizing that all citizens of the bioregion have a right to shape the decisions about the future of their place. For example, citizens assembled might play an important role early in the BFF strategy process. Later on, BFFs might host town hall meetings at regular intervals in order to hear about urgent investment needs directly from community members before making grant or investment decisions or to get feedback on the impact of investments.

Innovative social methodologies and tools for collective decision-making that may support the design and execution of broader governance structures include:

— Liquid Democracy, "a form of delegative democracy, whereby an electorate engages in collective decision-making through direct participation and dynamic representation."[225] The non-profit Liquid Democracy provides open-source tools to support such processes.
— Participatory budgeting through an Edge Prize-inspired model
— Emerging tech that allows for real-time preference signaling (such as Quadratic Voting and Conviction Voting).
— Novel voting delegation mechanisms (e.g. Neural Quorum Governance).[226]
— "Two Eyed Seeing" - a concept from the Acadia and Eskasoni Nations integrating Indigenous wisdom and Western Science.[227]
— Systems for sourcing and privileging contextual data based on social relationships of trust. For example, the opinions of trusted subject-matter experts and place-based representatives can be highlighted in the discussion of issues, which may support finding common ground and weighing of trade-offs. If using a voting system, their votes could carry more weight.[228]
— Polis, "a real-time system for gathering, analyzing and understanding what large groups of people think in their own words, enabled by advanced statistics and machine learning."
— RadicalxChange, a platform that provides tools that support participatory and pluralistic funding, voting and ownership structures.
— Convergent Facilitation, "a decision-making process designed to build trust across differences and integrate what's important to everyone involved."

225 Wikipedia: Liquid democracy
226 Block Science: Introducing Neural Quorum Governance
227 More details here: Two-Eyed Seeing: Current approaches, and discussion of medical applications.
228 This can be done without the use of digital technology, and many Web3 efforts are underway to support such efforts; In their 2022 paper, Etheruem Co-founder Vitalik Buterin and others "illustrate how non-transferable "soulbound" tokens (SBTs) representing the commitments, credentials, and affiliations of "Souls" [i.e. unique, identity-protected individuals] can encode the trust networks of the real economy to establish provenance and reputation." (Olhaver, Weyl, and Buterin: Decentralized Society: Finding Web3's Soul)

5.4 Key aim: Work to shift power imbalances

Shifting power imbalances requires BFF management and board members to see, understand, and commit to addressing these imbalances among themselves, with citizens in the bioregion, and between financial capital holders and regenerators. To do this, they must embrace this work as a collective learning and unlearning – recognizing how their worldview and life experience have shaped them. For those holding substantial financial capital or financial and legal expertise, their ways of thinking, communicating, and acting, both consciously and unconsciously, are likely to have been crafted in part by learning how to "succeed" in navigating dominant systems of power. These learned traits may present challenges in a diverse group orienting around alternative value systems, especially in conversations of money and governance. Thus, it is critical that BFFs intentionally work to foster a healthy learning culture with a shared commitment to engaging in discussions about shifting power imbalances openly, humbly, and with care. Employing professional facilitators and educators, along with broader engagement with the BioFi Community of Practice (see attribute #12 in Section 4.1), can help establish and maintain this culture.

BFFs can also take steps to structure governance to prevent incentives that might put profits over purpose and compromise the BFF's ability to serve the Bioregional Regeneration Strategy. For example, operating governance can be separated from governance of the distribution of profits, so that those overseeing operations are not tempted to drive profits over purpose.

5.5 Key aim: Work with existing authorities

BFFs and Bioregional Organizing Teams can partner and support existing public work that is aligned with the Bioregional Regeneration Strategy and receives aligned public funding to educate and advocate to local authorities in areas where they see gaps in public programs; mobilize resources for critical activities when local authorities are failing to do so; and act as a 'partner state' over time.[229]

Partner state – Multi-stakeholder cooperatives or commons-based institutions responsible for the management and provision of certain public goods, common assets, or services that were once the responsibility of state governments, which instead provide funding and performance evaluation to partner states.[230]

229 Credit to Lawrence Grodeska of the Bay Delta Trust.
230 P2P Foundation Wiki: Partner State

While bioregional governance, capacity building resources, and financing facilities are under development, national and sub-national authorities continue to hold the majority of these resources and management responsibilities. Therefore, knowledge of public programs and procedures can support BFF management and boards in effectively raising and allocating financial capital or other resources through existing publicly-funded programs. For example, in the United States, knowledge of how to access public finance allocated through the Inflation Reduction Act will be critical. BFFs can also work with authorities to collaboratively develop strategies for devolving decision making around resource allocation to bioregional entities. This has been done with watershed authorities in many places globally, including Washington and Oregon in the US, New Zealand, and Australia. Similarly, Costa Rica has Territorial Councils.

5.6 Key aim: Build right relationship with other BFFs across regions and scales

Bioregionalism is about appropriate alignment with the natural systems and cultures of a region. The understanding that bioregions are interdependent with each other and contain within them many scales of natural systems and cultures is fundamental to achieving appropriate alignment. For example, rivers often cross multiple bioregions that each have fractal watersheds and distinct cultural regions, all of which are interdependent with the river. Appropriately allocating financial resources to support the regeneration of the river and its interdependent regions simply cannot be done by a single institution. For BFFs to effectively fulfill the vision of planetary regeneration, they must be able to govern in *right relationship* with each other. In some cases BFFs may form relationships of solidarity, deciding to share resources — and their governance — towards interdependent aims. In other cases, BFFs may identify the need to invest in the creation of additional BFFs at higher or lower scales so that resources can be governed and distributed fractally. These are only two possibilities; there is no theoretically ideal prescription that can be offered today for what these right relationships should be, as it will depend entirely upon the emergent capacity in each area. At this early stage, however, it is critical that BFFs are designed with this fundamental entanglement in mind, and that they seek to build relationships of trust with other relevant BFFs and emerging Bioregional Hubs, such that healthy conditions for gradual experimentation towards shared, interoperable governance in right relationship are established.

6. Innovative Mechanisms for Financing Bioregional Regeneration

6. Innovative Mechanisms for Financing Bioregional Regeneration

There are a range of innovative financing mechanisms that we believe can help BFFs achieve their objectives. Many of the themes explored in this book are aligned with the values and patterns driving the decentralized finance or "DeFi" movement. The authors believe that the potential of existing protocols, tools, technologies, and templates in the Web3 space to bolster the bioregional movement and supercharge grassroots regeneration, has – as yet – not been realized. Additionally, there is potential for further innovation, building on what has been learned in Web3 to date and what we have laid out with the objectives, attributes, and templates of BFFs. The BioFi x DeFi intersection provides fertile soil for experimentation. In this section, we explore a range of innovative financial tools and approaches (in the DeFi space and beyond) that we believe could help capitalize Bioregional Financing Facilities, enable participatory capital allocation, and support the transition to regenerative bioregional economies. Some areas we would like to see further innovation and experimentation include: bioregional Nature-based Currencies, bioregional participatory capital allocation (including through Quadratic Voting or Quadratic Funding), and the construction of Ecological Institutions for ecosystems or species to support their regeneration and sovereignty.

6.1 Web3-based eco-credits, Decentralized Autonomous Organizations, and Ecological Institutions

Web3-based eco-credits, Decentralized Autonomous Organizations (DAOs), and Ecological Institutions present innovative tools for financing bioregional regeneration efforts. Web3-based eco-credits, built on blockchain or Holochain[231] platforms, provide a transparent and traceable mechanism for validating ecological health. They can measure and trace such indicators as carbon sequestration, biodiversity indices, erosion mitigation, water conservation, social prosperity and wellbeing, and cultural integrity indicators like Indigenous ancestral stewardship. (see case study on Regen Network below). These eco-credits can be tokenized and traded on decentralized marketplaces, allowing stakeholders to invest in bioregional regeneration initiatives. It is important to recognize that these eco-credits are not primarily designed to "offset" destructive activities, as in the case of conventional carbon credits. They can play a much more flexible role in recording the community-determined value of a set of regenerative actions, and they can identify the value flows of biodiversity and ecosystem services in need of preservation or regeneration and validate effective action taken. Eco-credits can support the shift to more pluralistic approaches to assessing value within a bioregion. This enables a more transparent view of financial beneficiaries so buyers can make more informed choices that align with economies rooted in equity and commons stewardship.

The joint ownership and authorship of eco-credits is made possible through decentralized protocols in the form of blockchain-powered DAOs. DAOs can be understood as an evolution of commons, combining digital governance with common pool resource management. They enable decentralized decision-making and resource allocation within a community, leveraging smart contracts, to automate the distribution of funds for bioregional regeneration projects based on predefined criteria and community consensus. Through DAOs and Web3-based eco-credits, communities can mobilize financial resources in a transparent, accountable, and decentralized manner. Examples of DAOs innovating to support regeneration include Gitcoin, Kolektivo, and Big Green DAO.

Ecological Institutions use decentralized protocols to enable the creation of novel legal and economic actors, which would not be possible in a conventional centralized system of ownership, sensing, and governance. These Institutions enable non-conventional ecological actors, like non-human organisms, ecosystems, and even whole bioregions, to own their own currency, deeds, and information held on their unique blockchain address (See more in the Regen Network case study below).[232]

---

231 While similar to blockchain in using cryptography to create a distributed ledger for decentralized data management, Holochain is designed to empower peer-to-peer coordination and agreement customization while yielding greater efficiency and scalability by avoiding blockchain's dependence on a single universal system state across all participating computers. (HOLO: Here's Holochain in 100, 200, and 500 words)

232 Regen Foundation: Ecological Institutions → Protocols to Grow Autonomous and Convivial Ecological Actors

Regen Network and Eco-Credits - A Novel Funding Mechanism for Regeneration

By: Austin Wade Smith

About the Regen Network

Established on the belief that land stewards and local communities should define what eco-social regeneration looks like in their context, the Regen Network is an open source technology stack and blockchain dedicated to the redefinition of value, away from extraction, towards planetary regeneration. At the core of the project, is the belief that the instruments used to align finance with environmental wellbeing must be owned and governed by communities practicing regeneration. One of the primary instruments in achieving this are eco-credits, a novel funding mechanism that can support the protection of ecosystems and the stewardship practices which regenerate them. An eco-credit can be understood as an evolution of ecosystem service credits used in climate finance, like carbon credits, with several critical differences. Credits function like a discrete unit of value – fungible, non-fungible, or a combination of both – within a regenerative economic paradigm. Unlike philanthropy or impact investing, which allocate resources to critical habitats and people who need it most, regenerative economics redefines value at its root, arguing that ecosystems and their steward relationships produce value while alive and intact through their life-sustaining ecosystem functions, not just as commodities and raw materials.

Composition

Eco-credits move past carbon-tunnel vision to represent a more holistic definition of biocultural health. Carbon drawdown, while extremely important, is only one parameter in a myriad of factors that define healthy and

Carbon-tunnel vision – A myopic perspective that ignores the multiple interdependent socio-ecological system crises that we face to focus only on carbon emissions, and/or focuses solely on carbon emissions reductions as the key climate change response. Phrase coined by Dr Jan Konietzko, Maastricht University.

prosperous ecosystems.

— Eco-credits are multidimensional attestations of ecological health which may include:

— Carbon sequestration

— Biodiversity indices

— Practice - based methodologies of ecosystem regeneration

— Erosion mitigation

— Water conservation

— Social prosperity and wellbeing

— Cultural integrity like Indigenous ancestral stewardship

Attesting to data is a way to validate a piece of data and is comparable to signing a legal document – implying the contents of the data are accepted to be true by the attestor to the best of their knowledge.

Governance

The dynamic composition of eco-credits reflects the belief that regeneration looks like different measures, indices, and practices in different places. Eco-credits are reflections of their biocultural context. Rather than top-down prescriptions of what regeneration looks like across different contexts endemic to climate finance, the composition of eco-credits must reflect the people, bioregion, and a larger story of place. The definition and creation of an eco-credit is coauthored by the larger group of stakeholders through governance processes:

— The primary author of the terms and composition of an eco-credit is the bioregional community directly responsible for the stewardship.

— Indigenous Peoples and Local Communities (IPLCs), ecosystem guardians and protectors must hold the primary authority for what biocultural indicators mark the composition of a credit.

— This bottom up definition of value is corroborated with external stakeholders, like the scientific community, as well credit purchasers.

A process of co-authorship for the definition of value beginning with stewards themselves means the identity and wellbeing of the communities doing the direct work of restoring and protecting ecosystems are centered in the design and development of eco-credits.

Definition through decentralized protocols

The joint ownership and authorship of eco-credits is made possible through decentralized protocols in the form of DAOs. DAOs can be understood as an evolution of commons, wedding digital governance with common pool resource management. They are a hybrid of digital knowledge commons and biospheric commons. DAOs can be bioregionally defined; in bioregional DAOs, the members who govern the DAO are bound by a particular region and may include the grassroots communities directly responsible for the regenerative work like IPLC's, local stewards, community boards, and guardians. DAOs may also be defined by association as guild DAOs, where members who govern the DAO are affiliated by shared knowledge and expertise – like scientific peer communities, supply chains, and impact verifiers. Designing the governance model between bioregional and guild DAOs allows different stakeholders to interact in a facilitated manner to govern the composition, roles, and terms of eco-credits. This is particularly important for the co-authoring of credits between originators and purchasers. It also allows all aspects of the creation of eco-credits to be transparent as appropriate, auditable, and thus continuously accountable to the claims and attestations they define.

Ecological Institutions

Additionally, the use of decentralized protocols enables the creation of novel legal and economic actors, which would not be possible in a conventional centralized system of ownership, sensing, and governance. Decentralized protocols enable non-conventional ecological actors, like non-human organisms, ecosystems, and even whole bioregions to own their own currency, deeds, and information. Ecosystems are in effect autonomous funds or trusts of information and currency that disperse resources towards different stakeholders or initiatives based on the satisfaction of contractual conditions. These entities, broadly referred to as Ecological Institutions, are an integration of regenerative economics enabled by blockchains and DAOs with the rights of nature movement, proposed by the emerging field of Earth law. Legal personhood and other designations allow organisms, ecosystems, and whole bioregions to own their own currency, data, and contracts in digital form. This means non-humans are able to legally possess digital currencies, digital files, and data sets, as well as digital copies of contracts and deeds. The design and definition of Ecological Institutions is an area for significant potential research, which integrates social governance practices with data inputs in the form of oracles. Oracles can be understood as ecological sensing systems which deliver data about the state of ecosystems and organisms as inputs into software systems, controlling the behavior of algorithms based on conditions in the environment. Ecological Institutions may issue, own, or coordinate the creation and circulation of eco-credits using a stack like the Regen Network. A comprehensive introduction to this topic can be found in the paper, Ecological Institutions by Austin Wade Smith, Regen Foundation, and Earth Law Center.

Programmable circulation

The relationship between eco-credits and decentralized protocols allows finer control over the terms and conditions of credit sales. Originators of eco-credits are able to specify to whom credits can or cannot be sold, as well as the terms of their fungibility or expiration. This allows the nature of the credit circulation to be programmable by the originators. We broadly refer to the ability to control how credits are sold, to whom, and the terms of their resale as programmable circulation, because unlike conventional financial systems, eco-credits issued and exchanged on blockchains, allow originators of credits to specify the conditions of how eco-credits are transacted.

While enabled by decentralized protocols of ownership and governance, decentralized protocols are not required. The principle of community ownership around the terms and definition of regeneration at a local level lies at the heart of what an eco-credit is. As such, they may be implemented across a wide range of systems, which do not run on top of decentralized ledger technologies like blockchains.

Regen Network works to scale joint trust agreements between originators and purchasers around context-specific regenerative action in the form of high integrity eco-credits. The Network supports an international community of practitioners and project developers designing and issuing eco-credits through the Regen Network app. Monthly eco-credit Builder Labs support and catalyze credit development, and are a good entry point into learning more about the relation of eco-credits to BFFs.

6.2 (Digital) Nature-based Currencies

Bioregional Banks could issue complementary Nature-based Currencies that base their value on the health and vitality of the local ecosystems - the ecological wealth - in a given bioregion. While most currencies in circulation today are no longer linked to physical assets such as gold, these new currencies would be tied to natural assets – fostering a symbiotic relationship between local economies and ecosystems. With this form of bioregional, asset-backed currency, BFFs could issue tokens representing natural assets like clean water, wild animal populations, or biodiversity conservation – incentivizing regenerative practices and the responsible stewardship of natural assets. Nature-based Currencies could also be backed by a basket of bioregional eco-credits. Ongoing research on the application of active inference[233] in the design of Nature-based Currencies can inform prototypes by bioregions. By integrating ecological indicators of health into monetary systems, BFFs can enable a shift in theory of value within the bioregion and beyond. For more information on digital Nature-based Currencies, we recommend reading Nature Based Currencies: Integrating natural capital in advanced monetary systems, a white paper by Open Earth Foundation.[234]

6.3 Local Market Networks and Bioregional Vouchers

While not necessarily a novel solution, Local Market Networks are potentially powerful ways to resource bioregional transitions toward regenerative economies. These networks are decentralized systems connecting producers, consumers, and investors within a bioregion. Emphasizing local sourcing, production, and consumption, the networks can take various forms, including farmers' markets, Community-Supported Agriculture (CSA) programs, online platforms for local goods, and community-based cooperatives. Local Market Networks aim to strengthen local economies, reduce environmental impact by minimizing transportation and supporting regenerative practices, and foster community resilience by promoting relationships between producers and consumers locally. They often prioritize transparency, ethical sourcing, and community engagement over traditional market dynamics such as competition.

Local Market Networks can also include innovative approaches like Bioregional Community Voucher systems as a form of community currency.[235] These systems promote local economic resilience by circulating currency within the community, facilitating transactions between residents and with local businesses. Unlike conventional currency, these vouchers are tied to a specific bioregion, encouraging value

233 Friston et al.: Federated inference and belief sharing
234 Additional resources and examples include: Kolektivo: Primer on Natural Capital Currencies: Silvi: TreeForwards; Ernesto van Peborgh: Living Capital Design: The Rise of Nature-based Currencies; Single.Earth: World's First Nature-Backed Currency MERIT
235 Examples include the Community Asset Vouchers program developed by Grassroots Economics.

exchange within the bioregional economy and supporting bioregional regeneration efforts. Such community currencies enable the two essential functions of money (i.e. serving as a standard of value and facilitating exchange), promoting quick circulation and discouraging its utilization as a store of value or a medium for speculation. They foster a sense of community ownership and solidarity, empowering residents to actively participate in shaping the future of their bioregion. They can also be used to avoid the undesired financialisation of value flows.

6.4 Bioservices Banks

A Bioservices Bank[236] is designed to integrate ecological services into the local financial system by turning them into financial assets. By issuing bills of exchange pegged against a stable currency and underwritten by third parties, the bank monetizes ecological services, creating a self-sustaining engine for financing ecological action. A Bioservices Bank operates by issuing notes equivalent to a national currency, backed by the value of ecological services. These notes become liquid in the market once the underwritten ecological services are matched with liabilities or financed through various methods. This system effectively transforms environmental conservation into a bankable service, creating a perpetual financing mechanism.

A pivotal element of this concept is the integration of a system where landowners and other actors can attribute their future rights to ecological services — for example the carbon sequestration rights of their land to the bank. This process, functioning similarly to assigning rights, allows these stakeholders to contribute their future ecological assets to the bank. In exchange for this contribution, they receive equity in the Bioservices Bank. This mechanism ensures that stakeholders directly benefit from the bank's capitalization and investments made by the bank or other agents in ecological projects. Thus, it creates a mutually beneficial relationship, aligning the interests of individual landowners and other actors with the broader goals of transitioning to regenerative bioregional economies.

A key feature of the proposed bank is its reliance on automation and transparent governance. The verification of ecological services, transaction processes, and banking operations would be fully automated, utilizing digital sensors and transparent frameworks. This ensures efficiency, accountability, and public trust. The governance structure is designed to avoid conflicts of interest. It suggests an independent oversight mechanism, separate from the banking institution's administrative body. This is crucial for maintaining impartiality and enhancing credibility.

236 Credit to Raj Kalia and Indy Johar of Dark Matter Capital Systems.

6.5 Participatory grant-making through Quadratic and Conviction Voting

Place-based participatory grant-making allows members of bioregional communities both to submit projects and vote on the ones they believe best serve the regeneration of the bioregion. Project proposals and votes are submitted via an app or platform which builds on both Quadratic Voting and Conviction Voting mechanisms.

In the case of participatory grant-making for bioregional regeneration, projects proposed by the community will need to align with the Bioregional Regeneration Strategy. Once a project gains sufficient community support, it advances to the stewardship phase, where stewards, who also serve as bioregional trustees, collaborate with project leaders to finalize submissions for funding consideration. Successfully approved projects receive funding. They then document expenses and project completion status and upload relevant information onto the selected platform to enable transparency and accountability.

Engaging bioregional stakeholders in proposing and voting on projects which they feel best support the Bioregional Regeneration Strategy allows the community to be empowered and connected. This helps foster a sense of purpose, connection, and belonging to place. Since the projects are carried out on a rolling basis, the funding can be administered on a similar basis.

Participatory grant-making through quadratic and Conviction Voting is currently being applied and piloted in the Golden Bay Bioregion in New Zealand (see Case Study 7 below).

237 Lalley and Weyl: Quadratic Voting: How Mechanism Design Can Radicalize Democracy
238 Jeff Emmett: Conviction Voting: A Novel Continuous Decision Making Alternative to Governance

Golden Bay and the Wellbeing Protocol – Participatory Grant-making through Quadratic and Conviction Voting in Practice

By: Reggie Luedtke

About Mohua 2042

Mohua 2042 is a Bioregional Trust located in the bioregion of Mohua/Golden Bay, Aotearoa/New Zealand. Mohua 2042 convened 60+ members of the local community in a process to create a strategic and inspirational vision for the bioregion over the next 20 years. During the gathering, blank posters around 9 key themes were placed around the venue and people collaborated in adding to and refining each of these. As a next step the trustees converted the posters into a 65 page strategic vision document for the bioregional trust.[239] The document was well received by the local government and has been published on the local district council website, under Mohua 2042.

Next, the trustees needed to decide how to carry out the execution of the strategy, and how to fund it. It was decided that the combination of purpose-owned companies, which exist for the benefit of the community and bioregion, would be supported along with a participatory grantmaking process – where anyone in the community could propose and vote on ideas. The Wellbeing Protocol team, a not-for-profit organization building technology-based infrastructure, was asked to set up a trial and developed an app that bioregional stakeholders could use for proposals and the voting process.

To positively constrain the types of projects which could be approved, the strategic vision was adapted into a constitution; all of the projects proposed and approved needed to fit with the constitution and vision. Once initial funding was secured from the local Tasman District Council, a kickoff meeting for Mohua Wellbeing 2042 was organized.

Launching the Trust

During the kickoff, community members learned both how the app functioned, and shared the projects they believed were valuable in advancing the goals set out in the strategic vision document and constitution. They also learned about other potential local projects, and the members who were present voted on projects using the app. The Wellbeing Protocol team demonstrated that projects which receive a certain number of up-votes would be approved to move to the next stage through *Quadratic Voting*. By this method, rather than using 10 percent

---

239 Mohua 2042: Strategy Document

of their tokens to give one up-vote, a member could use 40 percent of their tokens for two up-votes or 90 percent of their tokens for three up-votes. This allowed community members to cast their votes according to how passionate they were about a project. The up-votes would also be buffered using the Conviction Voting approach, such that the full power of the vote only set in after the vote was not moved or changed to another option.

Once a project receives enough up-votes from the community, the bioregional trustees – who are stewards within the app – can choose to move the project to the next phase but this is only possible if the project matches with the constitution, which is viewable by anyone within the app. Prior to moving the project to the next phase it is also reviewed in terms of its budget and feasibility, and stewards can make suggestions for changes to the project proposers during this time. The projects that make it to the final phase are then voted on again by the community. The amount of funding the project requires compared to the amount of money in the community funding pool determines the up-vote threshold the project must meet to be approved.

Moving to implementation

As of March 2024, four projects have progressed to the final proposal phase. Once a project is approved, the stewards work with the project lead to transfer the approved funding amount. As the project evolves, photos and videos related to the progress of the project are uploaded to the app for anyone in the community to view. In the first phase of funding, individual project costs ranged from NZD 200 to 1,000. The next phase involves securing ongoing funding to top up this community funding pool, ideally by local government and local companies. Initial funding was sourced by the local government and a few leads have been established with companies that have verbally committed to allocating 10 percent of their profits to community projects that support bioregional wellbeing. One advantage of the rolling approach is that capital can be added as trust is built that the community can collectively propose, steward, and execute on valuable projects.

The plan is also to help steward community-benefit companies that are steward-owned, i.e. owned by their purpose. These companies would be required to tithe 10 percent of their profits to Mohua Wellbeing, and would receive help with their incubation from local community business advisors as well as receiving community or purpose oversight from the Mohua 2042 Bioregional Trust. Mohua 2042 is a charitable non-profit, and the trust deed allows trustees to serve in an oversight capacity for purpose-owned companies in an unpaid capacity.

6.6 Quadratic Funding and Equity Crowdfunding as proxies for capital allocation

Crowdfunding is a financing instrument that allows ordinary citizens to participate in funding projects that are subjectively important to them. In the special case of equity crowd-funding, participating individuals gain shares of the funded project or business in return for their money. Place-based Equity Crowdfunding thus allows local stakeholders to participate in the success of the local regenerative economy, and simultaneously weaves even stronger connections in this local economy. At the same time, aggregated data from such place-based crowdfunding platforms could help funders and investors who are not as immersed in the local context to understand which projects locals consider worthy and promising. This helps them to overcome knowledge gaps, and investment decisions can be made more in alignment with what local people think best contributes to the Bioregional Regeneration Strategy. This approach operates on the premise that locals know best what is required for holistic regeneration, and where the likelihood of financial success is highest. This way, more money can find its way to the right regeneration projects in a bioregion. By surfacing tacit grassroots knowledge, place-based Equity Crowdfunding can act as a conduit, bridging the often-cited gap between those intimately acquainted with the needs of local regeneration and capital holders wanting to finance it.[240]

Another mechanism that is currently tested to amplify community voices and knowledge in financial resource allocation is Quadratic Funding – an idea that emerged as an extension of Quadratic Voting as described above.

In the context of building regenerative bioregional economies, this approach can empower grassroots movements, Indigenous communities, and local stakeholders to propose and implement initiatives aligned with the Bioregional Regeneration Strategy. Beyond magnifying small investments, Quadratic Funding, similar to Quadratic Voting, incentivizes collaboration and fosters a sense of

Quadratic Funding - By allocating funds based on a quadratic formula that magnifies the impact of many small investments from the community (similar to crowdfunding) through a so-called 'matching pool' that is resourced by larger capital providers, Quadratic Funding encourages widespread participation and fosters a diverse array of projects that resonate with local communities. Projects that receive a given amount of community funding from a broader base of individuals receive more match funding than those that receive the given amount from only a few community investors.[241]

---

240 Credit to Durukan Dudu.
241 Quadratic Funding (QF) - Unlocking the power of community funding. See (Buteren et al. 2020) for the seminal articulation.

collective ownership, ensuring that resources are allocated to projects with broad-based support and high potential for long-term regenerative impact. Since 2019, Quadratic Funding pioneer Gitcoin DAO has channeled over $60 million from 4.2 million unique donations to fund open-source Web3 digital infrastructure and social and ecological impact projects, including $3.9 million towards "climate solutions." An example of a funder leveraging Gitcoin for regeneration, is Ma Earth's recent 2024 grant round, which supported regenerative land projects.

6.7 Retroactive Public Goods Funding (RetroPGF)

Another model for funding regenerative projects is the Retroactive Public Goods Funding (RetroPGF) approach developed by the Optimism Collective. This model is based on the idea that it is easier to agree on what *was* useful in the past than what *might* be useful in the future. The approach aims to enable distributed but not fully decentralized capital allocation to public goods[242] projects (similar to Quadratic Voting and Quadratic Funding). In the case of RetroPGF - which is initially focused on funding software development - badge holders vote on projects and funding is allocated based on the median score projects receive. Through this approach, the community can select criteria for people with specialized expertise. These specialists then do the necessary research and analysis to determine which projects created the greatest community benefits. The RetroPGF structure provides possible exit liquidity for public goods projects, which opens up a market for early investment in those projects. In the case of RetroPGF, revenue from the use of open source software funds that work retroactively. This approach to the governance of capital allocation could support regenerative projects – particularly in areas like ecological regeneration that also require a sufficient level of technical expertise, whether Western or Indigenous, and where revenue is hard to capture directly at the project level. One of the major challenges with this approach is that it requires projects to have access to seed funding at the outset. Thus, it will likely not work well in low-income communities.

6.8 Web3 flow funding and dynamic token issuance mechanisms for living, adaptive economies

Traditional grant models and discrete funding can put the focus on securing operational funding, reducing the amount of time organizations spend on performing mission-related work. For regenerative economies to flourish, resource allocation must more closely resemble the living systems they aim to mirror in information and

---

242 In this book, we primarily refer to public goods as 'common assets.'

economic systems. Flow funding has been identified as an innovative mechanism for this purpose, and with blockchain and novel digital currency issuance mechanisms, funding flows can be automated, integrated, and expressed as highly adaptive economies that can contract and expand based on needs and value creation in the network.

One such mechanism making use of flow funding – bonding curves – holds great potential for the implementation of BFFs. Bonding curves[243] are a new tool in the Web3 space that tie two or more elements of a system together through mathematical relationships encoded into smart contracts. They provide an economic invariant between the supply of tokens and the reserve assets backing their value, making token price deterministic and providing guaranteed liquidity for tokens. Adjusting the circulating supply based on demand dampens the volatility and couples with the demand for the token's utility. Bonding curves and primary market token issuance lay the economic foundations for new tools that can address some of the major challenges of distributed economic systems, such as bootstrapping small economies, providing necessary exchange liquidity, facilitating demand-responsive dynamic token supply, and continuous fundraising. Bonding curves have also been 'augmented' with the addition of common pool treasuries or even prediction markets, to improve the collective signaling capacity of these new tools for social and ecosystemic benefit.

6.9 Place-based Bioregional Tithing, voluntary taxation, and Business Improvement Districts

Bioregional Tithing, voluntary taxation, or taxation-like initiatives, such as Business Improvement Districts (BIDs) offer a promising avenue for financing bioregional regeneration. BIDs provide a defined area within which businesses elect to pay an additional fee in order to fund projects within the district's boundaries. By harnessing the collective financial contributions of businesses, property owners, and residents within a specific geographic area, BIDs can generate a dedicated pool of funds to support initiatives that aim to support regeneration and achieve what is set out in the Bioregional Regeneration Strategy. Voluntary taxation mechanisms like BIDs provide a means for stakeholders, including organizations and individuals, to directly invest in the health and resilience of their local ecosystems, fostering a sense of ownership and responsibility within the community. Additionally, they enable collaborative partnerships between public and private entities, leveraging resources and expertise from both sectors to drive meaningful ecological improvements at the bioregional level. Combined with participatory budgeting (such as outlined in Section 6.5) Bioregional Tithing can help communities mobilize financial resources in alignment with their shared values and priorities. One inspiring precedent at the bioregional scale is the Shuumi Land Tax on Ohlone territory in the East Bay of San Francisco.

243 Jeff Emmett et al.: Exploring Bonding Curves: Differentiating Primary and Secondary Automated Market Makers

6.10 Advance Market Commitmentsfor bioregional regeneration

Similar to offtake agreements, Advance Market Commitments (AMCs) constitute a promise to purchase or financially support a product upon its successful development. Governments and private foundations commonly offer AMCs to incentivize the creation of vaccines or treatments. In return, pharmaceutical companies agree to supply a specified quantity of doses at a predetermined price. This funding approach is employed when the expenses associated with research and development are deemed prohibitive for the private sector without assurance of a minimum volume of sales. In the space of bioregional regeneration, AMCs can be used as investment funds committing financial capital to projects that promise future ecological value and regenerative asset creation, but are risky or expensive to initiate. Using this tool, financial resources would be guaranteed to ventures, for example regenerative food startups, that meet certain ecological impact criteria, providing a stable market for their future development.

6.11 Profit Pooling and whole economy health as triggers for investor returns

Building resilient bioregional economies relies on a strong connectivity between local businesses. In these economies, the financial health of one organization is inextricably interlinked with that of others and with the whole ecosystem – much like in the web of life in biology. With a Profit Pooling agreement, participating businesses agree to contribute a defined fair and equal percentage of their monthly or annual profits to a common insurance pool. This pooling of excess profit ensures that if any participating business faces cashflow or profitability issues due to external and uncontrollable circumstances, it can access funds to stabilize its operations. Profit Pooling has long been utilized in large global corporations to ensure healthy support between their various subsidiaries; its implementation within local economies could yield profound benefits that are currently untapped. By bolstering the resilience of individual businesses, Profit Pooling cultivates resilient or even anti-fragile enterprise ecosystems, fortifying the fabric of local economies against external shocks.[244]

Data that is generated from the usage of profit pools in a regenerative local economy could inform the timing and size of investor returns in a single company as part of that ecosystem or an investment portfolio. Tying the payment of returns to ecosystem health incentivizes holistic investment strategies that prioritize bioregional regeneration, keep invested money circulating in a local economy, and prevent financial extraction.

6.12 Obligation Clearing (also known as netting) and Mutual Credit as a liquidity- saving mechanism

The practice of debt clearing is centuries old, with origins in 14th century Italian banking practices. Now, its resurgence using Web3 technologies and interdisciplinary research that integrates graph and monetary theory offers new possibilities in leveraging payment graphs and cycles (second order dynamics) rather than money itself.[245] The basic concept is to create greater economic efficiency and reduce the need for liquidity by clearing debts within a network, where participant's obligations cancel each other out without money or a single token changing hands. Paired with Mutual Credit in the form of loans on complementary currency backed by future production, these clearing loops can save businesses up to 50 percent of their need for cash to settle those debts. This could offer BFFs and corollary organizations significant savings in operating costs and provide shelter in high interest rate environments.[246]

244 Inspired by Graham Boyd's book *Rebuild*.
245 Obligation Clearing and Mutual Credit are explained and being actively developed by Informal Systems and Sardex, a monetary network and commercial credit circuit based in Sardinia.
246 For more information see Fleischman et al.: Liquidlty-Saving through Obligation-Clearing and Mutual Credit: An Effective Monetary Innovation for SMEs in Times of Crisis.

7. Additional Case Studies: Stories of Bioregional Organizing and Bioregional Finance in Action

7. Additional Case Studies: Stories of Bioregional Organizing and Bioregional Finance in Action

The case studies in this chapter tell diverse stories about how dedicated social processes are combined with thoughtful technological innovations to create strong foundations for BFFs. While each story is substantial as a standalone case study, their real power is found in the synergies between them, and how these linkages give rise to cascading benefits in the bioregions served by these projects and organizations. In these examples, Regenerate Cascadia (Case Study 9) emerged from the Inaugural Edge Prize (Case Study 8), which used Hylo (Case Study 10) as a platform for convening leaders to consider potential beneficiaries. As a set of independent but interlocking narratives they represent a powerful collective case study in how creative efforts across bioregions are resourcing each other and amplifying the global movement.

The Edge Prize – Scaling What's Possible by Supporting and Connecting Regenerative Innovators

By: Edward West

About the Edge Prize

The Edge Prize, represents a new methodology for growing a bioregional community by hosting a distributed online accelerator and prize challenge. The goals of The Edge Prize methodology are to:

— Convene a group of extraordinary entrepreneurs, leaders, and innovators throughout a bioregion working on regenerative projects that benefit the lands, waters, and people of the bioregion — "The Edgewalkers."

— Invite them into a supportive community of reciprocity, mentorship, workshops, and collaboration.

— Amplify their stories, in order to bring resources, collaboration, partnerships, and inspire others to start their own regenerative initiatives — in their bioregion and beyond.

— Build from these stories a public-facing library of "what's working" to help scale and accelerate regenerative practices worldwide.

Benefiting communities and ecosystems

The inaugural Edge Prize, piloted in Salmon Nation in 2023, was created by Applied Alchemy and the Terran Collective, and sponsored by Salmon Nation Trust and the Magic Canoe. The 2023 Edge Prize invited individuals and organizations doing something that benefits their community and surrounding ecosystems, offering dozens of cash prizes, ranging from $500 to $20,000. Individuals and organizations stewarding projects in areas as diverse as Food and Agriculture, Health, Culture and Education, Water, Energy, Community Finance and Development, Water, Ecosystem Restoration, or Governance sectors were invited to apply, attracting a diverse and accomplished collection of 130 leaders and entrepreneurs throughout Salmon Nation. Overall, USD 80,000 were distributed to deserving impactful projects in Salmon Nation bioregion, with USD 60,000 of that allocated by the community themselves in a participatory funding process that supported all participating Edgewalkers to get to know each other's work.

All applicants were invited to create a brief written description of their work, as well as a short video describing their work. These formed the basis of a public open-source library of bioregional solutions. Applicants, along with subject matter experts, voted to allocate the prize money to the most compelling applicants. Applicants were also invited into an online community, encouraged to discover and learn about each other's work, and were given access to capacity-building support from mentors and subject-matter experts. The overall structure and format of the Edge Prize encouraged Edgewalkers to collaborate with each other, and numerous self-organizing partnerships emerged during the program. In one example, two Edgewalkers partnered with each other to convene the first Edge Prize-inspired event series and movement building strategy: Regenerate Cascadia.

The Edge Prize concept is a template for a broader, open-source movement to catalyze critical regenerative innovation in bioregions globally, fitting into a template of bioregional transformation on an evolutionary trajectory toward regenerative innovation.

Regenerate Cascadia – Coordinated and Coherent Bioregional Organizing

By: Taya Seidler, Clare Attwell, Brandon Letsinger, and Sheri Herndon

About Regenerate Cascadia

Regenerate Cascadia is a capacity-building organization and a social movement and developing a vision and framework to administer a regeneration fund for Cascadia, a bioregion located along the upper Pacific Rim of North America stretching from Southeast Alaska to Northern California, and as far east as the Yellowstone Caldera. A central goal of Regenerate Cascadia is to grow capacity cohesively across the scales of landscapes, ecoregions, and bioregions – something that currently does not exist locally or globally – as part of a multi-generational strategy for the long-term health of the Cascadia bioregion. Regenerate Cascadia is addressing the complex challenges in funding connected landscape outcomes across a bioregion through a whole-systems approach that: prioritizes the central role of place-based stewardship; ensures decision-making is held by those at the local level; develops trust-based networks that hold the integrity of the work; and uses a nested scale structure to facilitate information flow, representation, and learning across the whole system.

Activating a bioregional movement

Regenerate Cascadia was formed by Brandon Letsinger and Clare Attwell in April 2023 during the first ever Salmon Nation Edge Prize, where their vision to activate a bioregional movement in Cascadia won the Edge Prize for Innovation in Systems and Governance. After months of planning with 100+ local community organizers on both sides of the Canada-US border, they partnered with the Design School for Regenerating Earth to co-facilitate a month-long Bioregional Activation Tour. They traveled to 14 communities around Cascadia during October 2023, hosting presentations that asked, "How do we regenerate the Cascadia bioregion?". They met with more than 1000 individuals, including Indigenous knowledge keepers, regenerative leaders, groups, community artists, and elders across Oregon, Washington, and British Columbia through presentations, workshops, site visits, and strategy sessions. This was followed by an online summit that brought together 50+ presentations in a 'Festival of What Works', and concluded with an Open Space Unconference from November 3-12, 2023, where participants cocreated working groups for Regenerate Cascadia. The vision resonated strongly with many communities across the bioregion. Jay Bowen, an elder of the Skagit people who opened the Summit, articulated the following statement in the opening ceremony: *"Gathered before us are the most important people in the world. It may be a small group right now, but in a few short years, there's going to be a long line of people waiting to get involved in this very important movement that is overseeing the welfare of our communities."*

Beyond this, Regenerate Cascadia has succeeded in meeting the core challenge participatory events often struggle with – maintaining momentum and continuous engagement among participants. They have an active Telegram channel of 121 members sharing thousands of messages through 39 subchannels covering specific topics and guilds, organizational infrastructure discussions, local communities' individual channels, media and communication, inter alia. The community is thriving and members are actively engaging with each other. The Regenerate Cascadia community of 'regenerators' has since co-developed a digital platform to support the work; they continue to collaboratively take in feedback and refine this prototype as their ideas and needs evolve.

A digital landscape

The digital platform includes a structural framework (see Figure 11.) that prioritizes community-led work within a landscape, while thoughtfully aggregating place-based projects into larger coordination structures. A 'front door' website is an easy entry point for people to learn more, join as a member, donate to specific projects, and get more involved. Projects and communities each have a landing page that serve as a focal point for local news, resources, and events. These are curated by participating communities and are indexable by search engines. The digital platform provides an online space to connect within a landscape and across watersheds at the nested scales of ecoregions and the Cascadia bioregion. The platform includes a comprehensive 'back end' suite of tools and resources to support local project work, including (i) education and onboarding; (ii) an information commons and searchable directories; (iii) a regenerative movement map and relational database; and (iv) comprehensive data, measurement, evaluation and reporting capabilities. All Regenerate Cascadia programs are part of an integrated 501(c)3 nonprofit administrative backend to provide accounting, receive grants, raise funds, deliver timely financial reporting, and maintain legal compliance.

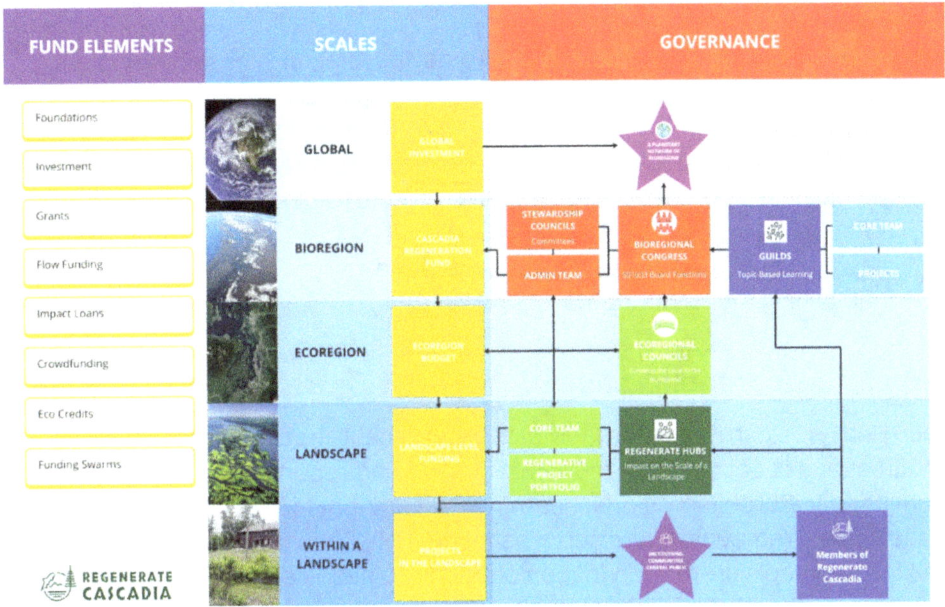

Regenerate Cascadia's living structural framework can be viewed as a system for the coherent flow of resources - educational, financial, inspirational, and cultural - that supports ongoing bioregional regeneration outcomes and learning. The framework enables capital to be distributed from a large bioregional fund into smaller landscape-level funds that deliver resources to decentralized projects according to the needs of ecoregions and landscapes. This ensures governance power is held by those closest to the work through trust-based networks of relationships that connect and align diverse projects within a landscape-level vision and strategy. The framework provides a comprehensive intermediary between local communities and funders. This enables effective cooperation, coordination, and governance across the bioregion to optimize strategic outcomes.

Representing diversity

A key tenet of the framework is the commitment to the representation of diverse voices at all scales, including those of ecosystems and keystone species, ensuring that feedback loops from across the whole system enable collective intelligence to inform future actions. This supports the whole system to see itself (co-sense), learn (co-presence), and iterate (co-create), enabling connected *and* concurrent local and bioregional agency to solve problems at the appropriate scales. Regenerate Cascadia's structures are built with one of the movement's core goals in mind – to prototype a series of replicable transformational templates that return 'right relationship' to the Earth as a central organizing premise for finance, while evolving how we live and work together cooperatively across scales.

A core foundation of Regenerate Cascadia are 'Regenerate Hubs', which hold the governance capacity to manage a fund for a discrete landscape across diverse stakeholders. Regenerate Hubs operate in several ways, including:

— working with local communities and weaving relationships to develop a long-term vision aligned with the overall bioregional vision of Regenerate Cascadia;
— identifying and engaging voices that need to be present;
— maintaining a portfolio of regenerative projects within their defined landscape areas;
— stewarding an annual landscape budget; and
— maintaining team coherence.

Structured for regeneration

Each Hub has a core team that facilitates/helps establish conditions for cooperation and trust and is accountable for administrative and reporting requirements. Each landscape features Bioregional Learning Centers that facilitate the cocreation of place-based frameworks and serve as foundational education spaces for sense-making and decision-making in the community. These centers monitor, evaluate, and manage the dynamic flow of an information commons using shared metrics for social, cultural, and ecological impact that supports robust fund reporting and continuous learning. Hubs primarily collaborate with members of Regenerate Cascadia from within a particular landscape, and are represented by a network of Ecoregional Councils – governance bodies responsible for creating ecoregional budgets that maintain the connections between local and bioregional scales.

Regenerate Cascadia's structural framework serves several other core functions in supporting landscape leaders, including bioregional 'Guilds' made up of knowledge communities responsible for providing tools and resources around specific regenerative topics, and connecting learning and networks across landscapes. Hubs and Guilds undertake their own projects and activities while sharing news, updates, resources, directories, and events for a specific place or topic in a way that is meaningful for all participants. Regenerate Cascadia supports the Hubs and Guilds' core teams and services by administering a portion of all funds raised; providing opportunities to practice healthy budgeting and governance with small sums of money; and growing their decision-making and governance capacities ahead of receiving larger flow funding. Finally, the non-profit backbone of Regenerate Cascadia is maintained through 'Bioregional Stewardship Councils', which directly assist with communications, outreach, fundraising, finance, legal, and reporting requirements, and a Bioregional Congress – an assembly comprised of Guilds and Ecoregional Councils to govern a shared Cascadia bioregional vision.

Each of the structural components Regenerate Cascadia is collaboratively building are demonstrable templates that are adaptable, replicable, and scalable in other localities. They are significant, not only for a single bioregion, but as a living framework for movements emerging around the world. By connecting and resourcing those doing the work in their communities through the support of core backbone teams of bioregional weavers; providing knowledge and resource sharing through Guilds that weave between landscapes; and co-creating the digital infrastructure for coordination and communication, Regenerate Cascadia enables coordinated, coherent processes for bioregional learning and regeneration. This framework provides a governance model for bioregional funding, enabling capital to flow to where it is needed on the ground, and building the foundations for funding the transition to a regenerative economy.

CASE STUDY 10:

Hylo – A Coordination Platform for the Future of Bioregional Organizing

By: Clare Politano

About Hylo

Hylo is a community-led, open-source coordination tool for purpose-driven groups, with an emphasis on place-based organizing. The free web and mobile apps allow community members to deepen relationships and collaborate to get things done through discussions, requests, offers, resources, projects, events, geographic maps, direct messaging, and chat. All of this is offered without advertising or data-harvesting in a clean and simple user interface.

Hylo is for place-based organizing

Giving groups tools for local coordination is a particular focus for Hylo, because ecological regeneration and community care must happen in a place-based context. By using the geographic map, members can share and discover local events, resources, and collaborators. Groups can also define their geographic boundary and display that on the shared map, which also includes a layer for Native territories that can be toggled on and off. Hylo plans to add bioregions as the next map layer.

Bioregional coordination is already happening on Hylo

Several bioregions are using Hylo to support connection in their local landscape.

In 2023, Salmon Nation bioregion used Hylo to convene a community of local leaders, the "Edgewalkers," throughout Alaska, British Columbia, Washington, Oregon, and northern California for an initiative called the Edge Prize. The group gathered on Hylo for a series of online relationship-building and educational sessions, and many participants also met up in-person and made new local connections. The Edge Prize culminated in the Edgewalkers distributing $80,000 in prize money to deserving bioregional projects through a participatory budgeting process. The Edgewalkers used a different tech tool to conduct the co-budgeting exercise, and in the future this function will be built into Hylo.

After the convening, two Edge Prize participants founded a new bioregional group together, Regenerate Cascadia, which went on to organize an in-person bioregional activation tour, in-person event series, and online summit all dedicated to ecological regeneration and community resilience in Cascadia bioregion. This group remains very active on the ground in Cascadia bioregion.

Other bioregional groups using Hylo include the Bay Area Bioregion, Salish Sea, Sacramento River, Appalachia, Thames River Watershed, and Bioregional Weaving Labs. People use these groups to share local opportunities and information, meet collaborators, and coordinate action - like civic participation in public comments related to local environmental policy, or crowdfunding to support the return of land to Indigenous tribes. There is also a global community of practice, the Bioregional Commons, where place-based organizers from around the world are connecting to share and discuss resources relevant to bioregionalism and the transition to regenerative bioregional economies.

Tools for bioregional self-governance

Through a partnership with OpenTEAM, the Open Technology Ecosystem for Agricultural Management, Hylo is building tools to support the transition to regenerative agriculture and the participatory governance of purpose-driven, collaborative groups. These prosocial tools include space for groups to share their purpose and agreements, and prompt members to commit to them; administrative tools to curate and assign roles and responsibilities within the group; and coming soon, tools for proposals and decision-making. OpenTEAM is using these tools to manage collaboration among dozens of sub-awardees - networks of farmers and open-source technologists - working together to fulfill a $35M grant to the organization from the USDA to support the growth of climate-smart agriculture in the US.

Combined with Hylo's mapping features, these tools to support place-based collaboration and governance give bioregional groups the power to steward their landscape as a commons. This might, for example, mean the residents of a bioregion making proposals for restoration projects or local regenerative businesses, with other residents voting on which proposals to support and how to allocate resources among them. These tools can be powerful enablers of capital allocation for Bioregional Financing Facilities.

Hylo is stewarded by Terran Collective, a bioregional group in the California Bay Area whose purpose is to amplify collaboration among people regenerating communities and the planet. Terran's vision is for bioregional groups on Hylo to grow strong collaborative cultures and mature into bioregional DAOs – Decentralized Autonomous Organizations (see Section 4.7). A DAO is a collaborative organization where members decide together how to govern a shared resource or a commons. The aim of such a DAO would be to steward the wellbeing of the land and the people, with members participating in governance decisions to support this care. Decisions could enable the creation of land management agreements, the transition to local production and circular economies, advancement of ecological regeneration, and improvements in community resilience and climate adaptation.

CASE STUDY 11:

ReCommon – Regenerative Common Land Trusts

By: Alex Corren

About ReCommon

ReCommon is a US-based organization dedicated to building systems for regenerative community land acquisition and governance, using an adaptive bioregional framework.

ReCommon approaches this work on the "pattern-level" to create innovative yet grounded solutions that reflect foundational principles in nature. This approach is based on the understanding that there are common patterns present in most successful solutions, and that identifying and making those patterns accessible to others can greatly streamline place-based, on-the-ground action.

This work includes building governance protocols and legal templates that are designed to scale based upon natural patterns, such as land use patterns, community design patterns, and regenerative landscape intervention patterns. The groups that ReCommon works with then move from the pattern-level to the detail-level by adapting these protocols and templates to their place-based projects and communities – rendering them increasingly decentralized and interoperable, which cultivates systemic resilience.

Hybrid entity structure

ReCommon's hybrid entity structure serves as an integrated bridge between impact investment capital and long-term regenerative stewardship of land in Trust by place-based bioregional communities. There are three core sister entities are:

ReCommon Foundation - 501(c)3 nonprofit, cultivating Bioregional Nodes, governance and stewardship of land in Trust

ReCommon Trust - impact investment trust fund, acquires land to be stewarded and governed by Bioregional Nodes and other aligned entities

ReCommon Labs - cooperative that builds digital tools to support the coordination, acquisition, and governance of land held in Trust

These diverse entity structures are able to work closely together towards a common goal while leveraging all pathways of capital formation. The Foundation accepts tax-exempt donations of all kinds and applies for grant funding, the Trust issues shares to investors for the acquisition of land from investors, and Labs accepts a blend of investor and non-investor members to build the ReCommon ecosystem.

Adaptive bioregional governance

ReCommon's place-based governance framework is called the **Regenerative Community Land Trust** (aka *RCLT, RegenCLT*), which builds upon core principles and functionality of the **classic CLT model** while expanding on it with ecological design principles codified into bylaws, leaseholds, and other documents. This model of land tenure serves as the foundation for how the land is managed, accessed, and stewarded by the community.

The distinct governance bodies that are responsible for the long-term stewardship of land in trust **correspond to ecoregions** and are called **Bioregional Nodes**. They oversee the agreements for use of the land, manage the *Bioregional Node Treasury*, and submit proposals related to use of funds, and use of land.

Land is held in Trust and is governed by Bioregional Nodes. Leaseholders access the land via long-term renewable leaseholds, and have direct ownership in the structures, businesses and activities that happen on the land. Each Node has five key stakeholder categories. Each category has equal weight – 20 percent – regardless of the number of members

— *Stewards*: leaseholders with direct stewardship responsibility for land in Trust

— *Elders*: members that represent rights of nature and Indigenous wisdom

- *Patrons*: Commons Credit holders, investors into land held in Trust

- *Partners*: aligned organizations that are working in and/or with the Node

- *General Members*: members located in the Node, with no other qualifiers

This structure allows for larger and smaller coordination bodies to form organically, honoring the complexity of relationships within and across landscapes and cultures.

Securing land for the bioregional commons

ReCommon Trust raises capital to build a distributed bioregional network of land holdings through the issuance of shares known as Commons Credits. CCs directly correlate to property acquired by the Trust, and are backed by the value of the land. Patrons – the owners of CCs – have a seat at the table in RCLT governance in the Bioregional Node that contains the property.

Governance of the land held in Trust is explicitly delegated to stewardship entities. Bioregional Nodes, via ReCommon Foundation, are the default stewardship entity, but the Trust has the flexibility to work with any place-based organization that exists specifically to support the multi-generational care of land.

The Foundation is a significant shareholder in the Trust, which means that when profits are generated – by scalable leasehold fees, etc. – and are distributed to shareholders, the Bioregional Node Treasuries are direct recipients of a portion of those profits. This serves as the foundation of a regenerative flywheel for resilient bioregional economies, where land in Trust generates revenue that is redistributed to the community for ongoing support of ecological bioregional initiatives.

Regenerosity – Flowing Capital to Grassroots Regeneration by Cultivating Trust

By: Faith Flanigan and Ruth Andrade

About Regenerosity

For over 15 years, the Buckminster Fuller Institute, Lush Spring Prize, and UNDP's Equator Prize have identified, spotlighted, and funded more than 400 leading and upcoming grassroots organizations in the regenerative movement that are delivering programs at the nexus of climate, ecology, livelihoods, and sovereignty. Regenerosity emerged in 2019 as a collaborative between these prize programs designed to bolster the critical role philanthropy has to play during these challenging times by leveraging this track-record and experience. Regenerosity works to continually grow partnerships, flow resources, and facilitate learning for regenerative grassroots organizations.

To achieve this, Regenerosity thinks systemically. From the understanding that regeneration is about creating more capacity and capability to create conditions conducive to life, Regenerosity supports a developmental culture throughout all the elements of our theory of change by:

— Supporting grassroots, community-led organizations in threatened or degraded landscapes through capacity development grants, and by inviting members of the communities Regenerosity works with to design participatory trust-based programs according to their needs.

— Bringing grantee organizations together in regional peer-to-peer learning circles and supporting their connection to other networks and funders.

— Bolstering the critical role of philanthropy by engaging funders in the concepts of trust-based and regenerative philanthropy, providing experiences of connection to nature (in partnership with Be the Earth Foundation), and attracting further funding for grassroots organizations in ways that are more trust-based.

— Creating and promoting grassroots-led stories to share the impact and inspire the larger movement.

— Developing Regenerosity into an organization that embodies those principles in governance and creates opportunities for its own growth.

Regenerosity's vision is a world where the power of gifting and collaboration can nurture thriving communities and grassroots initiatives as they steward ecosystems towards vibrant health.

Regenerosity's theory of change

Regenerosity works across scales through all of their programs. They weave action-focused collaboration between grassroots organizations, funders, and key actors to develop human capacity to be in right relationship with all living systems by centering:

— **Place-based Impact**: Co-designing catalytic programs with grassroots organizations based on long-term relationships of trust. Flowing capital and resources to these organizations so they can grow their impact and potential to become regional hubs of regenerative practice.

— **Network Collaboration:** Bringing organizations together through regional communities of peers. Organizations join learning circles in and across cohorts for peer-to-peer learning, storytelling, and strategy development.

— **Movement Building:** Spotlighting evidence and grassroots-led stories that inspire the larger movement. Engaging with funders and key actors to influence the field of regenerative philanthropy and further attract interest and resources for the growth of the grassroots regenerative movement.

Regenerosity's core programs

Regenerosity's core programs are based on shifting the power dynamics of philanthropy, catalyzing the work of their partners, and deeply listening and sharing their stories.

Seeds Flow Funds

The Seed Flow Funds are an experiment in trust-based philanthropy that puts the design (and direction) of the fund and decision-making about how the money gets spent in the hands of community leaders. The two current funds support "Indigenous Women in Brazil" and "East African Youth & Women in Permaculture".

In each of these funds, $3,000 is distributed to individuals and groups to lead changes in their communities. So far, 13 indigenous women in 12 states across Brazil and 12 mostly women permaculturists across 3 regions in Uganda and Kenya have delivered a diverse array of unique, context-dependent community initiatives. Currently 16 more women in Brazil are participating in the second cycle.

Blossom, capacity strengthening program

Blossom is a two-year program co-designed with grassroots partners who are working to regenerate threatened or degraded landscapes at the intersection of food sovereignty, livelihoods, and ecology. Through deploying participatory capital via a co-design process, Regenerosity is able to support their grassroots partners' growth and innovation.

The program develops partners' organizational capacity, leadership skills, and connections, and supports their prototyping of models so that local organizations can grow into thriving regional hubs. The 2021-2023 cohort enabled thousands of members of Indigenous and local communities to increase food security and secure sustainable incomes while protecting and regenerating their traditional lands; scaling regionally and/or nationally while partnering with government offices and large NGOs; and scaling their programs through additional funding received through Regenerosity's support.

Regenerosity has delivered over $1M USD to 11 projects over 2.5 years, including supporting:

— 2,500 direct beneficiaries who saw a 76% increase in household income with partners YICE Uganda and KAFRED in Bigodi National Park

— a 100% increase in daily household meals in Nakivale Refugee camp with the participants of the food program with YICE Uganda

— a 30% increase in water availability for biodiversity and livelihoods through Tarun Bharat Sangh across 5 watersheds in India.

Pollinate storytelling series

Liberation Agriculture is a film series exploring what true regeneration cultivates. Far too often, narratives around regeneration only go soil deep. With the intersections of ecological collapse and systemic oppression becoming increasingly clear, Regenerosity is sharing stories that interweave the struggle to reclaim ecosystemic health and the struggle for collective liberation.

Nurture Funder Community of Practice

The Nurture Funder Community of Practice is an aligned community of funders that are learning, sharing, and experimenting with allocating financial capital in ways that are trust-based, coherent, and inclusive, in order to address social and environmental challenges from their roots.

Regenerosity takes an experimental approach that aims not only at sharing knowledge, but also create a call-to-action environment, through helping to evolve the capacity of funders for redistributing power, upgrading methodologies, and reframing governance structures; creating collaborative prototypes for alternative types of funding; and generating stories that inspire other funders to transform their practices.

Regenerosity believes in the power of shifting catalytic capital through trust-based, participatory practices, deep listening, and putting the voices of their partners at the forefront. They have catalyzed over 1.5M dollars to grassroots projects and continue to iterate and grow their programs.

8. Next Steps and Call to Action

8. Next Steps and Call to Action

– Rick Rubin

Bioregional Finance is an idea whose time has come. There are already many remarkable organizations, projects, and people working to actualize the spectrum of ideas and recommendations laid out in this book. We are grateful to them for inspiring us and feeding into this document.

With the publication of this book, the authors and our many collaborators will now move from research and template design to designing, building, and implementing BFFs through partnerships with Bioregional Organizing Teams and by catalyzing broader action in Bioregional Finance. We invite stakeholders from around the world, working across disciplines and sectors, to engage with us and with each other to support the decentralization of financial resource governance, the design of project portfolios for systemic change, and the transition to regenerative economies. We recognize that while there is no single solution to the polycrisis, Bioregional Finance can catalyze a global place-based movement that shifts value structures, and enables each of us to contribute to healing the Earth and culture in our unique ways.

In *Table 12* below we lay out some potential actions for key categories of actors.[247] While no two bioregions will follow the same path, we hope that through shared learning and prototyping we can rapidly advance the field of Bioregional Finance in an emergent, evolutionary way. While many of these actions may on the surface look like to-do list items to check off, we suggest that they are all – including the most technocratic and technical – recommendations to form and nurture relationships of care, trust, healing, reciprocity, clear communication, and mutual learning. We look forward to embarking on this journey with all of you. The forthcoming BioFi Community of Practice on Hylo will be a key place for us all to engage.

247 These actions are not intended to be prescriptive and are not linear. We understand bioregional regeneration to be a complex, dynamic flow of actions and relations across multiple nested scales within a landscape and hope for these actions to support that process. We encourage you to consider that by reading this book, you are already an active participant in this movement, whether or not you identify with one of these categories. We encourage you to be curious about actions and relationships not listed that may be right for you to engage in.

Table 12. Actions for advancing Bioregional Financing Facilities

ACTORS	POTENTIAL ACTIONS
Bioregional Organizers	<ul><li>Connect, engage, align, and organize diverse actors in your bioregion and continually work to identify voices missing from the process[248]</li><li>Establish relationship with aligned local Indigenous communities early in the organizing process[249]</li><li>Prioritize building relationships of care, trust, and long term commitment before formal community organizing</li><li>Start a thorough, participatory, and iterative bioregional mapping process</li><li>Invite Indigenous communities to contribute to a story of place through participatory mapping processes[250]</li><li>Develop Bioregional Hubs to build capacity in the bioregion</li><li>Connect with organizers in other bioregions to form relationships and networks of mutual learning and support[251]</li><li>Develop a Bioregional Regeneration Strategy</li><li>Prototype and iterate participatory, inclusive governance structures for effective bioregional connectivity and representation</li><li>Run a project incubator: prepare projects and organizations for investment by helping them assess and locally source their multi-capital needs; *financial capital may not be what is most needed now*</li><li>Prioritize projects and develop project portfolios best suited for initial funding</li><li>Experiment with facilitating financial flows through shared governance and document your learnings</li><li>Connect with the BioFi teams and/or experts in your bioregion to design, implement, and evolve BFFs</li><li>Develop an integrated MRV strategy</li><li>Learn out loud: Publicly share the story of efforts and learnings as they unfold</li><li>Join the forthcoming BioFi Community of Practice on Hylo</li></ul>

248 See 3.1 Bioregional organizing and value creation for a list of key actors. Exercise sensitivity to the place-specific context impacting Justice, Equity, Diversity, and Inclusion (JEDI) within a place

249 Some communities and First Nations may have cultural liaison officers available to advise on engagement protocols, culture, and history.

250 As the first peoples of the land, their stories, including place names and language, are invaluable to the bioregional mapping process.

251 Bioregional Weaving Labs (Europe), Design School for Regenerating Earth (Global), and Regenerative Communities Network (Global) are three of many great places to start.

Regenerators and Indigenous Communities, Nations, and Tribes	> Tell the story and share the vision for the transition to a regenerative economy in your place in a way that demonstrates the wisdom and expertise in the unique stewardship role you hold. Invite and support others in doing the same > Connect with aligned projects, organizations, or Indigenous groups in the bioregion and consider developing an integrated or at least coordinated approach – leverage synergies > Develop project or organizational proposals for your vision > Share your multi-capital and financial capital needs with bioregional organizers > Work with bioregional organizers to develop a phased funding approach illustrating what types of financial capital are needed at each stage of the work and what activities those resources will be used for; seek expert support where needed > Work with bioregional organizers to design and collect project data and develop an integrated MRV strategy > Share project progress updates transparently and frequently, showcasing locally and globally what is possible
Investors	> Invest in capacity to understand bioregional, systemic approaches to regeneration so that they are better equipped to assess and engage with this new category of investment > Build private equity funds focused on regeneration of the biosphere that can deploy capital into Bioregional Investment Companies > These funds should be underpinned by risk management philosophies that enable dynamic, forward-looking, and holistic risk assessment, consider value-at-risk, and have a strong impact mandate > Work closely with other financial capital providers to ensure an integrated capital stack approach > Work with Bioregional Hubs and Bioregional Organizing Teams to construct systemic investment portfolios in line with Bioregional Regeneration Strategies > Experiment with more innovative financial mechanisms to better deploy financial capital in service of building resilient bioregional and regenerative economies > Consider investing in revolving or evergreen fund structures or structures that enable an exit to community > Embark on a personal, team, or organizational exploration of what concepts of value, wealth, risk, and return mean to you, your team, or your firm in this pivotal moment in human history

Philanthropists	>	Support the design, build, and implementation of BFFs through the BioFi Project, Dark Matter Capital, or other organizations working on BFF creation
	>	Start capitalizing BFFs through a strategic, integrated capital stack approach, in collaboration with other financial capital providers
	>	Explore more trust-based, participatory, post-capitalist, philanthropic approaches that support systems change and healing and reconciliation[252]
	>	Further explore the roots and responsibilities of philanthropic capital and how it can be deployed in the most catalytic way
Policymakers (nation state level)[253]	>	Explore policies that can drive decentralization of financial resource governance to achieve global climate and nature goals, and to avert and mitigate further ecological, economic, and social collapse
	>	Take steps to better integrate risks of destruction of life on Earth into decision-making on proposed projects, policies and regulations, including through developing and applying valuation, metrics, and decision-support tools[254]
	>	Engage in economic policy reform to align incentives with regenerative practices (e.g., through tax and subsidy reform and possible introduction of Common Asset Trusts, payments for ecosystem services, environmental permits, etc.), especially at the bioregional scale
	>	Consider financial regulation that drives a dynamic, forward-looking, and holistic assessment of risk and supports the localization of risk assessment
	>	Work with Bioregional Organizing Teams and BFF management to collaboratively develop strategies for devolving resource allocation decision-making to bioregional entities
	>	Push for the Global North to Global South funding flow to support Global South countries in meeting the targets under the Rio Conventions to flow directly to BFFs rather than through a multilateral fund
	>	Set up a technical assistance fund to support Bioregional Organizing Teams and Indigenous nations (or consortiums of nations) to design, build, and operate BFFs
	>	Invest in a portfolio of BFFs through a bond fund
	>	Provide guarantees to enable Bioregional Investment Companies and Bioregional Banks to raise return-seeking financial capital

252 Some aligned resources include: Flow Funding, Post Capitalist Philanthropy, and the Six Principles of Trust-Based Philanthropy.

253 Further recommendations for financial and economic policymakers available here: An Overview of Nature-Related Risks and Potential Policy Actions for Ministries of Finance: Bending The Curve of Nature Loss.

254 e.g., through implementing or supporting the development of natural asset/capital accounting, developing alternatives to gross domestic product (GDP), and developing nature loss scenarios.

Policymakers (local level)	>	Implement the actions described above for national policymakers that local policymakers also have jurisdiction over
	>	Work with Bioregional Organizing Teams and BFF management to collaboratively develop strategies for devolving resource allocation decision-making to bioregional entities
	>	Create local authorities, bonds, and taxes to directly support landscape, bioregional and watershed scale regeneration
	>	Take steps to cultivate a bioregional perspective (holistic, ecologically-intersectional, Indigenous-informed, systems-level) when considering policy and program development and implementation
	>	Seek deeper and more frequent cross-jurisdictional, multi-sectoral, multi-stakeholder collaboration on issues of bioregional importance and purview
	>	Prioritize funding and capacity-building for initiatives that explicitly pursue their work through a holistic, intersectional bioregional lens
Multilaterals and Development Agencies	>	Work with client countries to design and implement BFFs
	>	Decentralize financial resource governance to BFFs when possible
	>	As new public resources are mobilized – for example those promised under the Kunming-Montreal Global Biodiversity Framework – structure them to flow to BFFs rather than to a global fund and then to national governments[255]
Web3 practitioners	>	Work to apply existing Web3 technology and to develop new tools and protocols where needed to innovate at the BioFi x DeFi intersection – particularly in the areas of capital raising, participatory capital allocation, MRV, governance, relational trust networks, complementary or Nature-based Currencies, Ecological Institutions, Rights of Nature, and wallets for ecosystems or species
	>	As much as possible, seek partnership with "on-the-ground" regenerators and communities who are facing contextually-specific challenges and can guide iterative experimentation
Innovators, Technologists, and Futurists	>	Develop new financial and governance tools/instruments, business models, and legal structures that can support the legibility of both the local and global (real) value of biocultural regeneration and support the transition to regenerative economies
	>	Continue to design and innovate integrative, cost-effective MRV solutions deliverable/contributable by place-based regenerators
	>	Further iterate and improve the concepts of BFFs

255 This is particularly important for getting financial resources to Indigenous nations and tribes.

Designers, Economists, and Financial Services Consultants	<ul><li>Support Bioregional Organizing Teams to design and implement BFFs and oversee iterative improvements</li><li>Support bioregions in developing and implementing appropriate capital raising and participatory capital allocation approaches</li><li>Work on complementary or nature-based currency experiments</li><li>Share learnings openly and widely in the BioFi Community of Practice so that others may benefit from it</li></ul>
Storytellers, Artists, and Designers	<ul><li>Invite local artists, storytellers, and designers early on into the process[256]</li><li>Use art, storytelling, and other forms of creative expression to engage and reflect the local communities' vision for a regenerative, bioregional economy – supporting a sense of common purpose and identity</li><li>Form artist collectives to work together to create art that fuels a movement in the bioregion</li><li>Submit collective proposals for grants to the Bioregional Trust once it is set up</li><li>Form a national or global fund to resource artists building the bioregional movement</li><li>Connect with local regenerators or Indigenous tribes to discover opportunities for connective tissue between place-based "old story" and artistic vision for "new story" culture creation</li></ul>

256 Due to historical and ongoing marginalization, it is particularly important that, where possible, these contributors are paid for their time and creative work.

Academics	> Partner with a Bioregional Organizing Team to conduct strategic research to support the development of a Bioregional Regeneration Strategy, BFF, or Bioregional Hub > Support the development of an integrated MRV platform and strategy for BFFs and Bioregional Hubs > Support Bioregional Organizing Teams in systems mapping and identification of leverage points that can inform BFF investment strategies > Write about BFFs and bioregional efforts in academic journals or other publications. > Speak about case study examples at conferences to help spread the word and raise the profile of these efforts > Publically engage in debates, podcasts, or interviews about bioregional philosophy and tools (such as finance) > Organize meetings or conferences on bioregional themes > Interface with policymakers and other stakeholders to weave connections and facilitate information flow > Share research with bioregional communities > Listen to bioregional communities and help them share their stories with other bioregions and the broader planetary community

9. Conclusion

9. Conclusion

- Ilya Prigogine

Islands of Coherence - Ilya Prigogine, a renowned theoretical physicist and chemist, used the concept of "islands of coherence" to describe emergent phenomena in complex systems, particularly localized regions within a complex system where coherence or order emerges spontaneously amidst overall disorder or randomness. These islands of coherence are characterized by temporary stability or organization that arises due to nonlinear interactions and feedback processes within the system.

With this book, we aim to catalyze nothing less than Bioregional Financing Facilities sprouting up in every bioregion on Earth. They can take in capital from an extractive and destructive economic system and compost it to grow new, regenerative, bioregional economies that eventually do not require external capital at all, but can autonomously engage in economic reciprocity and solidarity with neighbors both near or far. In this way, Bioregional Financing Facilities can channel life-giving nutrients and energy to, and potentially between, the islands of coherence emerging amidst increasing disequilibrium. They can support us in reanimating the economy and putting finance in service to life and Indigenous wisdom.

BFFs can help us return to seeing ourselves as an integral part of the living, breathing Earth, and our economic actions and underlying perceptions of value as steps toward or away from a regenerative future. We have been stuck for too long thinking about what is possible within the bounds of economic and financial systems that have us locked into a path of mutually assured destruction. Creating institutions that can effectively meet the polycrisis will require bold envisioning of the possible.[257] And critically, a remembering that it's all intelligent, it's all alive, and it's all connected. Our financial architecture must serve this recognition.

We believe that there is an order to the changes now emerging from the disorder of our current social and economic systems. Ecosystems regenerate through

---

257 More on the analysis behind why human survival requires imagination in Iain McGilchrist's books: *The Master and the Emissary* and *The Matter With Things*.

phases of resource exploitation, conservation, release, and reorganization and our socio-economic systems can do the same.[258] Just as clouds gather and disperse, so too has capital gathered and is finding its way to flow back to life, including its human stewards.[259]

<hr>

258 "During the slow sequence from exploitation to conservation, connectedness and stability increase and a capital of nutrients and biomass (in ecosystems) is slowly accumulated and sequestered. Competitive processes lead to a few species becoming dominant, with diversity retained in residual pockets preserved in a patchy landscape. While the accumulated capital is sequestered for the growing, maturing ecosystem, it also represents a gradual increase in the potential for other kinds of ecosystems and futures. For an economic or social system, the accumulating potential could as well be from the skills, networks of human relationships, and mutual trust that are incrementally developed and tested during the progression from exploitation to conservation. Those also represent a potential developed and used in one setting, that could be available in transformed ones." (Resilience Alliance: Adaptive Cycle)

259 Inspired by the Emerald podcast episode On Clouds and Cosmic Law.

Glossary

Anti-fragility – The quality of a system, entity, or process that allows it to not only withstand — but actually benefit and grow stronger from — stress, volatility, and uncertainty. Unlike fragile systems, which break under stress, or robust systems, which withstand stress without changing, anti-fragile systems thrive and improve in response to challenges and disruptions.

Biocultural regeneration – A holistic and interconnected approach to revitalizing and restoring ecosystems, biodiversity, and cultural practices in a given spatial context. It recognizes the interdependence of nature and culture, emphasizing the importance of Indigenous and traditional knowledge and practices in stewarding ecosystems.

Biodiversity – Biodiversity or biological diversity is the variety and variability of life on Earth. Biodiversity is a measure of variation at the genetic (genetic variability), species (species diversity), and ecosystem (ecosystem diversity) level.[260]

Bioregion – A region defined by unique physical characteristics (climate, topography), ecological characteristics (such as soil, flora, fauna, and fungi), cultural characteristics (such as language, art, and identity), and their interconnections. There are many differing definitions of the scale and boundaries of bioregions,[261] and this book celebrates this diversity as a critical insight about the lack of any firm boundaries in ecosystems and the need to work with neighbors in bioregional organizing.

Bioregional Hub – A community-led institution that functions as a gathering place (physical and/or virtual), resource center, and facilitator of various regeneration-related activities, initiatives, and networks within a bioregion. While Bioregional Hubs can offer educational and capacity building programs, much like Bioregional Learning Centers do, their focus extends to facilitating the flow of multiple forms of capital (intellectual, social, cultural, etc.). They cohere and strengthen a synergistic bioregional collaboration network by fostering connections and partnerships, and catalyzing projects and initiatives that align with the Bioregional Regeneration Strategy. See 3.3 Bioregional Hubs for detailed description.

Bioregional Learning Center (BLC) – An educational hub for gathering and synthesizing knowledge about local ecology and culture.[262] Centers typically focus on education, research, and skill-building related to the specific ecological, cultural, and social aspects of a bioregion. They offer various programs, workshops, mutual learning exchanges, and courses that focus on topics such as ecology, permaculture, sustainable living practices, Indigenous knowledge, and local history. The primary goal is to provide opportunities for individuals and communities to deepen their

260 UNEP: What is biodiversity?
261 One Earth: What is a bioregion? 22 ways to define a bioregion
262 Joe Brewer: What is a Bioregional Learning Center?

understanding of the unique characteristics and challenges of their bioregion while equipping them with the knowledge and skills necessary for regenerative living and stewardship in place.

Bioregionalism – A socio-political and ecological philosophy that advocates for the alignment of economic activity, ecological management, and governance with the natural systems and cultures of "bioregions," defined by unique physical, ecological, and cultural characteristics, and their interconnections. Bioregionalism suggests that the invisible and visible regenerative efforts occurring across multiple scales (individual, family, neighborhood, community, organization, ecoregion, global) can be anchored and organized in large, bioculturally coherent landscapes that federate through affinity, solidarity, and reciprocity to fulfill planetary potential.[263]

Bioregional Financing Facility (BFF) – A community-owned institution that applies a participatory, transparent, and place-based approach to driving the decentralization of financial resource governance, design of project portfolios for systemic change, and the transition to a regenerative economy. While a BFF specializes in facilitating the flow of financial capital between regenerative projects, community members, and investors, it also works in close relationship with a Bioregional Hub to facilitate the flow of all capital types (e.g social, intellectual, cultural) in holistic support of bioregional regeneration. See 4. Designing and Implementing Bioregional Financing Facilities for detailed discussion, templates, and case studies.

Bioregional Organizing Team – A team of local stakeholders that initiates a bioregional regeneration and governance process, activates other stakeholders, builds networks of relationality and trust, and facilitates the collective regeneration efforts. See 3.1 Bioregional organizing and value creation for detailed discussion.

Bioregional Regeneration Strategy – A co-created, 20-100+ year or multigenerational plan for regenerating a particular bioregion, including a guide to the worldviews, values, processes, and principles recommended in approaching the work. Strategies are ideally built upon comprehensive mapping and systemic analysis and employ long-term thinking. See 3.1 Bioregional organizing and value creation for detailed discussion.

Bioregional Tithing – A program through which citizens residing or organizations operating in the bioregion opt to "tithe" by donating a certain amount annually or monthly (based on their income or profits) to the Bioregional Trust to support regeneration of the bioregion they are tasked with stewarding. This program recognizes that while all humans are meant to be stewards of the lands and waters of their place, some are better placed to do this work directly, while others can support them with financial resources. Inspiration can be taken from the Ohlone Sogorea Te' Land Trust and its calculator for the voluntary Shuumi Land Tax.264

Biosphere – The thin life-supporting stratum of Earth's surface, extending from a few kilometers into the atmosphere to the deep-sea vents of the ocean. It is composed

263 This is articulated in the vision, mission, and goals of the Regenerative Communities Network.

of living organisms and nonliving factors from which the organisms derive energy and nutrients. The biosphere supports all life on Earth, estimated at 3 to 30 million species of plants, animals, fungi, single-celled prokaryotes such as bacteria, and single-celled eukaryotes such as protozoans.[265]

Carbon-tunnel vision – A myopic perspective that ignores the multiple interdependent socio-ecological system crises that we face to focus only on carbon emissions, and/or focuses solely on carbon emissions reductions as the key climate change response.[266]

Cascading benefits – A term coined by Buckminster Fuller used to describe how benefits from one well-designed change in a system can create enabling conditions for other beneficial changes.

Common assets (also referred to as commons) – A type of resource that is collectively owned, used, or engaged with by a group of people. Commons can range from local resources like forests, fisheries, and urban spaces, to global resources like the biosphere, atmosphere, digital networks, and data. Elinor Ostrom's work challenged the traditional notion that commons are inevitably subject to degradation or overuse ("the tragedy of the commons"), and instead demonstrated through empirical studies that communities are capable of developing effective rules and institutions to sustainably manage and govern commons over the long term.[267] "*Commoning*" and "*re-commoning*" are also coming into increasing use as verbs to describe the practice of forming and governing new commons or recovering historical commons from a present privatized state.

Community organizing, weaving, and activation – The processes of gathering, facilitating connection between, and empowering community towards a shared purpose and vision. The Bioregional Weaving Labs consortium outlines five core Weaving Practices: Helping systems see and sense themselves; Cultivating trust-based relationship; Aligning on a shared purpose and vision; Facilitating collective (un)learning; Fostering (experimental) action.[268]

Complementary currencies – A form of currency or exchange medium that operates alongside the national currency system, providing a means of transaction and value exchange within a specific community or network. They are designed to complement rather than replace national currencies and "to facilitate transactions that otherwise wouldn't occur, linking otherwise unused resources to unmet needs, and encouraging diversity and interconnections that otherwise wouldn't exist."[269] Complementary currencies can take various forms including local currencies, time-based currencies, rewards programs, or digital/blockchain-based tokens.

264 The Sogorea Te' Land Trust received a $20 million Shuumi Land Tax contribution in early 2024 - the single largest known cash gift to a Native land trust in history.
265 Britannica Biosphere
266 Phrase coined by Dr Jan Konietzko, Maastricht University.
267 Elinor Ostrom: *Governing the Commons: The Evolution of Institutions for Collective Action*.
268 Bioregional Weaving Labs: Weaving
269 Bernard Lietar: Scientific Evidence of Why Complementary Currencies are Necessary to Financial Stability

Conviction Voting – An approach to collective decision-making where individuals continuously express their preferences for the proposals they wish to support. They may change their preferences at any time, but the longer they maintain their support for a specific proposal, the greater the "strength" of their conviction becomes. This gives community members with consistent preferences more influence than short-term participants who may only seek to sway a single vote.[270]

Decentralization – The distribution of decision-making authority and management responsibilities away from a centralized or top-down authority and toward a larger group of diverse representatives, aiming to improve the efficiency, effectiveness, and responsiveness of information processing, coordination, and decision-making (notably, resource allocation).

Eco-credits – Attestations (i.e. validations) about ecological state which prove regeneration is occurring, has occurred, or will occur. It is our recommendation that eco-credits are based on community-developed and governed definitions of regeneration that are rooted in local context and include a composition of ecological factors (rather than a single, non-local parameter, such as carbon).[271]

Ecological integrity – The ability of an ecosystem to support and maintain ecological processes and a diverse community of organisms.[272]

Ecoregion – A relatively large area of land or water that contains a geographically distinct assemblage of plant and animal communities. Ecoregions can generally be understood as encompassing biome subtypes (e.g. a grassland prairie biome can include multiple different grassland ecoregions — tall grass, short grass, etc.).

Ecotones – A transition area between two ecosystems where they meet and integrate. It may be narrow or wide, and it may be local (the zone between a field and forest) or regional (the transition between forest and grassland ecosystems). An ecotone may appear on the ground as a gradual blending of the two ecosystems across a broad area, or it may manifest itself as a sharp boundary line.[273]

Emergence – "Emergence is the way complex systems and patterns arise out of a multiplicity of relatively simple interactions." It is these "simple interactions" – from how we relate to the thoughts in our own heads, to how we show up in our relationships, to how we exist as local communities – that create the patterns that give rise to our ecosystems and societies.[274]

Financial sector – The segment of the global economy composed of institutions and markets that facilitate the flow of funds between savers, borrowers, and speculators managing financial assets and liabilities. It differs from the real sector, which involves the production and exchange of tangible goods and services.

270 Jeff Emmett: Conviction Voting: A Novel Continuous Decision Making Alternative to Governance
271 Adapted from input from Regen Foundation.
272 IPBES: Ecological Integrity
273 Wikipedia: Ecotone ("ecosystem" has been substituted for "biological community")
274 adrienne maree brown: Emergent Strategy

Financialization – A trend in which financial instruments and markets exert dispro-portionate influence over real economic activities and policy, prioritizing short-term speculative gains for the financial sector over long-term productivity and health in the real sector.

Fractal – A pattern comprising parts, each of which is a reduced-scale copy of the whole, displaying self-similarity across scales. In nature, fractals can be observed in patterns such as snowflakes, mountain ranges, and the branching of trees, blood vessels, and watersheds.

Gaia Hypothesis – Introduced in the early 1970s by James E. Lovelock and Lynn Margulis, the Gaia Hypothesis posits that Earth and its biological systems behave as a single, global entity with closely controlled self-regulatory negative feedback loops that keep the conditions on the planet within boundaries that are favorable to life. This way of looking at global ecology and evolution differs from the classical picture of ecology as a biological response to a menu of physical conditions.[275]

Indigenous – produced, growing, living, or occurring natively or naturally in a partic-ular region or environment.[276]

Indigenous peoples – A term holding immense complexity that is best defined within specific context.[277] However, for general interpretation throughout this book, we suggest the term be understood as members "of a community retaining memories of life lived sustainably on a land-base, as part of that land-base,"[278] particularly peoples practicing non-colonial knowledge systems rooted in relationships of reciprocity with more-than-human life, and as a term of self-identification used by those with "a special relationship with their traditional territory and an experience of subjugation and discrimination under a dominant cultural model."[279] *Note: In some geographic contexts, 'First Nations' is used as a more specific term.*[280]

Investment – For this book we have chosen to use the terms "investment" and "investing" to describe all processes of providing financial resources. This builds on an understanding that all forms of financial capital provision (equity, debt, donations, grant-making, etc.) ideally yield returns, as in the traditional notion of "investment." However, sometimes these investments are designed to return financial capital and at other times additional or other forms of capital (see "Multi-capital"). "Investment" can also be used to describe the provision of non-financial capital, although this book does not apply this meaning.

---

275 ScienceDirect: Gaia Hypothesis
276 Merriam-Webster: Indigenous
277 We encourage great care with this term and caution against simplistic categorizations that ignore historical contexts of interrelatedness between peoples, and between all peoples and the entire land-base of Earth. We encourage deep listening and relationship-building with sources of Indigenous knowledge and dialogue in your contexts.
278 This quotation is sourced from Tyson Yunkaporta's book Sand Talk: How Indigenous Thinking Can Save the World, which is an excellent resource for engaging with the depth and complexity of this term.
279 Wikipedia: Indigenous peoples
280 'First Nations' is often used to identify Indigenous peoples of Canada (who are neither Inuit nor Métis) and to identify people with familial heritage from, and membership in, the ethnic groups that lived in Australia before British colonization.

Islands of coherence – Ilya Prigogine, a renowned theoretical physicist and chemist, used the concept of "islands of coherence" to describe emergent phenomena in complex systems, particularly localized regions within a complex system where coherence or order emerges spontaneously amidst overall disorder or randomness. These islands of coherence are characterized by temporary stability or organization that arises due to nonlinear interactions and feedback processes within the system.

Kinship – Encomposses a complex and interconnected understanding of relationships, identity, and responsibilities within human and more-than-human communities. It is not merely a biological or legal concept, but encompasses spiritual, cultural, familial, and historical dimensions.

Land Back – Also referred to with hashtag #LandBack, is a decentralized campaign by Indigenous Australians, Indigenous peoples in Canada, Native Americans in the United States, other Indigenous peoples, and allies alike, that seeks to reestablish Indigenous sovereignty, with political and economic control of their ancestral lands. Land Back promotes a return to communal land ownership of traditional and unceded Indigenous lands and rejects colonial concepts of real estate and private land ownership.[281]

Living in relationship to place – Having an intentional, embodied, and perhaps spiritual connection and responsibility to specific lands, ecology, and place-based culture. In contrast, many people in modern culture may experience a "placelessness" – a disconnection from geographic roots due to factors like globalization, technological change, and dominant culture that considers humans as separate from nature.

Living system – Living systems, as contrasted with nonliving complex systems – such as the stock market, computer simulations, or car traffic patterns – are characterized by the following set of key features: complexity, self-organization, interdependence, nested hierarchies, dynamic balance, and the emergent properties of cognition, adaptation, and autopoiesis – the capability of a system to produce and maintain itself by producing its own parts.282

Monitoring, reporting, and verification (MRV) – A process that ensures accuracy, reliability, and transparency in reporting and measurements. The goal of MRV is to verify that the data and information presented in reports, statements, or performance measurements are truthful, consistent, and compliant with applicable standards and regulations.

More-than-human life – A phrase that intentionally values all living beings and elements of the natural world as interconnected and integral to life. This concept emphasizes the agency, consciousness, and relational significance of non-human entities.

Multi-capital/Multicapitalism – A framework that acknowledges and values different forms of capital beyond traditional financial capital. A wide diversity of multi-capital frameworks and definitions – including Indigenous concepts – have been proposed in recent years to offer language for breaking out of the perception that money is the only form of capital flowing around and through us.

Natural assets – The stocks of natural resources and ecosystems that provide essential services and benefits to Gaia, society, local economies, and the global economy. These assets include forests, wetlands, fisheries, clean air and water, biodiversity, and other elements of the natural environment that contribute to the well-being of life and economic prosperity.

Nature – Perhaps an undefinable term (e.g. where does it end?) it is mostly used in this book to refer to the organic world (plants, fungi, animals (including humans), ecosystems) as well as world features (hydrology, geology, climate) that western science does not generally consider organic or alive, yet are being increasingly recognized as interdependent with the organic world (see Gaia Hypothesis). Within the context of other knowledge systems, it includes categories such as Mother Earth and systems of life, and it is often viewed as inextricably linked to humans, not as a separate entity.[283]

Nature-based Currencies – A type of complementary currency that bases its value on the health and vitality of the local ecosystems – the ecological wealth – in a given bioregion. While most currencies in circulation today are no longer linked to physical assets, such as gold, communities deploying these new currencies can use natural capital as a reserve asset to mint the financial capital needed to protect ecosystems and support the livelihoods of their local stewards.[284]

Partner states – Multi-stakeholder cooperatives or commons-based institutions responsible for the management and provision of certain public goods, common assets, or services that were once the responsibility of state governments, which instead provide funding and performance evaluation to partner states.[285]

Place – Where geographic reality and human culture intersect. It is the foundation for culture and economy.[286]

Planetary boundaries – A scientific framework that presents a set of nine biophysical thresholds, "within which humanity can continue to develop and thrive for generations to come." Crossing boundaries increases the risk of generating large-scale abrupt or irreversible ecological changes.[287]

Polycrisis – "A time of great disagreement, confusion, or suffering that is caused by many different problems happening at the same time so that they together have a very big effect," (Cambridge Dictionary, n.d.). Polycrisis is often used interchangeably with "*Metacrisis*", although some assert that "*meta-*" offers a preferable distinction by denoting the interdependence (rather than mere multiplicity) of crises and the worldviews/values that may be generating these crises.[288]

282 Fritjof Capra & Pier Luigi Luisi: The Systems View of Life: A Unifying Vision
283 IPBES: nature
284 Inspired by Open Earth Foundation: Nature Based Currencies
285 P2P Foundation Wiki: Partner State
286 Credit to Capital Institute
287 Stockholm Resilience Center: Planetary Boundaries
288 Rowson, Jonathan: Prefixing the World

Public good – In economics, a "public good" refers to anything that is both non-excludable and non-rivalrous, meaning people cannot be barred access, and one person's use doesn't degrade another's.[289] Street lights, public databases, and open-source patents or code are all examples. Public goods are different from common assets, which can be rivalrous and made excludable through governance.

R Values – Jan Hania (Tuwharetoa, Raukawa-ki-teTonga, Te Atiawa of Aotearoa/New Zealand and the Principal of Strategy Development for Biome Trust) uplifts the "R values" of relationality, reciprocity, responsibility, respect, reverence, regeneration, redistribution, and reconnection – noting that language must be contextualized and place-based.[290] The authors also uplift re-membering, restorying, rewilding, and rematriation.

Real sector – the part of the global economy that produces goods and services, rather than the part that consists of financial institutions and services.

Regeneration – The process of a system regaining its needed energies, resources, and relationships to vitalize and sustain. Contrasted with "*sustainability*", which is oriented towards preserving and minimizing negative impacts, regeneration is oriented towards restoring and revitalizing systems that have been degraded.

Regenerator – The individuals, communities, organizations, and networks actively engaging in biocultural regeneration efforts. The specifier "on-the-ground" refers to those working in consistent, embodied, and intimate relationship with ecosystems and landscapes.

Returns – The outcomes (normally assumed to be positive, but could include negative) generated for investors, stakeholders, and human and more-than-human community across multiple forms of capital as a result of investments or actions.

Rights of nature – The recognition that our ecosystems – including trees, oceans, animals, and mountains – have rights just as human beings have rights. Rather than treating nature as property under the law, rights of nature acknowledges that nature in all its life forms has the right to exist, persist, maintain, and regenerate its vital cycles. And we – the people – have the legal authority and responsibility to enforce these rights on behalf of ecosystems. The ecosystem itself can be named as the injured party, with its own legal standing rights, in cases alleging rights violations.[291]

Right relationship/ right relation – As an aspirational quality or state of relationality that can only be encountered in a unique web of relations and biocultural understanding, it is not possible to offer a comprehensive and specific definition of this term. Generally, however, "right relationship" connotes a harmonious way of relating that is active, reciprocal, consensual, and sustainable (or regenerative) across dimensions of past, present, and future, with respect to humans, more-than-human-life, lands, and waters. The term is most often used to refer to Indigenous ways of relating. Therefore, we

289 Wikipedia: Public good (economics)
290 The Regeneration Will Be Funded (Podcast): Jan Hania
291 Global Alliance for the Rights of Nature: What are the Rights of Nature?

recommend learning about relationality directly from Indigenous sources and relationships, as translation across languages and worldviews risks eroding its essential meaning.292

Stewardship – The responsible and ethical relating, tending, and nurturing of land, resources, and ecosystems for the benefit of present and future generations of human and more-than- human communities. Stewardship emphasizes a holistic approach that prioritizes the well-being of the entire ecological system over individual ownership rights, focusing on sustainability, resilience, and regeneration of natural capital.[293]

Steward-ownership – A corporate ownership structure that presents an alternative to shareholder value primacy. It ensures that companies prioritize their long-term purpose over short-term profits – by legally enshrining two principles of Self-Determination and Purpose-Orientation.[294]

Story of place – A holistic narrative that integrates the history, ecology, culture, and potential of a specific location, guiding sustainable design and development processes rooted in community stewardship and alignment with living systems principles. *Note: Story of Place® refers to a specific educational concept and service offering of the Regenesis Group.*[295]

Traditional ecological knowledge (TEK) – The ongoing accumulation of knowledge, practice, and belief about relationships between living beings in a specific ecosystem that is acquired by Indigenous people over hundreds or thousands of years through direct contact with the environment, handed down through generations, and used in life-sustaining ways. It encompasses the world view of a people, which includes ecology, spirituality, human and animal relationships, and more.[296]

Transcontextual – The recognition that complex systems do not exist in single contexts, but rather are formed between multiple contexts that overlap in living communication and among living systems. "Warm Data" can be defined as: Transcontextual information about the interrelationships that integrate a complex system.[297]

Quadratic Funding – By allocating funds based on a quadratic formula that magnifies the impact of many small investments from the community (similar to crowdfunding) through a so-called 'matching pool' that is resourced by larger capital providers, Quadratic Funding encourages widespread participation and fosters a diverse array of projects that resonate with local communities. Projects that receive a given amount of community funding from a broader base of individuals receive more match funding than those that receive the given amount from only a few community investors.[298]

292 For an in-depth academic discussion of relationality from Indigenous perspectives, please see Matt Wildat & Daniel Voth: Indigenous relationality: definitions and methods
293 A note of caution for spanish speakers: steward is often translated as 'mayordomo' – a term originating from colonial structures of domination and control of land and people. 'Cuidador/a' or 'guardiano/a' are closer to the intended meaning.
294 Purpose Economy: What's steward-ownership?
295 Regenesis Group: Story of Place
296 U.S. National Park Service: Traditional Ecological Knowledge

Quadratic Voting – A method of collective decision-making where individuals assign votes to reflect both the direction and intensity of their preferences. Participants can allocate more votes to express stronger support for specific options, allowing them to "purchase" additional votes on a particular matter, thereby aligning the voting outcome with the highest willingness to pay, rather than solely the preference of the majority. Payments for votes can be made using either artificial or real currencies, such as voting tokens distributed equally among voting members or fiat and complementary currencies with actual economic exchange value.[299] (Lalley and Weyl, 2018)

Wealth – True wealth is not merely money in the bank. It must be defined and managed in terms of the well-being of the whole, achieved through the harmonization of multiple kinds of wealth or capital, including social, cultural, living, and experiential. It must also be defined by a broadly shared prosperity across all of these varied forms of capital. The whole is only as strong as the weakest link.[300]

Weaving – Weaving is the practice of cultivating meaningful relationships, within, between and across socio-ecological systems. It connects people, projects, and places in synergistic and purposeful ways to help cohere fragmented change-making efforts. It seeks to strengthen the socio-ecological fabric and the system's resilience by addressing the vital and relational aspects of trust, common meaning, capacity for learning, and capacity for self-organization.[301]

Web3 – In contrast to the current internet era (Web2) characterized by centralized platforms and services where user data is controlled by a few large corporations, Web3 represents an emerging internet that is decentralized, enabled by blockchain technology, where users have greater control over their data, identities, and interactions through peer-to-peer networks and protocols.

Worldview – "A set of presuppositions (assumptions which may be true, partially true or entirely false) which we hold (consciously or subconsciously, consistently or inconsistently) about the basic makeup of our world."[302]

297   The International Bateson Institute: Warm Data Labs
298   Quadratic Funding (QF) – Unlocking the power of community funding. See (Buteren et al. 2020) for the seminal articulation.
299   Lalley and Weyl: Quadratic Voting: How Mechanism Design Can Radicalize Democracy
300   Capital Institute: The Field Guide to a Regenerative Economy
301   Hussain et al.: Socio-Ecological Resilience: 'Weaving' to scale Nature-based Solutions
302   Definition by James Sire, referenced in D.C. Wahl: Design for human and planetary health: a transdisciplinary approach to sustainability

About the Authors

Samantha Power

Samantha Power is a Co-Founder and the Director of the BioFi Project and the Founder and Principal Consultant of Finance for Gaia. She is a Regenerative Economist, Futurist, and Bioregionalist based in Oakland, CA on the ancestral land of the Ohlone people. Samantha believes we need to build a new layer in the global financial architecture to halt the sixth mass extinction and she is dedicating her life to doing just that.

For 15 years now, Samantha has been asking "How do we change where money is flowing so that it supports, rather than destroys, life?" This question has taken her to many different geographies, communities, and institutions — from rapidly disappearing rainforests across Southeast Asia, women's community lending circles in Myanmar, the US Treasury Department, the UN, the World Bank, as well as the ecological and social impact investing community.

Ultimately, it landed her amidst the redwoods in the San Francisco Bay Area, where Samantha took stock of what she had learned trying to change financial flows from the top down. She began deepening her listening to the people she saw doing the most urgent work in the world right now: regenerating the Earth's lands and waters. She learned that the Indigenous land stewards, regenerative farmers, community builders, and regenerative systems designers from around the world were not able to access the financial resources needed to support their critical work, and imagined a set of new bioregional-scale financial institutions and infrastructure, strategically coordinated to change ecosystems and economic systems at scale.

Samantha channeled what she learned into a new book: *Bioregional Financing Facilities: Reimagining Finance to Regenerate Our Planet.* The book makes the case for, and explains how to build systems and infrastructure to shift capital to place-based regenerators to achieve global climate and nature-related goals, while enabling the transition to regenerative economies. To turn this vision into a global movement, Samantha co-founded the BioFi Project — a collective of practitioners supporting bioregions around the world to design, build, and implement BFFs inspired by the templates laid out in the book.

Prior to her work on Bioregional Facilities, while working at the World Bank, Samantha played a leading role in developing the institution's 'nature finance' agenda and co-authored one of the early reports on this topic in 2020, *Mobilizing Private Finance for Nature*. She then went on to advise the Coalition of Finance Ministers for Climate Action on the economic and financial risks of destroying the biosphere, the UN Convention on Biological Diversity of resource mobilization, and the UN Decade on Ecosystem Restoration on innovative approaches to financing large-scale landscape regeneration.

Samantha holds a Master's degree in International Affairs and International Economics from Johns Hopkins School of Advanced International Studies and a Bachelor's degree in International Economics from Louisiana State University. She is an advisor to the sustainable investment firm Ethic, and the Open Future Fund, as well as an Ambassador for the Capital Institute. All of Samantha's work is informed by her listening to the Earth.

Leon Seefeld

Leon Seefeld is leading Strategy to Operations as well as the project portfolio of Dark Matter Capital Systems – the unit within Dark Matter Labs focussed on building the capital markets for urban and bioregional transitions to regenerative and resilient economies. In addition, he leads the financial innovation work of the Bioregional Weaving Labs consortium in Europe and is the Co-Founder and Executive Director of reframe.ventures, a consultancy firm focussed on regenerative business model innovation.

With a background in systems thinking and complexity science as well as international business management, Leon has a strong curiosity for those structural and systemic shifts that help us respond as best as possible to the undeniable collapse that is currently underway. He is a profound thinker and deeply appreciates the importance of the inner work, complementing our outer striving for change. Apart from a genuine passion for his work on transformation topics, he likes to spend time in the outdoors and is a passionate wildlife and nature photographer.

The book Bioregional Financing Facilities: Reimagining Finance to Regenerate Our Planet is a product not of Leon as an individual author but of the countless conversations he was fortunate to have with brilliant people at Dark Matter Labs, Bioregional Weaving Labs, and beyond. Following from the conceptual work of the book, Leon is committed to helping bioregional stewards across the world with the arguably more difficult piece: The practical implementation and constant iteration of new financial mechanisms genuinely in service to regenerative life.

Prior to working at the nexus of finance and systems change as well as finance and bioregional regeneration, Leon has gained a breadth of experience across the topics of (Social) Entrepreneurship and (Social) Innovation, Sustainability (Strategy) Consulting and Corporate Purpose Consulting, International Development, Personal Development and Sustainability Education as well as complex multi-stakeholder alliance work in various contexts (including the national and bioregional scale).

Leon holds a Master's degree in Strategic Leadership towards Sustainability from Blekinge Institute of Technology in Karlskrona, Sweden, covering topics from science-based sustainable development, systems thinking, and complexity theory to the systemic, participatory, innovative, and personal dimension of future-fit leadership. Before, he earned his Bachelor's degree in International Management from Lancaster University, in Lancaster, UK, and ESB Business School in Reutlingen, Germany.

Acknowledgments

Advisors

Stuart Cowan, Ph.D. (Buckminster Fuller Institute)
Edward West (Applied Alchemy / The BioFi Project)
Indy Johar (Dark Matter Labs / Dark Matter Capital Systems)
Raj Kalia (Dark Matter Labs / Dark Matter Capital Systems)
Jan Hania (Biome Trust)
Matthew Monahan (Biome Trust / Ma Earth)
Karl Burkart (One Earth)
Justin Adams (Ostara)

Note: While the advisors provided important guidance on the development of the report, the authors did not ask them to endorse the text in full.

Research Assistance and Glossary

Tyler Wakefield (Interdependent)

Design & Illustration

Arianna Smaron (Dark Matter Labs)
Madelyn Capozzi (Dark Matter Labs)

Cover Art

Aaron Brodeur (Applied Alchemy)

Editing

Nick Paul (nicewriting)
Tyler Wakefield (Interdependent)
Taya Seidler (Applied Alchemy)

Production Coordinator:

Edward West (Applied Alchemy)

Book Layout

Onur Alka (bookdesign.berlin)

Case Studies

Alex Corren (ReCommon)
Alana Peterson, Kalah Duncan, and India Rose Matharu-Daley (Spruce Root)
Austin Wade Smith (Regen Foundation)
Clare Politano (Hylo)
Edward West (Edge Prize)
Faith Flanigan and Ruth Andrade (Regenerosity)
Isabel Carlisle (Bioregional Learning Centre South Devon)
Keoni Lee (Hawai'i Investment Ready)
Reggie Luedtke (Golden Bay Bioregion & Mohua 2042)
Sarah Prosser and Karin Müller (Bioregional Weaving Labs)
Spencer Beebe, Ian Gill, Christopher Brookfield, Cheryl Chen, and Edward West (Salmon Nation)
Taya Seidler, Clare Attwell, Brandon Letsinger, and Sheri Herndon (Regenerate Cascadia)

This work benefited from guidance and technical support from the Buckminster Fuller Institute Design Lab under the "Bioregional Resilience and Regeneration" track.

It received financial
support from:

And in-kind support from:

Other Acknowledgements

We would like to give special thanks to Tyler Wakefield for his beautiful contributions bringing heart and wisdom to the book, to Stuart Cowan and Edward West for their incredible contributions throughout the envisioning, writing, and publication process, to our editor Nick Paul who went above and beyond in his efforts to make our messages as clear and compelling as possible, and to Matthew Monahan and Jan Hania for their early trust in the vision for this work and their wise counsel as it came to life.

While Leon Seefeld was the primary Dark Matter Labs author, his contributions built on the wisdom, thinking, and previous work of the broader Dark Matter Labs team. In particular the advisors to the report, Raj Kalia and Indy Johar, as well as Emily Harris substantially influenced the writing and thinking that went into this book.

We would also like to acknowledge the thoughtful, generous contributions from the following friends and colleagues: Aaron Brodeur, Analise Roland, Ashoka Finley, Atherton Phleger, Christopher Lindstrom, Clare Politano, Cory Brown, Cristina Valverde, David Hodgson, Durukan Dudu, Evan Steiner, Faith Flanigan, Félix de Rosen, Jeff Mendelsohn, Jessica Zartler, Johny Mair, Jörgen Anderson, Josiah Cain, Kaitlin Archambault, Karie Crisp, Kevin Bayuk, Lawrence Grodeska, Louis Fox, Matt Jorgensen, Nicolas Rotundo, Reggie Luedtke, Scott Morris, and Taya Seidler.

We would like to express our gratitude to Bioregional Weaving Labs and Regenerate Cascadia for their respective contributions to the field in developing and refining the template for a thorough multi-stakeholder process and the phases of bioregional regeneration. Additionally, the members of the Planetary Regeneration Alliance, EcoWeaving, Regen Network, Regen Foundation, Applied Alchemy, Buckminster Fuller Institute, One Earth, Biome Trust, Ma Earth, Open Future Coalition, Open Civics, Indigenous Knowledge Systems Lab, AIME Mentoring, and Ripple of Impact teams all provided collective inputs that were meaningful in shaping this work.

We would also like to express our excitement and enthusiasm for what is emerging as one of the direct results of this book coming to life: the creation of The BioFi Project, co-founded by Samantha Power and Edward West, which will offer resources, capacity building, training, and thought leadership for Bioregional Organizing Teams intending to design, build, and implement their own Bioregional Financing Facilities inspired by this book. Dark Matter Labs will also offer support to Bioregional Organizing Teams on their journey toward a next generation of financial architecture and resource governance.

The authors bow in gratitude to our family, friends, and colleagues not named here who supported us in developing this work. We acknowledge our deep entanglement with them, and with the more-than-human life in the places in which we wrote this. There are many books, articles, podcasts, and pieces of music that inspired us and influenced our thinking for which we are grateful. Samantha would like to give a special nod to Rick Rubin's book The Creative Act: A Way of Being for supporting her writing process.

References

Almond et al. (2022) *Living planet report.* Banson. Available at: https://livingplanet.panda.org/en-US/.

Aminetzah, D. et al. (2022) *Nature in the balance: What companies can do to restore natural capital.* McKinsey & Co. Available at: https://www.mckinsey.com/capabilities/sustainability/our-insights/nature-in-the-balance-what-companies-can-do-to-restore-natural-capital (Accessed: May 2, 2024)

Bongaarts, J. (2019) IPBES, 2019. *Summary for policymakers of the global assessment report on biodiversity and ecosystem services of the Intergovernmental Science-Policy Platform on Biodiversity and Ecosystem Services.* Population and Development Review, 45(3). Available at: https://doi.org/10.1111/padr.12283.

Boston, P.J. (2008) *Gaia Hypothesis.* Encyclopedia of Ecology, Five-Volume Set, 1–5, pp. 1727–1731. Available at: https://doi.org/10.1016/B978-008045405-4.00735-7.

Boyd, G. (2020) *Rebuild: the Economy, Leadership and You.* Evolutesix Books.

brown, a.m. (2017) *Emergent Strategy.* AK PRESS.

Buller, A. (2022) *The Value of a Whale: On the Illusions of Green Capitalism.* Manchester, England: Manchester University Press.

Burckart, W. & Lydenberg, S. (2021). *21st Century Investing: Redirecting Financial Strategies to Drive Systems Change.* Berrett-Koehler Publishers.

Buterin, V., Hitzig, Z. and Weyl, E.G. (2019) *A Flexible Design for Funding Public Goods.* Management Science 65(11), pp. 5171–5187. Available at: https://doi.org/10.1287/MNSC.2019.3337.

Carson, R. (1962) *Silent Spring.* Mifflin.

Chancel, L. et al. (2022) *World Inequality Report 2022.* Available at: https://doi.org/10.4159/9780674276598.

Convention on Biological Diversity, CBD (2022) *Indigenous Communities Protect 80% Of All Biodiversity.* Available at: https://www.cbd.int/kb/record/newsHeadlines/135368 (Accessed: May 25, 2024).

Cook, S.J. and Holliday, S.C., 2024. Insuring Nature's Survival: The Role of Insurance in Meeting the Financial Need to Preserve Biodiversity. Washington, D.C.: World Bank Group. Available at: Available at: http://documents.worldbank.org/curated/en/099850304272234140/IDU02b17904f04af504b8f087f708041ff6d79d4

Costanza, R. et al. (2021) *Common Asset Trusts to effectively steward natural capital and ecosystem services at multiple scales.* Journal of Environmental Management. Available at: https://doi.org/10.1016/j.jenvman.2020.111801.

Cox, T. (2024) *Pollination plans blended regenerative agriculture fund worth billions « Carbon Pulse,* Carbon Pulse. Available at: https://carbon-pulse.com/261073/ (Accessed: May 2, 2024).

Crystallin M., Moren P. and Boissinot J. (2022) *Finance Ministries, Central Banks and Supervisors Recognize Nature-Related Risks and Commit to Deepening Their Understanding.* Coalition of Finance Ministers for Climate Action. Available at: https://www.financeministersforclimate.org/node/697.

Daggers, J., Hannant, A. and Jay, J. (2023) *Impact Investing: Systemic Investing for Social Change.* Stanford Social Innovation Review. Available at: https://ssir.org/articles/entry/systemic_investing_for_social_change.

Davis, F. et al. (2024) *Landmark UN report: The world's migratory species of animals are in decline, and the global extinction risk is increasing.* UNEP. Available at: https://www.unep.org/news-and-stories/press-release/landmark-un-report-worlds-migratory-species-animals-are-decline-and.

Emmett, J. and Zartler, J. (no date) *Exploring Mycofi | Mycelial Design Patterns for Web3 and Beyond.* Available at: https://greenpill.network/pdf/mycofi.pdf.

Emmett, J. (2019) *Conviction Voting: A Novel Continuous Decision Making Alternative to Governance | Giveth. Medium.com.* Available at: https://blog.giveth.io/conviction-voting-a-novel-continuous-decision-making-alternative-to-governance-aa746cfb9475 (Accessed: May 6, 2024).

Evison, W., Low, L.P. and O'Brien, D. (2023) *Managing nature risks: From understanding to action.* Available at: https://www.pwc.com/gx/en/strategy-and-business/content/sbpwc-2023-04-19-Managing-nature-risks-v2.pdf (Accessed: May 6, 2024).

FAO and FILAC (2021) *Forest governance by Indigenous and tribal peoples. An opportunity for climate action in Latin America and the Caribbean, Forest governance by Indigenous and tribal peoples. An opportunity for climate action in Latin America and the Caribbean.* Available at: https://doi.org/10.4060/cb2953en.

Fischer, H.W., Chhatre, A., Duddu, A. et al., 2023. *Community forest governance and synergies among carbon, biodiversity and livelihoods.* Nature Climate Change, 13, pp.1340–1347. Available at: https://doi.org/10.1038/s41558-023-01863-6

Fleischman, T., Dini, P. and Littera, G. (2020) *Liquidity-Saving through Obligation-Clearing and Mutual Credit: An Effective Monetary Innovation for SMEs in Times of Crisis.* Journal of Risk and Financial Management 2020, Vol. 13, Page 295, 13(12), p. 295. Available at: https://doi.org/10.3390/JRFM13120295.

Fortune, 2024. *Carbon colonialism in Africa.* Available at: https://fortune.com/2024/04/07/environment-carbon-colonialism-africa/

Friston, K.J. et al. (2022) *Designing Ecosystems of Intelligence from First Principles.* Collective Intelligence, 3(1). Available at: https://doi.org/10.1177/26339137231222481.

Friston, K.J. et al. (2024) *Federated inference and belief sharing.* Neuroscience & Biobehavioral Reviews, 156, p. 105500. Available at: https://doi.org/10.1016/J.NEUBIOREV.2023.105500.

Fullerton, J. (2015) *Regenerative capitalism: How universal principles and patterns will shape our new economy.* Capital Institute Think Tank. Available at: https://capitalinstitute.org/wp-content/uploads/2015/04/2015-Regenerative-Capitalism-4-20-15-final.pdf.

Gabay, A. (2024) *International hesitancy to adopt environmental regulations threatens Indigenous rights.* Mongabay. Available at: https://news.mongabay.com/2024/04/international-hesitancy-to-adopt-environmental-regulations-threatens-indigenous-rights/ (Accessed: May 2, 2024).

Graeber, D., Wengrow, D. and Wodzicki, L. (2022) *The Dawn of Everything. A New History of Humanity. Cromohs*, 25. Available at: https://doi.org/10.36253/cromohs-14216.

Graeber, D. (2011) Debt: *The first five thousand years.* Melville House.

Haberl, H. et al. (2020) *A systematic review of the evidence on decoupling of GDP, resource use and GHG emissions, part II: synthesizing the insights.* Environmental Research Letters, [online] 15(6), p.065003. Available at: https://doi.org/10.1088/1748-9326/ab842a.

Hannant, A. et al. (2022) *Design Foundations for Systems Capital.* p. 66. Available at: https://research-repository.griffith.edu.au/bitstreams/358707a2-ff62-4171-9e13-55e89da87475/download (Accessed: May 3, 2024).

Harari, Y.N. (2015) Sapiens: *A Brief History of Humankind.* Vintage.

Harris, E. (2023) *Towards multivalent currencies, bioregional monetary stewardship and a distributed global reserve currency.* Dark Matter Labs. Available at: https://provocations.darkmatterlabs.org/towards-multivalent-currencies-bioregional-monetary-stewardship-and-a-distributed-global-reserve-dac459dc844e (Accessed: May 6, 2024).

Harris, E., Johar, I. and Lorenz, M. (2024) *Life-Ennobling Economics.* Dark Matter Labs. Available at: https://lee.darkmatterlabs.org/#Shifts (Accessed: May 3, 2024).

Hussain, S. et al. (2022) *Socio-Ecological Resilience: 'Weaving' to scale Nature-based Solutions.* Available at: https://bth.diva-portal.org/smash/record.jsf?pid=diva2%3A1669345&dswid=-8354.

Jeffery, T., Kurtz, D. and Jones, C.A. (no date) *Two-Eyed Seeing: Current approaches, and discussion of medical applications.* British Columbia Medical Journal. Available at: https://bcmj.org/articles/two-eyed-seeing-current-approaches-and-discussion-medical-applications (Accessed: May 3, 2024).

Kaufmann, R. (2023) *The Gaia Attractor. A planetary AI copilot network to overcome the Metacrisis. Medium.com.* Available at: https://rkauf.medium.com/the-gaia-attractor-41e5af33f3b7 (Accessed: May 2, 2024).

Keynes, J.M. (1936) *The general theory of employment, interest, and money, The General Theory of Employment, Interest, and Money.* Available at: https://doi.org/10.1007/978-3-319-70344-2.

Kimmerer, R.W. (2013) *Braiding Sweetgrass.* Milkweed Editions.

Klomp, K. and Oosterwaal, S. (2021) *Thrive: Fundamentals for a new economy.* Atlas Contact, Uitgeverij.

Lalley, S. and Weyl, E.G. (2017) *Quadratic Voting: How Mechanism Design Can Radicalize Democracy.* SSRN Electronic Journal [Preprint]. Available at: https://doi.org/10.2139/SSRN.2003531.

Landua, G. (2024) *To Credit, or not to Credit.. What's in a name?.* Medium.com. Available at: https://medium.com/regen-network/to-credit-or-not-to-credit-de48ba7da8c4 (Accessed: May 2, 2024).

Lenton, T.M. and Latour, B. (2018) Gaia 2.0 – *Could humans add some level of self-awareness to Earth's self-regulation?.*

Lietaer, B. (2022) *Scientific Evidence of Why Complementary Currencies are Necessary to Financial Stability.* Available at: https://bernard-lietaer.org/wp-content/uploads/2022/07/2010-Scientific-Evidence-of-Why-Complementary-Currencies-Are-Necessary-to-Financial-Stability-Lietaer-annotated.pdf (Accessed: May 6, 2024).

Lovelock, J. (2020) Novacene: *The Coming Age of Hyperintelligence.* The MIT Press.

Lukomnik, J. & Hawley, J.P. (2023). *Moving Beyond Modern Portfolio Theory: Investing That Matters.* Oxford University Press.

Manning Bancroft, J. (2023) *Hoodie Economics Changing Our Systems to Value What Matters.* Hardie Grant Books.

Marks, S. (2022) *The Foundation Review.* Available at: https://doi.org/10.9707/1944-5660.1636.

Mazzucato, M. (2020) *The value of everything: Making and taking in the global economy.* New York: Public Affairs.

Maentz, J. (2024) *State of Funding for Tenure Rights and Forest Guardianship DONOR FUNDING FOR INDIGENOUS PEOPLES, LOCAL COMMUNITIES, AND AFRO-DESCENDANT PEOPLES IN TROPICAL FORESTED COUNTRIES (2011-2023) State of Funding for Tenure Rights and Forest Guardianship Rights and Resources Initiative / Rainforest Foundation Norway-2.* Available at: https://rightsandresources.org/wp-content/uploads/2023-State-of-Funding_Brief-EN.pdf (Accessed: May 6, 2024).

Meadows, D., Randers, J. and Meadows, D. (no date) *A Synopsis: Limits to Growth: The 30-Year Update.* The Donella Meadows Project. Available at: https://donellameadows.org/archives/a-synopsis-limits-to-growth-the-30-year-update/ (Accessed: May 2, 2024).

Meadows, D. (1983) *History of the ideas underlying the Ballaton Group.*

NGFS (2023) *NGFS Recommendations toward the development of scenarios for assessing nature-related economic and financial risks.* Available at: https://www.ngfs.net/sites/default/files/medias/documents/ngfs_nature_scenarios_recommendations.pdf.

NGFS (2023) *Nature-related Financial Risks: a Conceptual Framework to guide Action by Central Banks and Supervisors.* Available at: https://www.ngfs.net/sites/default/files/medias/documents/ngfs_conceptual-framework-on-nature-related-risks.pdf.

Nunes, R. (2021) *Neither Vertical nor Horizontal: A Theory of Political Organization.* London: Verso.

Ohlhaver, P., Weyl, E.G., and Buterin, V. (2022) *Decentralized Society: Finding Web3's Soul.* Available at SSRN: https://papers.ssrn.com/sol3/papers.cfm?abstract_id=4105763.

van Peborgh, E. (2023) *Living Capital Design: The Rise of Nature-based Currencies.* Medium.com. Available at: https://ernesto-87727.medium.com/living-capital-design-the-rise-of-nature-based-currencies-1ac50f5649cd (Accessed: May 3, 2024).

Pimm, S.L. et al. (2014) *The biodiversity of species and their rates of extinction, distribution, and protection.* Science, 344(6187). Available at: https://doi.org/10.1126/SCIENCE.1246752/SUPPL_FILE/PIMM.SM.PDF.

Pistor, K. (2019) *The Code of Capital: How the Law Creates Wealth and Inequality.* Princeton University Press.

Power, S., Dunz, N. and Gavryliuk, O. (2022) *An Overview of Nature-Related Risks and Potential Policy Actions for Ministries of Finance: Bending The Curve of Nature Loss.* Available at: https://www.financeministersforclimate.org/sites/cape/files/inline-files/Nature-Related%20Risks%20for%20MoFs%20-%20Bending%20the%20Curve%20of%20Nature%20Loss.pdf.

Rights and Resources Initiative, 2020. *Who Owns the World's Land?* The Second Edition. [online] Available at: https://rightsandresources.org/who-owns-the-worlds-land-2nd-ed/

Radtke, H.L., Young, J. and van Mens-Verhulst, J. (2016) *Aging, Identity, and Women: Constructing the Third Age.* Women and Therapy, 39(1–2), pp. 86–105. Available at: https://doi.org/10.1080/02703149.2016.1116321.

Ragusa, A. et al. (2021) *Plasticenta: First evidence of microplastics in human placenta.* Environment International. Available at: https://doi.org/10.1016/j.envint.2020.106274.

Recio, E. and Hestad, D. (Dr.) (2022) *Indigenous Peoples: Defending an Environment for All.* International Institute for Sustainable Development. Available at: https://www.iisd.org/articles/deep-dive/indigenous-peoples-defending-environment-all (Accessed: May 2, 2024).

Resneck, J. et al. (2022) *The Roadless Rule is supposed to protect wild places. What went wrong in the Tongass National Forest?.* Grist. Available at: https://grist.org/project/accountability/tongass-national-forest-roadless-rule-loophole/ (Accessed: May 6, 2024).

Reuters. (2024) *Amazon Fund for rainforest received $640 million in new pledges in 2023.* https://www.reuters.com/sustainability/climate-energy/amazon-fund-rainforest-received-640-mln-new-pledges-2023-2024-02-01/

Richardson, K. et al. (2023) *Earth beyond six of nine planetary boundaries.* Science Advances, 9(37). Available at: https://doi.org/10.1126/sciadv.adh2458.

Rockström, *J. et al.* (2023) *Safe and just Earth system boundaries.* Nature 2023 619:7968, 619(7968), pp. 102–111. Available at: https://doi.org/10.1038/s41586-023-06083-8.

Roland, E. and Landua, G. (2015) *Regenerative Enterprise: Optimizing for Multi-capital Abundance.* https://www.regenterprise.com/.

Rowson J (2023) *Prefixing the World.* Perspectiva. Available at: https://perspecteeva.substack.com/p/prefixing-the-world (Accessed: May 2, 2024).

Rubin, R. (2023) *The Creative Act: A Way of Being.* Penguin Publishing Group [Preprint].

Sanchez-Moyano, R. and Simms, S. (2023) *Understanding CDFI Financial Data: A Primer for New Investors - San Francisco Fed.* Available at: https://www.frbsf.org/research-and-insights/publications/community-development-research-briefs/2023/12/understanding-cdfi-financial-data/ (Accessed: May 2, 2024).

Schelske, O. et al. (2020) *Biodiversity and Ecosystems Services Index: measuring the value of nature. SwissRE*. Available at: https://www.swissre.com/institute/research/topics-and-risk-dialogues/climate-and-natural-catastrophe-risk/expertise-publication-biodiversity-and-ecosystems-services.html#/ (Accessed: May 2, 2024).

Shames, S. and Scherr, S.J. (2023) *Mobilizing finance across sectors and projects to achieve sustainable landscapes: Emerging models 1000 Landscapes for 1 Billion People*. Available at: https://landscapes.global/wp-content/uploads/2023/08/Integrated-Landscape-Finance-Shames-Scherr-August-2020.pdf.

Stockholm University (2022) *It's raining PFAS: even in Antarctica and on the Tibetan plateau rainwater is unsafe to drink*. Stockholm University. Available at: https://www.su.se/english/news/it-s-raining-pfas-even-in-antarctica-and-on-the-tibetan-plateau-rainwater-is-unsafe-to-drink-1.620735

Strawser, C.C. and Brown, M.S. (2023) *The 2023 DAF Report*. NPTrust. Available at: https://www.nptrust.org/reports/daf-report/

Thayer, R.L., 2003. Life Place: Bioregional Thought and Practice. Berkeley: University of California Press.

The Club of Rome (2023) *The Limits to Growth+50*. Available at: https://www.clubofrome.org/ltg50/

Ma Earth (2023) *The Regeneration Will Be Funded: Trust in Place at Taranaki Mounga - Jan Hania (Biome Trust) on Apple Podcasts* (no date). Available at: https://podcasts.apple.com/us/podcast/the-regeneration-will-be-funded/id1706728107?i=1000637533272 (Accessed: May 2, 2024).

Trosper, R.L. (2022) *Indigenous Economics: Sustaining Peoples and Their Lands*. University of Arizona Press.

UK Gov (2021) *Final Report - The Economics of Biodiversity: The Dasgupta Review*. GOV.UK, HM Treasury.

UNCCD (2022) *Global Land Outlook, United Nations Convention to Combat Desertification - Assessment of Climate Change in the Southwest United States: A Report Prepared for the National Climate Assessment* [Preprint]. Available at: https://www.unccd.int/resources/global-land-outlook/global-land-outlook-2nd-edition (Accessed: May 6, 2024).

UN Decade on Ecosystem Restoration Finance Taskforce. (2022) *Scaling Up Ecosystem Restoration Finance: A Stocktake Report*. The World Bank. https://documents1.worldbank.org/curated/en/099955011092213526/pdf/P17770602aad4701309adb08b084c12888c.pdf

UNEP (2023) State of Finance for Nature 2023: *The Big Nature Turnaround - Repurposing $7 Trillion to Combat Nature Loss*. Available at: https://www.unep.org/resources/state-finance-nature-2023 (Accessed: May 6, 2024).

Vaarde, T.H. (2023) Social Forestry; *Tending the Land as People of Place.* Synergetic Press.

Wahl, D.C. (2006) *Design for human and planetary health: a transdisciplinary approach to sustainability.*

WIT Transactions on Ecology and the Environment, Vol 99. [online] Available at: https://www.academia.edu/84594072/Design_for_human_and_planetary_health_a_transdisciplinary_approach_to_sustainability .

Wahl, D.C. (2020) *Bioregional Regeneration for Planetary Health.* Medium.com. Available at: https://medium.com/activate-the-future/bioregional-regeneration-for-planetary-health-6b28e5e14e21 (Accessed: May 2, 2024).

Wahl, D. (2016) *Designing regenerative cultures.* Nucl. Phys., 13(1).

WEF (2023) *Nature-Positive Industry Sector Transitions.* Available at: https://www.weforum.org/publications/industry-transitions-to-nature-positive-report-series/ (Accessed: May 6, 2024).

van Westen, R.M., Kliphuis, M. and Dijkstra, H.A. (2024) *Physics-based early warning signal shows that AMOC is on tipping course.* Science Advances, 10(6). Available at: https://doi.org/10.1126/sciadv.adk1189.

Wildcat, M. and Voth, D. (2023) *Indigenous relationality: definitions and methods.* AlterNative, 19(2). Available at: https://doi.org/10.1177/11771801231168380.

WMO (2023) 2023 *Shatters Climate Records, With Major Impacts.* World Meteorological Organization [Preprint]. Available at: https://wmo.int/news/media-centre/2023-shatters-climate-records-major-impacts (Accessed: May 6, 2024).

World Bank. (1996) Decentralization and Biodiversity Conservation. Washington DC. Available at: https://books.google.com/books/about/Decentralization_and_Biodiversity_Conser.html?id=InW5AAAAIAAJ

World Bank Group (2023) *Mobilizing Private Finance for Nature: A World Bank Group Paper on Private Finance for Biodiversity and Ecosystem Services.* Available at: https://elibrary.worldbank.org/doi/abs/10.1596/40393

Yau, A. (2024) *How Can Impact Investors Enable Systems Change? Exploring the Theory and Practice of an Emerging Field.* SSRN Electronic Journal [Preprint]. Available at: https://doi.org/10.2139/SSRN.4707922.

Organizational Overviews and Contact Information

The BioFi Project

The BioFi Project is a collective supporting bioregions to design, build, and implement Bioregional Financing Facilities (BFFs) that connect financial resources with regenerators. We partner with bioregional organizing teams and Indigenous communities across North America and around the world to apply the BFF templates and capital raising and allocation approaches laid out in this book.

The BioFi Project team is made up of practitioners in the areas of economics, finance, governance, bioregionalism, ecology, regeneration, and social justice. The BioFi Project establishes partnerships with bioregions and then engages in a listening process; supports asset mapping; identifies which BFF is best to start with; designs a detailed proposal for a BFF; and supports the bioregion with capital raising, capital allocation, and governance implementation. At the global level, the team also shares the concepts laid out in this book, stewards a community of practice, builds relevant software tooling, and supports eco-credit co-design facilitation. The BioFi Project is a fiscally sponsored project of BFI, a 501(c)(3) tax exempt non-profit organization.

Samantha Power
samantha@biofi.earth
www.biofi.earth
Oakland, CA

Dark Matter Capital Systems

Dark Matter Laboratories (Dm) is a not-for-profit working to: (a) Demonstrate a new civic and commons economy; and (b) Build the open – financing, contracting, and governance – tools, instruments, and mechanism for the mass adoption of this economy. We analyze the shifts required in the underlying 'dark matter' – monetary, economic, governance, regulatory, and policy systems – to make a future of mutual thriving possible, and we work with partners across the planet to demonstrate these alternatives in neighborhoods, cities, and bioregions. We share our insights openly for mutual learning and catalytic collaboration.

A new theory of value is inherent to all our doing. Our vision is of a world with massive shared investment in civic and commons goods, and a new landscape of public luxury and private sufficiency as well as shared efforts to regenerate the natural world and human well-being. In our view, novel approaches to financing bioregional regeneration, such as the Bioregional Financing Facilities discussed in this book, are an important means to this end. Hence, Dm will continue to work with bioregional regenerators, demonstrating what is needed yet currently perceived as the edge of the possible.

Leon Seefeld
leon@darkmatterlabs.org
www.darkmatterlabs.org
London, UK